Revd James and Dr Mary Philip

A fitting tribute to a good and godly man which vividly elaborates the biblical thrust and power of his ministry, with its twin emphases on prayer and the teaching of the Word, and ranges over subjects as diverse as the mission of the church, medicine and faith, Calvin, worship, preaching and prayer.

I hope that all who read this volume will be encouraged to serve Christ and his Church with the same relentless zeal, dedication and ability.

Dr Brian Moore
Former Minister, West Kirk, Belfast, 1971-2001

It is both a delight and privilege to represent a multitude of thankful Christian people in welcoming this 80th birthday *Festschrift* for the Revd James Philip.

The editors are to be congratulated on having assembled such a sparkling array of contributors, whose rich diversity of background, experience, expertise, age, gender (just!), and evangelical history, bears eloquent witness to the breadth and depth of James Philip's influence. He stands before us pre-eminently as a preacher of the Word of God, rigorously expounded and searchingly applied. The relevance of the model of his ministry hardly needs underlining at a time when on both sides of the Atlantic the pulpit has simply lost its way.

There can be few greater satisfactions given on earth than to have laboured in the Word of God among a loving, praying congregation, in the context of a lost and yet hungry society, and to find God at work through it all. Such has been James Philip's experience, and the grateful multitude whose lives are ineffaceably richer because of having been touched by it will find in this volume much to warm their hearts, inform and challenge their minds, and motivate their prayers.

The one dimension tantalisingly absent from these pages is a deeper exploration of the personal hinterland of James Philip's ministry, the inner struggles and battles which underlay the manifest fruitfulness of his years (for pain is ever the price of power in the spiritual order). However, like one of his supreme mentors, John Calvin, James does not 'readily speak about himself', and so with that we will probably need to be content until the Great Unveiling.

As one who like many has tried to apply the core principles learned at Holyrood in a vastly different human and social context, and discovered (delightedly) that they are transferable, I happily join the chorus of thanksgiving to God, which this collection represents, for his faithful child, James Philip, a servant of the Word of God.

Dr Bruce Milne
Author and Conference Speaker,
Formerly Pastor, First Baptist Church, Vancouver

Seldom, if ever, have I read a *Festschrift* – a celebratory writing – of such interest and relevance. Its four principal divisions – *The Making of the Man, The Holyrood Years, The Wider Mission* and *Perspectives: Biblical, Theological, Church-Historical* – provide a fitting tribute by twenty-four contributors to a remarkable ministry of 40 years at Holyrood Abbey Church in Edinburgh. They also give an insight into Scottish Evangelicalism in the twentieth century, with significant lessons for the twenty-first.

A genuine sense of God-glorifying indebtedness pervades all the contributions. This is done without looking back to the past with unhelpful nostalgia but with a desire to sound a positive note for the future. Determined to learn lessons from such a significant ministry, it is recognised that they require a twenty-first century application.

Jim Philip's ministry is a telling and powerful example of the usefulness to which God may give one man's ministry, principally in one place, although the Gardenstown years were an important preparation for the long ministry at Holyrood Abbey Church. We are not in a position to suggest all the reasons for the amazing worth of such a ministry, but some are obvious because of their biblical nature. As the apostles determined to give themselves to prayer and the ministry of the Word, so did Jim Philip. Besides personal and private prayer, he ensured that the church prayer meeting was at the heart of the life of God's people at Holyrood. His preaching was marked by the seriousness of one who knew that he spoke always in the presence of God and with great responsibility for people's souls. It was prophetic in that it spoke to the times and issues of the day. Not one part of the Scriptures was neglected in the course of systematic exposition. It highlighted the transcendence of God and the accountability of men and women.

Complementary to the preaching ministry of Jim Philip were sermon tapes, and the widely used Daily Bible Reading Notes. The regular writing of the notes was a massive task and responsibility with telling benefit to many, not only within the Holyrood congregation but elsewhere and especially to missionaries. Helpful reference is made to his love and concern for those in training for the ministry and those serving overseas. One chapter is significantly, and rightly, entitled 'A Man of Weight', and the point made that much of the finest theology in Scottish Calvinism has come from the pens of parish ministers like Jim Philip.

All of the chapters providing biblical, theological, and church-historical perspectives are articles of substance. Perhaps especially relevant are those that relate to the contemporary debate about the nature of worship, and its place in the church.

This book deserves a wide readership since the wisdom of the past needs to be appropriated in the present. Many centuries ago, Christians spoke about 'standing on the shoulders of giants', recognising that those who have gone before have much to teach and pass on. Young ministers will prove it inspiring and instructive. Established preachers and ministers will find it confirming and encouraging. Church missionary committees will see ways of making missions important to their congregations. Church members will recognise afresh the importance of coming together for corporate prayer.

I measure the benefit and usefulness of a book often by the number of things of which I want to take note, and there were many! Perhaps the best tribute I can give is that it made me wish that I could start all over again!

Derek Prime
Author and Conference Speaker
Former Pastor of Charlotte Chapel, Edinburgh

Like Charles Simeon's half-century in Cambridge, James Philip's forty years of ministry in Edinburgh midwifed an era of strong congregational Evangelicalism in a national church that needed renewal. Like his older peer, William Still, James Philip maintained a faithful, unfashionable, whole-Bible, whole-church, whole-counsel-of-God preaching pastorate, evangelical and Reformed, humane and mature, full of grace and of God, igniting both heads and hearts in the knowledge and love of Jesus Christ. This book is a fine tribute to a great ministry, the impact of which, please God, will long continue.

Prof. J I Packer
Regent College, Vancouver

Confession is good for the soul. I was expecting this book to yield an uneven read of essays purporting to be connected but each displaying such independence and variation in quality a review might question the value of publication.

I was wrong!

Alas, I have never known the subject of the book, never heard any of his sermons, nor read one of his books. But exposure to these essays besides giving me an insight into the ministry of the Revd James Philip left me with deep regret that I had never benefitted from his Edinburgh pulpit.

Here in this book are a series of skilfully woven tributes each coming from a different perspective and succeeding in giving a portrait of the ministry of Mr. Philip. The material is interesting, often fascinating and there is an occasional flash of brilliant insight into the mystery of preaching.

I do not lightly tell my homiletics class to purchase a particular volume. Students are invariably hard up! This little volume will be the exception which proves the rule. Amongst other things it succeeds in giving us a picture of a contemporary preacher doing what preachers should – communicating the Word of God clearly, with unction and authority. 'True Preaching', D M Lloyd Jones said, 'is logic on fire.' James Philip illustrated this. I was challenged by what I read and can but pray my own attempts at preaching will be improved as a result.

Dr Tony Sargent
Principal, International Christian College, Glasgow

Here are twenty-two heart-warming tributes to a man who exercised one of the most influential ministries in the Scottish Church during the second half of the twentieth century. James Philip's weekly exposition of the Word of God was experimental and compelling, leading congregations into a sense of awe at God's presence, and inspiring them to engage in fervent missionary intercession for every country in the world. *Serving the Word of God* contains the testimonies of a few of the hundreds of men and women who were equipped by James Philip's unique ministry to serve Christ in Scotland and around the world.

Fergus Macdonald
General Secretary, United Bible Societies

SERVING THE WORD OF GOD

Celebrating the Life and Ministry of

JAMES PHILIP

Minister Emeritus
Holyrood Abbey Church, Edinburgh

Edited by David Wright and David Stay

Mentor
and Rutherford House

© Christian Focus Publications 2002

ISBN 1 85792 745 1

Jointly published in 2002 by
Christian Focus Publications, Geanies House,
Fearn, Ross-shire, Scotland, IV20 1TW
and
Rutherford House, 17 Claremont Park,
Edinburgh, Scotland, EH6 7PJ

www.christianfocus.com

Cover design by Alister MacInnes

Printed and bound in
Finland by WS Bookwell

Contents

Part 4 - Perspectives: Biblical, Theological, Church-Historical

FOREWORD

A Man of Prayer and the Word of God

'We will give ourselves to prayer and the ministry of the Word'
(Acts 6:4)

Like all the contributors to this book I owe James Philip a debt
that I can scarcely begin to repay. I remember, for example,
what followed the 'prayer and share time' on the opening
evening of one New Year Crieff Fellowship. I had been
agonising for weeks over the approach of a vacancy committee,
and after I had written to James Philip (my minister during my
student years in Edinburgh) with all the relevant material, we
had a chat about it in the quiet of the Hydro lounge. 'Well, what
do you think?', I asked. (For my part, I was really quite keen.)
He paused for a moment in his own inimitable way, looked at
me and said, 'No, Phil – that's not for you.' There and then the
matter was closed and I went to bed that night to sleep as I had
not slept for weeks (as did Lyn my wife). So when I was first
contacted by the Holyrood Abbey Vacancy Committee some
ten years later, you can surely imagine that the hardest thing in
all the world was to force myself not to pick up the phone
immediately to speak to the man whose wise counsel had been
sought and followed on that earlier occasion. I do not believe
that it was any coincidence that on the Saturday morning before
I left Ullapool to travel to Edinburgh to preach as sole nominee
for Holyrood a letter came from him, written from somewhere
in Africa just after he had received the news about my selection.
It was full of warmth and encouragement for a somewhat fearful
minister who could scarcely believe what was happening to
him – and it did make him take that journey to Edinburgh!

It is therefore with an enormous personal sense of privilege

9

and delight that on behalf of the Holyrood Abbey Kirk Session and congregation I introduce this book which pays tribute to a man we love and honour – a man of prayer and the Word of God. We look back on a life which has set us an example of godly zeal and humility in the service of Jesus Christ, we look up with gratitude and praise to God for all he has wrought in the lives of so many through his servant, and we look forward as we press on, labourers together in the ongoing work of the kingdom of God. What you read of in these pages is but the veritable tip of the iceberg; so much more could have been written by so many about this man. Though formally retired from his ministerial duties in his beloved Holyrood, Jim, as Minister Emeritus, is still very much at the heart of the work. With Mary, their presence in the congregation is a fragrance of Christ to all and a constant source of encouragement to this preacher Sunday by Sunday. We prize their friendship.

When James Philip came to Edinburgh from Gardenstown in 1958 he speaks of having had a 'restlessness of spirit'. Why was it that God had called him from a northeast fishing village, where so much fruit had been borne through the preaching of the gospel, to an east-end parish in the city of Edinburgh? This was the question that he asked again and again as he walked the streets of the parish in the evenings of those first months. The answer is that he was God's man for the hour – the man called by God to lay a foundation for a gospel work of eternal significance in Holyrood Abbey, in Edinburgh, in Scotland and beyond through prayer and the ministry of the Word of God. These were critical days for the work of the kingdom of God – as they were in the Acts of the Apostles, when the apostles pledged themselves to prayer and the ministry of the Word, just as James Philip would do in his day.

Whilst God was seeking to build the first church in Jerusalem, Satan was seeking to demolish it. He moved from persecuting and corrupting the church (see Acts 4:1f., 5:1f., 41-2) to dividing it. It was exactly what was needed, in that the great characteristic which gave the early church its impetus as it sought to bear witness to the Christ of the gospel was its single-mindedness in the truths of the gospel. 'All the believers were one in heart and mind' (Acts 4:32). This led to a unity of mind and heart amongst the believers, which in turn was the foundation of the remarkable work of those days.

In Acts 6 we read how this unity of mind and heart amongst the people of God was almost destroyed, and as a result, the work of God almost brought to grief. The initial problem was one that churches today would just love to be facing. It arose out of church growth. 'In those days when the number of disciples was increasing, the Grecian Jews among them complained against those of the Aramaic-speaking community because their widows were being overlooked in the daily distribution of food' (Acts 6:1). The Hellenic Jews for most of their days had lived in the Diaspora, in countries such as Turkey, Greece and Egypt, where they had absorbed Greek culture, spoke the Greek language, and read the Greek Scriptures. The Hebraic Jews had been born and bred in Judea, spoke Aramaic and read the Scriptures in the original Hebrew – and were proud of it! They considered themselves to be the real thing, and tended to look down on Hellenic Jews as second-class citizens. The latter felt it.

What happened? In response to the scriptural injunction that the orphan and the widow be looked after, the church was distributing food to the widows in the congregation who had no means of looking after themselves – and whilst the Hebraic widows got their full allocation, a number of Hellenic widows were being short-changed. What did they say? 'We are being discriminated against because of who we are.' Of course this was anything but the case. We are specifically told in verse 1 that these particular widows were 'overlooked'. So this was nothing to do with discrimination but rather everything to do with administration. Quite simply, the church was not coping with the numbers, and was not sufficiently organised. But the smallest of incidents – a look, a word, a lapse of memory, can sometimes cause the greatest of problems.

This problem was enormously serious, first because the church's very united existence was being threatened. We read that these Hellenic widows 'complained', literally they 'murmured'. This is such an expressive word – in fact, it is an onomatopoeic word. The very sound of the word expresses what they were doing. Can you not see these widows in their little group, whispering to each other, murmuring as they grumble and complain about the slight done to them? Before this happened they had been speaking about the church in terms of 'we', but now they were speaking of 'them' and 'us'. The church's very existence as a unified testifying company of believers was being threatened.

Secondly, the apostles' ministry was endangered. 'So the Twelve gathered all the disciples together' (Acts 6:2). We need to read between the lines here. One member said, 'In this business of distributing food we need people we can trust. The apostles should do it.' And they were probably right. But what did the apostles say? 'It would not be right for us to neglect the ministry of the Word of God in order to wait on tables' (Acts 6:2). They had recognised that the very future ministry of the church was at stake. What was Satan seeking to do here? Quite simply to distract the apostles from their great calling. 'We will give our attention to prayer and the ministry of the Word' (Acts 6:4). There was a ministry of the Word, and there was a ministry of tables. It was not a question of importance but rather of calling and priorities. If the apostles had listened to Satan's seductive voice, lacking the milk, bread and meat of the Word which builds up and makes strong, the church would have been left hungry and undernourished, and eventually would have died from spiritual malnutrition. As an institution it would have carried on, but in terms of a live, strong, vigorous testifying company of God's people, it would have died a death. In other words the very future of the apostolic ministry was at stake.

It was this very conviction that the future ministry and prosperity of the church was at stake that led James Philip at the outset of his ministry in Gardenstown to commit himself wholeheartedly to 'prayer and the ministry of the Word'.

How many hungry sheep there were in Edinburgh in those early days of the new Holyrood ministry who found themselves saying, 'Let's go to Holyrood Abbey and hear James Philip.' They came, heard – and never left. And under the ministry of the Word they came to see that at the heart of the work of the gospel and the kingdom is prayer – not supplemental to the ministry but fundamental. In the words of E.M. Bounds: 'Men are God's method. The church is looking for better methods; God is looking for better men. . . . He does not come on machinery, but on men. He does not anoint plans, but men – men of prayer.'[1]

The response of the apostles was decisive: 'Brothers, choose seven men from among you who are known to be full of the Spirit and wisdom. We will turn this responsibility over to them and will give our attention to prayer and the ministry of the Word' (Acts 6:3-4). What was the result? 'So the Word of God spread' (Acts 6:7). From sitting under the ministry of the Word of God, the people of God, equipped and strengthened, took that Word out and spread it abroad – the very thing that Satan had been trying to stop. 'So the Word of God spread. The number of disciples in Jerusalem increased rapidly, and a large number of priests became obedient to the faith' (Acts 6:7).

Surely this is what we long for in our praying in these days for men of the calibre of James Philip, with that settled and absolute conviction that the answer to a spiritually and morally bankrupt nation is a church revived through prayer and the ministry of the Word. 'Lord – raise up more James Philips!'

Philip Hair

---

1. *Power Through Prayer* (London, 1972), 9.

INTRODUCTION

Many members of Holyrood Abbey Church sat under James Philip's ministry for most if not all of his nearly forty years there. There are not many whose contacts predate that ministry. Yet two of the contributors to this work have links back to the days of his assistantship in Springburn Hill, Glasgow. There is even one church member in Holyrood who was baptised by him at Springburn Hill fifty-three years ago. Both editors have links with James Philip and Holyrood going back almost forty years, and many of the contributors have ties of similar duration. It is inevitable therefore that such long years of close fellowship have created a deep awareness of the worth of James Philip and the quality of his work, which should be marked in some significant way.

We are also aware of the great cloud of witnesses, in the ministry, on the mission field, in the professions, in the home and in other spheres of life, both in Britain and in many lands across the world, who owe an enormous debt to Jim. He was born on 11 January 1922. So when the idea of a 'Festschrift' (German, literally, celebratory writing) was first mooted, it seemed that through a volume of memories, tributes and studies, many, who would otherwise be unable to attend any normal celebration or gathering, would be able to share in the anniversary and pay their respects to God's servant.

The first meeting was held in March 2001, and preliminary confidential invitations were sent out. It was a great thrill to find that most of the proposed contributors agreed to our time scale, and so we made our plans accordingly. Fortunately most of the contributors were accessible by e-mail, which greatly simplified communication with one of the editors. Only a few gentle reminders were needed. Then wonderfully in mid-June the contributions began to come trickling in, a few hints were dropped here and there, and by the first week of July we had in our hands all those promised for the deadline. We have been particularly thrilled that one contributor who had gladly accepted our initial invitation but seemed likely to have to withdraw due to serious illness, has mercifully been restored and completed his chapter.

As the chapters have come in, it has become abundantly clear that this celebration is paying tribute to a man whose influence under God spanned the world. We felt that this was the church celebrating and paying tribute to God's servant, to whom an enormous debt of gratitude was owed. One or two tributes came from those who never sat under James Philip's ministry within the walls of Holyrood Abbey Church, but who, through his written ministry, conferences or the tape ministry, had been blessed, encouraged and equipped for the ministry to which they had been called. The fields of service covered by the contributors (who of course represent only a tiny selection of those significantly influenced by Jim's ministry) have been very wide: ministers for the gospel; nurses, doctors and consultants in hospitals worldwide; lecturers and professors; authors and church administrators; fishermen and tradesmen. Jim's ministry has been of the stature that not many decades ago would have been recognised by an Honorary D.D. of a Scottish university.

Those of us who have been members of Holyrood accepted almost unthinkingly the huge amount of effort that James Philip poured into his working week. Not that he was a workaholic. He was too human and loved his family too much for that. When his children needed him he re-arranged his work schedule so that Saturdays could be spent with the family. Mary Philip once said, 'Jim would never go upstairs one at a time, when two was so much quicker.' That attitude typified his service within the congregation. How else could he have preached two full sermons every Sunday, expounded a biblical passage for nearly an hour on a Wednesday, conducted the Saturday Prayer Meeting, produced Bible Reading Notes for three hundred and sixty-five days a year, ninety percent of the time with new material, and kept up a prodigious correspondence with missionaries across the world? Small wonder that eight hundred copies of the Congregational Record were mailed all over the world every month, in addition to the two to three hundred taken to every member of the congregation.

Such a wide-ranging ministry was not achieved single-handedly, and he would be the first to pay tribute to the dedicated band whose commitment was almost as single-minded as his. There were secretaries, typists, printers, assemblers, tape-recorder operators, mailing helpers, pastoral visitors, innumerable helpers and supporters, who played their part week by week, month by month, year by year; not to mention the prayer warriors whose commitment to intercessory prayer undergirded all that was done, at home and in many situations overseas. They were good followers, but this book pays tribute to their leader, a quiet, shy, modest man, never the 'big personality' such as some of God's servants have been. He would have said with John the Baptist, speaking of our Lord, 'He must increase, but I must decrease.'

Mention has been made of James's wife Mary, who after their marriage in November 1960 became a true help-mate in the work and ministry. A bachelor minister has many lonely battles and wounds to endure, which he can share with very few. Mary's partnership in life was also a great partnership in the gospel, and brought Jim additional strength, courage and comfort, in his ministry in the congregation and beyond. The coming of their two children, William and Jennifer, brought great joy to the Manse, and also to the congregation, and gave a new sensitivity to Jim's ministry to the children in the congregation. The children of those early years have now grown up, and have since brought their own families for baptism.

We want to pay special tribute to the Revd Philip Hair for his full support and encouragement throughout the planning and preparation of this work, to all the contributors for their willing and eager support, inevitably in the midst of busy lives, to the proof readers and also to Mr William Mackenzie of

Christian Focus Publications and his staff, whose total support and sympathy with our aims have made it all possible. Finally our grateful thanks to our loving heavenly Father whose help, guidance, strength and encouragement have been ours in abundant measure from the outset of the work.

D.F.W. D.G.S.
October 2001

CONTRIBUTORS

Eric Alexander Minister of St George's Tron, Glasgow 1972-97; previously of Loudoun East, Newmilns; a member of James Philip's Bible Class in Springburn Hill, Glasgow. Graduate of Glasgow University.

Martin Allen Minister of Chryston Parish Church, Glasgow, since 1977; previously Education and Training Officer for Scottish Gas. Graduate of St Andrews and Edinburgh and of Covenant Theological Seminary, St Louis.

Peter Balla Head of the New Testament Department, Faculty of Theology, Károli Gáspár Reformed University, Budapest, Hungary, and Associate Pastor at the Reformed Congregation at Szabadság tér (Freedom Square) in Budapest. Graduate of Reformed Theological Academy in Budapest and University of Edinburgh.

Monty Barker Adjunct Professor at Union Biblical Seminary, Pune; South Asia Institute of Advanced Christian Studies, Bangalore; and Jubilee Memorial Bible College, Madras, India; previously Consultant psychiatrist to the United Bristol Hospitals Trust and University Lecturer in Bristol, St Andrews and Dundee. Elder in Steeple Church, Dundee during the 1960s. Graduate of St Andrews University.

William Black Minister at Stornoway High Church since 1997; formerly minister of Durness Kinlochbervie and O.M.F. missionary in Korea. Graduate of Aberdeen and Edinburgh Universities.

Warren Beattie With OMF International, teaching Missiology and Biblical Studies at Discipleship Training Centre, Singapore;

previously in South Korea, teaching at a Christian university, and minister of an international congregation in Pusan. Graduate of Edinburgh University.

Nigel Cameron Executive Chairman, Centre for Bioethics and Public Policy, London; Dean, Wilberforce Forum, Washington, DC; Principal, Strategic Futures Group, LLC, Deerfield, Illinois; previously Warden, Rutherford House, Edinburgh 1981-91, and Associate Minister, Holyrood Abbey Church 1981-85. Graduate of Cambridge and Edinburgh Universities.

Marion Conacher Appointed a medical missionary of the Church of Scotland in 1963 to serve in India; on retirement thirty years later awarded the MBE for services to nursing and the community. Trained in Edinburgh Royal Infirmary and Glasgow Royal Maternity Hospital.

Sinclair Ferguson Minister of St George's Tron Church, Glasgow since 1998; previously Professor of Systematic Theology in Westminster Theological Seminary, Philadelphia. Graduate of Aberdeen University.

Bill Fraser General Practitioner in private practice in Swaziland; formerly served in Swaziland as Medical Director of prison services (1987–90) and as orthopaedic surgeon (1980–87) and in Zambia (1973–6). Member of the Royal College of Surgeons of England and Licentiate, Royal College of Physicians of London.

Philip Hair Minister of Holyrood Abbey Church, Edinburgh since 1998; previously minister of Lochbroom and Ullapool Church of Scotland. Graduate of Edinburgh University.

Ian Hamilton Minister of Cambridge Presbyterian Church (Evangelical Presbyterian Church in England and Wales); previously of Loudoun Church of Scotland, Newmilns, Ayrshire. Graduate of Strathclyde and Edinburgh Universities.

Douglas Kelly Professor of Systematic Theology at Reformed Theological Seminary, Charlotte, North Carolina, and previously at Jackson, Mississippi. Graduate of the Universities of North Carolina, Chapel Hill, Lyons, Edinburgh, and Tübingen.

Francis Lyall Professor of Public Law at the University of Aberdeen; for thirty years Clerk to the Deacons Court of Gilcomston South Church, Aberdeen. Graduate of the Universities of Aberdeen and McGill (Montreal).

Jeremy Middleton Minister of Davidson's Mains Parish Church, Edinburgh; previously at Kildrum Parish Church, Cumbernauld. Graduate of Edinburgh University.

George M. Philip Minister of Sandyford Henderson Memorial Church, Glasgow, from 1956 until retirement in 1996; James Philip's younger brother. Graduate of Aberdeen University.

William Philip Ministry Secretary of the Proclamation Trust, London; practised General Internal Medicine and Cardiology in Aberdeen, before training for the Church of Scotland ministry. James Philip's son. Graduate of Aberdeen University.

Kenneth Ross General Secretary of the Church of Scotland Board of World Mission; formerly Professor of Theology at the University of Malawi. Graduate of Edinburgh University.

David Searle Warden, Rutherford House, Edinburgh; previously minister of Newhills, Larbert Old, Hamilton Road Bangor Presbyterian Church, N.Ireland. Graduate of St Andrews and Aberdeen Universities.

David Stay Servicing Supervisor, Edinburgh Royal Infirmary, 1974-97; formerly Test Engineer Ferranti Ltd 1961-74. Member and Elder of Holyrood Abbey Church for many years. Editor of the Congregational Record and Co-ordinator of tape ministry. Higher National Certificate from Southampton University.

Howard Taylor Chaplain to Heriot-Watt University and lecturer in Moral Philosophy and the Science-Religion Interface; previously served in Malawi, then at Innellan and Toward in Argyll, and at St. David's Knightswood, Glasgow. Graduate of Nottingham, Edinburgh and Aberdeen Universities.

David Temple Superintendent of the Irish Mission of the Presbyterian Church in Ireland; formerly minister in Torry, Aberdeen, and Portglenone and Ballygomartin, Northern Ireland. Graduate of Trinity College, Dublin, and New College, Edinburgh.

James Watt Retired Bible Society representative for north-east Scotland; formerly self-employed fisherman and boatbuilder. Session Clerk in Gardenstown Church of Scotland for thirty years.

David Wright Professor of Patristic and Reformed Christianity at New College, University of Edinburgh, where he has taught since 1964. Graduate of Cambridge and Edinburgh Universities.

Part 1

The Making of The Man

James Philip the Man

George M. Philip

James Philip was not born into an academic or well-to-do family. There had been a James Philip, born in 1777, son of Alexander Philip and Isabel Mackenzie, in the parish of Garioch in Aberdeenshire. By 1850 the family had moved to Bankhead in the parish of Newhills some four miles from Aberdeen. In 1873 another James Philip was born who was to be the father of our James. He was clever at school and the headmaster was eager for him to go on in education but, because his father had died and someone had to bring in wages, he left school at the age of twelve to begin work as an apprentice in the lithographic printing department of the local paper mill in Bucksburn in the parish of Newhills. He retired from the same department sixty-two years later. When he was 24 he married the daughter of the mill manager. Their first child, James, lived only one month. A second child, John, was born in 1901 but James's wife died of tuberculosis in 1905.

The mother of our James Philip was Isabella Mackenzie, whose family tree can also be traced back to 1777. She was born in 1883 in Auchendoir, Aberdeenshire. Both her parents had died by the time she was nine and she was brought up by an aunt and uncle. She started work as a servant in Craig Castle and later in life she recounted to her children how Sunday evening Gospel services were held in the stone-flagged kitchen of the castle. Having moved to Aberdeen she was in the Salvation Army and it was while she was singing a solo at an open-air meeting that James Philip, not a church-goer, first saw her. They were married in 1917. Their first child died, then Moira was born, then James, and then George (the present writer). Neither parent went to church although for a time mother continued contact with Salvation Army week-day meetings. In his seventies father became a regular Sunday morning attender at Gilcomston South Church and had a great regard for the Revd William Still.

My brother James Philip, who was to become minister of Gardenstown and then of Holyrood Abbey Church, Edinburgh, was born in the village of Bucksburn on 11 January 1922. It was a dull, somewhat characterless village with little of cultural life. At the village school (1927-34) James was obviously clever, and so for secondary school, with the help of a bursary, he moved to Robert Gordon's College in Aberdeen, one of the best schools in the north-east (1934-9). This must have been quite a strain on the family's finances because money was always in short supply, but it was a matter of pride for his parents. He did well at school and he was also very gifted musically, although he resented the fact that music lessons were on a Saturday when others were at sport. The church Boys Brigade Company used him to the full for all manner of activities, for which he usually played by ear. While still a teenager he played the church organ at a series of meetings led by the Church of Scotland Evangelist, the Revd D.P. Thomson, and during that campaign he signed a decision card.

It was no surprise when James went to Aberdeen University and graduated M.A. in 1942. During his course he became persuaded of his call to the ministry but, not having declared that intention at the start, and since it was wartime, he was called up for service in the RAF as soon as he graduated. He tells of an early experience of being billeted on a farm in North Wales where no-one spoke English, but his difficulties were a source of amusement to him rather than complaint. In due time he saw active service overseas and finally was invalided home from Burma suffering from rheumatic fever. He resumed his studies for his Divinity course and it was during his time at University that his friendship with William Still began, a deep spiritual bond that lasted a lifetime. Right through his ministry James acknowledged his debt to the ministry, counsel, friendship and guidance of William Still, but few know the immense debt William Still owed in many ways to James in the early and continuing ministry in Gilcomston South Church, Aberdeen, when there was so much criticism and opposition from formal churchmen and evangelical Christians alike. The loyal, unflinching support James gave encouraged, guided and at times restrained that most gifted minister who needed reassurance more than most people realised.

James was licensed by the Presbytery of Aberdeen in January 1948 and served his Probationary period as assistant to the Revd Dr William Fitch in Springburn Hill Parish Church, Glasgow, a congregation of over 2000 members, many of whom seldom if ever attended church. During the ten-year ministry of Dr Fitch his first assistant was William Still, halfway through he had James and for the last year, the present writer. James was ordained as assistant by Glasgow Presbytery in February 1948.

On 21 December 1949 James was inducted to the parish of Gardenstown, a small but prosperous fishing village in Banffshire, with a congregation of 218 members. His years there revealed various aspects of his character, not least his patient, uncomplaining spirit and his astonishing dedication to the people and the work entrusted to him by God. In those days the minimum stipend was meagre, paid in two half-yearly instalments from Edinburgh, expenses largely non-existent and a car totally beyond his means. It took two buses to travel to Aberdeen for hospital visitation and regular visits were expected. In the congregation there were about fifty families with the surname West, and a similar number called Watt, so that naturally people were known by their 'by-names'. Such was James's pastoral capacity that he knew them all and how they were related.

His preaching in those days was, as it continued to be right through his ministry, biblical and expository and at times vivid and dramatic. One Sunday evening in the summer he preached on the judgement of Sodom and Gomorrah. At the end of the sermon he urged the people when they left the church to look across to the steep cliff face, where a great area of the gorse was burning fiercely with clouds of dark smoke, and to remember God's day of judgement and to be ready. That sermon and image have remained with me for fifty years. There were spells when not a Sunday went past without someone being converted. It was not without great cost, but the depth of the personal and spiritual battle was shared with only a few and is not for public curiosity. James knew a lot of what Paul meant when he said, 'I die daily.' On a lighter note it is good to remember that in those days a great many of the fishermen came to church on Sunday evenings dressed in their dark jerseys and sat upstairs in the gallery. Although they knew the gospel they were not believers but they sang the old Redemption Hymns with great gusto. When a man was converted the whole congregation knew at once because the next Sunday he would sit downstairs 'properly dressed', white shirt, collar and tie. The signs of saving faith are many and varied! The arrival in the village of a new school teacher was the start of a friendship of highest quality with Tom Swanston, a friendship that deepened significantly after Tom's conversion. It continued through Tom's call to the ministry and his subsequent powerful preaching in the West Church in Inverness and lasted right to the time of Tom's death.

I, for one, always believed Edinburgh was the place for my brother and it was no surprise when he was called to Holyrood Abbey Church, being inducted on 15 January 1958. The various aspects of the ministry there are spoken of in other chapters of this book. All through the forty years the diligence, consistency and care of his pastoral work continued, as did his biblical ministry. Two preachings every Sunday, again at the midweek service, a 'word' of exhortation at the Saturday Prayer Meeting, a full set of Daily Bible Reading Notes and an instructive pastoral letter each month, plus addresses at student meetings and a variety of other commitments signify a full and demanding life. In all his pastoral counselling there was both care and strict confidentiality, something which, alas, is not always given by ministers. Many of us envy his ability to recall detailed quotations from his wide reading in theology and biography and have been impressed by his going right to his bookshelves for the appropriate volume and the exact page. Unlike many ministers, old and young, he never made wild or extreme statements. He always believed that the truth of the Word of God made its own impact. There was a carefulness in his scholarship. In dealing with difficult and controversial topics he emphasised that in our affirmations we must go as far as Scripture clearly goes but no further. In discussions at gatherings of ministers you could watch him listening, taking it all in and eventually intervening with the words, 'Yes, but . . .' In many ways, although some recognised his worth, expressed it and gave thanks for it, in general terms in the evangelical world his calibre, contribution and influence were not fully acknowledged, especially by those who ought to have known better.

In Presbytery and General Assembly he played his part as he had promised in his ordination vows and in this he showed an example to other ministers. James Philip was quite clear that battles for the gospel have to be fought in the right places. In his years of service at a senior level in the area of the selection schools for candidates for the ministry, his biblical and theological position was respected because of its balance, integrity and human fairness. In that realm, as in others, he commended the gospel. For virtually half a century of comprehensive ministry, spoken and written, he went on with the dogged determination that was part of his character, not seeking a name for himself but being from beginning to end a man rightly described as valiant for the truth.

Of course, no article on the man and his ministry would be complete without reference to Mary his wife, who has been his loving partner, support and encouragement in every way. Mary Frances Moffat was born on 4 January 1935, the daughter of Unwin and Sheila Moffat (née Townsend). Her father was a great-grandson of Robert Moffat, the pioneer missionary in South Africa and David Livingstone's father-in-law. Mary trained as a doctor in Edinburgh and later specialised in psychiatry. James and Mary were married on 19 November 1960. If ever there was a life-long and romantic marriage it is theirs. God, who said it was not good for man to be alone, certainly brought this woman to this man and the human story of how it all came about is really quite thrilling. They are the ones to tell the story. With William and Jennifer and now six grandchildren we see what a real Christian family is. The love and respect they have for each other is a joy to behold and an example to all.

In many places world-wide there are those who stand up and give thanks to God for the man James Philip, his life, his ministry and his example of commitment to Christ and the gospel. In many ways he is a very private person, who does not easily let it be known just how sensitive he is and how deeply he feels things. Through all his ministry his faithfulness to God, his Word and his people was indeed costly. But that meant that countless people were ministered to in their need with great sensitivity and tenderness.

At his retirement gathering, with Holyrood Abbey Church full to capacity, I, as his younger brother, had the privilege of giving the closing address. After speaking of the grace of the man and the thoroughness of his ministry I quoted from Hebrews 13:7: 'Remember your leaders who have spoken the word of God to you, whose faith follow, considering the outcome of their conduct.' James Philip is a good man to copy.

The Gardenstown Years

James Watt

During 1949 the Church in Gardenstown, Banffshire, became vacant when the Revd J D Wallace, who had been minister for seventeen years, accepted a call to Abbotsford Chalmers Church of Scotland, Glasgow. The normal procedure for a vacancy was set in motion, an Interim Moderator appointed, a Vacancy Committee formed, and the search began. The spiritual state of the congregation at that time was rather encouraging; a number of young people had been converted and come into the fellowship. What kind of person was required to fill the vacant charge? It was felt we needed a younger man, someone who would relate to the new converts, yet mature enough to guide the fellowship forward, but most importantly, a man of God, someone who would preach the Word without fear or favour. Where could such a person be found? This was made a matter for earnest prayer by the Vacancy Committee and also by the congregation.

About this time some of the young people of the fellowship were visiting Gilcomston South Church, Aberdeen. It was there that some had come to faith in Christ, under the ministry of American Youth for Christ. Through this contact they had come to know the Revd James Philip, who was a great friend of the Revd William Still, minister of Gilcomston, and had been greatly influenced by Mr Still and his ministry. Mr Philip was assistant minister of Springburn Hill Church of Scotland, Glasgow. His time there being completed, he was ready for his first charge. To cut a long story short, he was contacted by the Vacancy Committee and was eventually asked to become sole nominee. In due course, he preached, was accepted unanimously and was inducted to the charge on 21 December 1949.

Thus began a new ministry in Gardenstown, and one that was to bear much fruit in the coming years. Looking back, we have great cause to give thanks to God for the coming of his servant.

The Early Days of his Ministry

It was not very long before it became apparent that the ministry of Mr Philip was going to have a profound effect upon the fellowship, indeed upon the community as a whole. Here was a man who was totally committed to the work of God in Gardenstown, and who would give his all to see that this would be accomplished. He was a person of great ability, both intellectually and practically. He also liked everything to be done properly and in an orderly way, taking an interest in every detail, and personally supervised every aspect of the work and life of the congregation.

Right at the outset of his ministry he initiated a monthly letter to the congregation, a letter of challenge and encouragement, to all who were involved, or should be involved in the work, with a kindly word to the older members, and especially to the sick. With the letter went a series of Bible readings and comments, prepared by himself, to encourage his people in the reading and study of God's Word. This was carried on right to the end of his ministry in Gardenstown, and proved a great inspiration and blessing to many.

What was the main thrust of his ministry? It soon became obvious that this consisted of two things, the systematic and faithful preaching of the Word, and prayer. He emphasised that the success or failure of the work depended upon these two things. So it was that people were encouraged, even urged, to attend every diet of worship, and also be at the prayer meeting, as these were the things that would nourish and build up people to Christian maturity, and make them effective in their Christian witness. James Philip's utter dedication and truly Bible-centred ministry soon resulted in fruit-bearing. In less than two years, over fifty people were added to the fellowship by profession of faith. In a congregation of approximately two hundred this was really amazing. Not that numbers are all important, but surely it bears testimony to the fact that the faithful ministry of the Word was bearing fruit.

Of course, very early in the ministry we realised that where God is working, Satan is also active. One of Mr Philip's many sayings was, 'The same sun that melts wax, hardens clay.' This soon became obvious in Gardenstown. A number of people who resisted the message left the fellowship, and went elsewhere, where the preaching was more to their liking.

Mr Philip also took charge of the Sunday School, and prepared a whole series of lessons covering both Old and New Testaments. These became a blessing to teachers and pupils alike, and continued to be used in Sunday School many years after he left Gardenstown. I can bear testimony to the fact that they were a great blessing to me, and a great help in understanding the Scriptures. During the many years I was superintendent of Sunday School I used Mr Philip's notes, as I could never find anything as suitable. Another great feature of his ministry was his talks to the children on Sunday mornings. He expounded stories like Bunyan's *Pilgrim's Progress* week by week, and both adults and children alike eagerly looked forward to this. These were the days of great blessing as the Spirit of God was working in the hearts of many people.

Consolidating the Work

One of the things Mr Philip continually emphasised was the importance of prayer, in the life both of the individual and of the fellowship. He encouraged all, both young and old, to be at the Saturday evening prayer meeting, and would say that the strength or weakness of this meeting was a good spiritual barometer to assess the state of the Church. People who had never prayed in public were encouraged to do so, and others who had been taking part were reprimanded for using too long prayers, or praying for too many things. He encouraged people to focus on one or two items, and then to pray specifically about them. He also said that prayer should be spontaneous, without long pauses between prayers, as this caused people's minds to wander to other things, and thus killed the spirit of the meeting. One of the things that was given priority was world mission. We were encouraged to take a deep personal interest in the work of many missionaries, and to support them both prayerfully and practically. It was by this means that the Church and fellowship were strengthened and built up spiritually.

There were of course disappointments. Some did not respond to the teaching of the Word, or showed little or no interest in prayer. Nevertheless, this was a time when God was working in Gardenstown and many lives were being changed and transformed.

One can remember well the joy and also the challenge it was to be in God's house on a Lord's day morning. The opening praise was sung so heartily, with hymns like 'Where high the heavenly temple stands'. Then came his opening prayer, so uplifting and vibrant, that one was brought into the very throne room of heaven. All this prepared the people for the ministry of the Word that was to follow. The feeling when one left the church was, 'It was good for us to be in the House of God.'

The preaching of the gospel on a Sunday evening was very special. People were conscious of the moving of the Spirit as he preached the Word, and made personal application of the message to his hearers, pleading in the words of Matthew 23:37, 'O Jerusalem, Jerusalem, you who kill the prophets, and stone those sent to you, how often I have longed to gather your children together, as a hen gathers her chicks under her wings, but you were not willing.' Thus he emphasised the privileges that Gardenstown had enjoyed, just like Jerusalem, and yet many had not responded to the message.

His quotations from many of the saints of former days were but a token of his literary knowledge, quoting from Samuel Chadwick, John Newton, Charles Finney, Samuel Rutherford, the Bonars, John and Charles Wesley, Amy Carmichael, D.L. Moody, C.H. Spurgeon, C.S. Lewis, and many others. Another aspect of his preaching was how many wonderful illustrations he used in the application of his message.

We have discussed James Philip's preaching and prayer, but what of his pastoral work? He was someone who gave himself wholeheartedly to the visitation of his flock, especially the older people, the housebound, and the sick. He had no car, and all had to be done on foot, walking up and down the Brae, and round the Bay to Crovie, to visit some of the elderly people who lived there. These visits were a great blessing and uplift to many a dear soul. Truly his whole life was given to the work that God had called him to, and God honoured him for his faithfulness.

As a preacher and teacher, he was much sought after, but very often would turn down invitations, because he believed that God had called him to Gardenstown, and it was there that the main thrust of his ministry had to be. One of the things that disturbed him a little was the fact that no one from the fellowship had offered for full-time Christian service, despite all the preaching and teaching they had received. After he left Gardenstown, there were a few who responded in this way, and no doubt one of the reasons they did so was because of his faithful Bible-centred ministry. Two young women went as missionaries to Africa, and one young man became a minister in the Church of Scotland. There were others who served God faithfully in other ways and bore a faithful testimony in what God had called them to do and be.

So as the years passed, the work quietened down. There were fewer conversions than in the early days, but God had consolidated the work, and in the fellowship there were quite a few who could bear testimony to a deep spiritual work in their lives.

The Final Years

To many it had become obvious that God had a greater sphere of service for Mr Philip than that of a minister in a small village church. About this time opportunity was given for two broadcast services from Gardenstown Church. In everything relating to the work of God Mr Philip insisted that it should be done to the best of our ability with prayerful and practical preparation. The date for these broadcasts was Sunday 1 July 1956. The morning service was broadcast on the BBC Home Service, the evening on the Overseas Service. Space allows the inclusion here of the text of only the evening sermon:

Evening Sermon

The Healing of the Lame Man (Acts 3: 1-9).

I wonder if you've ever noticed how disturbingly personal the Bible is? It declares that 'God so loved the world', yet it contains an amazing number of personal encounters between individual men and women and Christ. It is vague and rather comforting to be always speaking about the needs of humanity, for then you can always hide your own personal needs from view. But it is individual men and women that God deals with, and this story is a case in point. It is upon a man's personal needs that our attention is focussed, almost as if nobody else in the world needed help but himself. That is always how God deals with people – never mind the people round about you, He says, it is you I want to speak with.

Now it seems to me that God is speaking to you and to me tonight in this story. In the lame man at the gate of the temple, it may be that we have a disturbingly realistic picture of our own spiritual need.

Here is a man, lame from birth, with all that implies – a stunted boyhood, youth's hopes blasted, manhood withered. What a travesty of life, what a shadow of what might have been! A caricature of humanity! Do you think that was God's plan for his life? Never! God planned a *man,* whole, noble, fully developed, possessed of all his powers, but something went wrong. And so it is, the Bible says, with sin. God made man in His own image, but something has gone wrong, tragically wrong, sin has laid siege to man's soul, and life has become crippled and cramped, always falling short, always missing the mark. There is nothing so true in the life of man as the crippling power of sin.

Have you ever seen the remains of an ancient castle, standing gaunt and derelict in the highlands of Scotland? There it is, broken down and in ruins, but here and there we see traces of its former grandeur, a tower, or an arch, or a stately column, just enough to remind us of the noble building it once was. A ruin, yes, but a magnificent ruin. Man is like that. Here and there we can see the marks, faint suggestions and reminders of a glory that has faded. Oh, the crippling power of sin! I wonder if in this story there is a picture of your life? Christ once told a story about a lost coin. It bore the image and superscription of the king upon it; there was a job for it to do, a purpose to fulfil. But it was lost in the dust of the house, useless.

Is your life like that? You once bore the image and superscription of the King of kings. There was a purpose for your life, a job for you to do, but that purpose is unfulfilled, and God's plan for your life has not even begun. You are like the man in the story, a crippled and broken life. Listen! The good news of the gospel is that Jesus Christ can make men whole again, and Peter cries to us over the centuries, 'In the name of Jesus Christ of Nazareth, rise up and walk.' The apostle called for faith in Christ, and it was faith in Christ that brought wholeness to this broken life. And down the long years men have proved again and again that the power of Christ has remained unchanged. He is the same yesterday, today and forever.

> He breaks the power of cancelled sin
> And sets the prisoner free.

And there is no life so broken, so crippled or wasted, that it cannot be made whole by the Saviour of men, if only men have faith in Him. 'In the name of Jesus Christ of Nazareth, I say unto you, rise up and walk.'

But there is also a message here to many within the Church itself. The story seems to mirror the experience of many who have named the name of Christ and owned Him as their Lord. Here is a man, begging for a living. Do you think that was God's plan for his life? Do you think that is God's plan for any man in a world of plenty? Never!

Yet there he was, poverty-stricken and destitute. And there are many Christians today just like that man, begging for a living when they might be living like kings in the unsearchable riches of Christ. If there is one thing abundantly clear in our time it is that a great part of our failure in Christian work and witness is that we suffer from a poverty-stricken spiritual experience. It is not that we are lacking in methods and equipment – rarely has the Church been so magnificently equipped as today – it is that our souls are dry and parched instead of being like a well-watered garden. It is not that we are not working hard enough; we toil and labour at God's work, like Peter and the other disciples fishing all night with nothing to show for their labour. We have not learned that the secret of effectual service is not overwork but overflow. The story was told at the General Assembly last month about a girl who had thought of missionary service, but withdrew, because, she said, she did not think she had a faith worth passing on. Is that a picture of your life? Are you like that lame man, poverty-stricken in spiritual experience, begging for a living? Is God revealing to you in this story the basic problem in your life? I wonder what it is in your spiritual life that has made you like this? Does your lameness mean that you no longer walk with God? Do you sometimes sing

> Where is the blessedness I knew,
> When first I saw the Lord?

Is it that your devotional life has become dull and forced? Have you neglected God's Word and the place of prayer? Have idols, things or people, gradually and imperceptibly crept in, and drawn you away from the Lord? Ah, how easy it is to become impoverished in spiritual life, how easy to lose the glow, until we are reduced to poverty and make do on scraps when we used to live royally. Or is it perhaps that you have never known the vitality and power of the Christian life of victory?

Christ can change that state of affairs. He knows how desperately dissatisfied with your spiritual life you are. He knows the secret longings of your heart for a new lease of life and vitality. And he is willing and able to lift you to a new plane of life even now. 'In the name of Jesus of Nazareth, I say unto you, rise up and walk!'

The call is for faith. And there is the challenge. For real faith demands surrender; it means yielding wholly to Christ, in a new obedience and devotion, putting away everything that has hindered. Aye, there's the rub. It may not be possible to decide what circumstances had led to this poor man's lameness, but perhaps you know only too well what has led to yours.

Is this the truth of the matter? Are you like this lame man in your spiritual experience because in fact you have been holding out against God? He has not been allowed to have His way in your life. There is a resistance in your heart to His good and perfect will. You have refused the real challenge of discipleship, to take up the cross and follow Christ. Ah, the faith that appropriates all His fullness and brings men into victorious, abundant life, is a faith that puts Christ on a solitary throne in the heart. In the Christian life we die to live, die to sin and self, and all that competes with His Lordship. He will brook no rivals. If He is not Lord of all, He is not Lord at all. A missionary was once heard to give radiant testimony to the reality of the power of Christ in personal life, and when she had finished, someone whispered behind her to a companion, 'I'd give everything I had to have a testimony like that.' The missionary, overhearing the comment, turned and quietly said, 'That is exactly what it cost me.'

Is that your problem? Is that why you are begging for a living? We need to recall the story of the other lame man, in John's Gospel, at the pool of Bethesda. To him Jesus said: 'Wilt thou be made whole?' That is the challenge. And, in the quietness of this moment, Christ awaits your answer. Are you willing? Then, 'In the name of Jesus of Nazareth, I say unto you, rise up and walk!'

The response nationwide to the morning service was tremendous, the headlines in the press next day being: 'A Word to the Nation.' Letters were received from all over the country: Lerwick, Kirkwall, Evanton, Skye, Banff, Fraserburgh, Aberdeen, Stonehaven, Kincardine O'Neil, Ballater, Dundee, Perth, Fife, Kinross, Stirling, Glasgow, Airdrie, Motherwell, Larkhall, Lanark, Ayr, Edinburgh, Hawick, Stranraer, Belfast, Londonderry, Wigan, Lowestoft, Dorset. They came from all the different denominations: Free Church, United Free Church, Church of Scotland, Brethren, Episcopal, Methodist and Mission Halls. These letters came from people of all walks of life, expressing their appreciation for the blessing they received. With regard to the evening service, letters were received from various parts of the world: Jamaica, Peru, Trinidad, South Africa, Morocco, Cyprus, all expressing the great blessing received and the challenge from such a clear presentation of the gospel. Some of the letters came from missionaries whom we knew and prayed for. Some came from people who were passing through difficult times and expressed how they were blessed and encouraged by the message. Mr Philip's response was,

> For all this we give thanks to God. It is His doing, both the bestowing of blessing upon the many who heard, and also the prompting of so many kind letters of encouragement, and it ought to cheer us not a little at this particular point of our work and witness, that He should have given so liberally of His own grace. In the light of what has been done, and the blessing that has been ours in working for Him, we humbly say to God be all the glory.

Surely these words of James Philip give a true picture of the deep and profound commitment he had to the work of God, both in Gardenstown and indeed to the ends of the earth.

There is much more that could be said, but surely what has already been said is sufficient to give a deep and lasting impression of the nature of his ministry, and his total commitment to the work of God. Over the years many had come to faith in Christ and had been given a solid foundation upon which to build their spiritual lives. Others had been deepened in the faith and given a greater desire to live lives that would be both glorifying to God, and beneficial to the life of the fellowship. It may be that there were some who showed little response, but one thing is sure: this was not because they had not been amply taught the truths of the gospel.

Then in early 1958 he told us he had accepted a call to Holyrood Abbey Church in Edinburgh. It did not come as a total surprise, as many had felt for a while that his time in Gardenstown was drawing to a close. This however did little to soften the blow, that this man, who had so ably ministered and been our Pastor for the past eight years, was about to leave us to take up a fresh challenge in the work to which God had called him. Thus we came to the concluding days of a ministry that had had a profound effect upon Gardenstown as a whole, and upon the congregation of the Church in particular. Many people could bear testimony that their lives had been changed and transformed, all because of the ministry of this man of God who had been our minister for eight years. What was his own assessment of the years spent in Gardenstown? I conclude with his own words taken from his final letter to the congregation:

Of course there have been failures and mistakes. At the last we must all acknowledge ourselves to be unprofitable servants, and no one is more conscious than I am of unworthiness in this regard. And yet, even in the dark experiences of what might not have been but for our own sinfulness, is it not true that we have learned much, aye, and – such is the sovereignty of God – profited much. He who turns the wrath of man to praise Him also overrules our folly and turns it unto good. Great is His faithfulness! For all that ought not to have been in the past years we ask for forgiveness, and commit it to Him whose

41

mercy is greater than all our sin. . . .

And now I close. 'I take you to record this day that I am pure from the blood of all men. For I have not shunned to declare unto you all the Counsel of God. Take heed therefore . . . I commend you to God, and to the word of His grace, which is able to build you up, and to give you an inheritance among all them which are sanctified.'

Part 2

The Holyrood Years

'A Man of Weight'

Martin Allen

Thomas Chalmers, one of the greatest of the evangelical Scottish church leaders in the nineteenth century, apparently assessed the worth of an individual by raising one invariable question. Chalmers in his broad Fife accent (he hailed from Anstruther), would ask, 'Is he a man of wecht?' My contention is that James Philip was 'a man of wecht' or weight, substance, in respect of his definitive ministry of forty years in Holyrood Abbey. I want to explain and expand that contention by highlighting the 'weightiness' of Jim Philip's preaching content and style while trying to draw some lessons for the present and future generation of Scottish preachers.

In reflecting to start with on the content of the preaching, I recall the first time that I attended Holyrood Abbey Church and listened to James Philip. The year was 1964, the Sunday before Christmas, and it was an evening service. That day I had moved to Edinburgh to begin seven years' employment at the Scottish Gas Headquarters, after graduating from St Andrews University. The sermon text was John 1:14, 'The Word became flesh and dwelt among us.' The theme of the message was the meaning of the incarnation. Looking back over the thirty-five years and more, I still remember the impact made on an impressionable young Christian on the verge of his working career. My mind was stimulated, far beyond what I had been used to within the context of a church service. I was made to think about the biblical text and its meaning within the context of the prologue in John's Gospel and the wider backcloth of the New Testament teaching on the person and mission of Jesus Christ. I would be dishonest if I claimed that I recall the sermon points as if yesterday. However, I do remember the mental and spiritual exhilaration experienced in being exposed to solid living biblical content. Subsequently, I became a member of the congregation, and later an elder and shared in the work and witness of the Church in the 1960s and early 1970s, before receiving a call to the ministry as a result of the preaching ministry at Holyrood. My reflections in this chapter relate particularly to this period of time.

It hardly needs emphasising that the weightiness of James Philip's ministry was sourced in its biblical content. His preaching became well known for its systematic, expository, biblical nature. Along with many others, I can recall several series through individual books of the Old and New Testaments. Jim Philip was convinced of the validity of Calvin's maxim, namely, that 'The whole Bible is needed to make a whole Christian.' Most parts of the Bible were preached or taught at Holyrood Abbey over the years, on Sunday mornings and evenings or Wednesdays midweek. Many parts were expounded many times, especially Paul's Epistle to the Romans. Listening was no easy exercise. The preacher expected his hearers to have open Bibles and to follow the message from the text. The expositions were unstructured, in the sense that they contained no neatly arranged headings or sub-headings. James Philip instead allowed the Scriptures to express form and shape as he followed through the interpretation and explanation of the consecutive verses in the stated passage. Thus the demand made by preacher upon the people in the pews was considerable in terms of concentration and assimilation for a period of approximately three-quarters of an hour. This was justified, he believed, because of the eternal significance of the subject matter and also because of the strenuous preparation, involving time, energy and prayer.

The content was also weighty in that it was theological. James Philip personally delighted in the doctrines of Reformed theology and his obvious joy in preaching was to draw out such doctrines from the Scripture text and then expand and explain them. He firmly believed that all Christians should be 'theologians' to the extent that they should desire knowledge of God, through the truth of God, to the glory of God, which was the basic task of theology. He gave a remarkable series of expository sermons on the Westminster Confession of Faith at the Wednesday midweek fellowship, over one winter, in the late 1960s. This was a time when the status of the Confession and much of its content were under attack from influential committees in the Church. The preacher worked his way through it chapter by chapter and in these massive and marvellous lectures highlighted the riches and glories of Reformed and Puritan theology.

Over the years, the congregation became used to lengthy quotations from favoured theologians during the course of sermons. These included Calvin, James Denney, Emil Brunner and of course C.S. Lewis. Who can forget from the last mentioned dramatic readings of the story of the little Red Lizard (emphasising the necessity for mortification of sin) and the amazing anecdote concerning Mrs Fitchet (illustrating the dangers of legalistic pseudo-love). These quotations were hardly sound bites. The congregation had to listen carefully and at length, if they were to get the point. However, if they persisted, the point stuck.

The preaching content in the late 1960s was also weighty in that it was prophetic. A friend of mine, a theological student from a different denomination, used to refer to James Philip as the prophet. 'What was "the prophet" preaching on yesterday?', he would ask on a Monday morning. The nickname was not used altogether lightly, but with a respect which deepened over the years and contained the instinctive recognition of a dynamic characteristic of Jim Philip's preaching. This student and many of us sitting under the ministry were vividly aware of what we might call 'Thus saith the Lord' preaching! It was prophetic not primarily in the sense of being predictive of the future course of events, although that element was not absent, but rather, preaching that spoke to our times and to the issues of the day. I always felt that the preacher was in his element in expounding the major or minor prophets or the book of Revelation. He would most relevantly draw parallels between the scriptural life situation within the text and the current matters of concern in church and nation. General Assembly Sundays or rather the Sundays after the General Assembly were eagerly anticipated. Invariably, the atmosphere would be charged, as 'the prophet', in expounding the set Scripture passage, would apply the lessons to the woes and weals of the national church of our day.

Contemporary cultural matters were also addressed in many of the Holyrood sermons during the 1960s. Professor Callum Brown, in his recent book the *The Death of Christian Britain*, presents the thesis that the decline of the Christian church was not a slow line as is customarily held but a sudden thing from the 1960s onwards. 'In the 1960s, the institutional structures of cultural traditionalism started to crumble in Britain.'[1] Some readers may remember the '60s as the era of 'flower power', 'permissiveness' and the Beatles. It was the 'we've never had it so good' and 'wind of change' era in Prime Minister Harold Macmillan's famous or infamous words. It was also the 'Death of God' decade and the years when the Bishop of Woolwich's published views shocked traditionalists within the church. It was the period of the Profumo scandal which rocked the Macmillan Conservative government to the core. James Philip devastatingly brought God's Word to bear on all these issues and many more. He exposed the sin of church and nation, setting out the scriptural implications before highlighting the remedy. He could be amusing in his scathing denunciation of modern cultural changes in the world of art and music. When commenting on the modern 'musician', John Cage, who played his composition on a piano with the lid shut, James quoted the late Tom Swanston, 'He should be locked in one!'

This prophetic dimension of the pulpit preaching in Holyrood underlines the necessary relevance of authentic Bible teaching for the contemporary scene. It was this note among others which

1. Callum G. Brown, *The Death of Christian Britain* (London, 2000), 176.

drew many visitors to Holyrood in the 1960s and 1970s, not least crowds of University and College students.

A fourth note of the weighty content of Jim Philip's preaching ministry, it seems to me, was how it evoked response. That is to say the preacher always called for a response from the individual soul in respect of the word of salvation. This application of the message at a personal level invariably came at the end of the sermon, in the last five minutes or so. Sometimes the challenge or call to faith or obedience was given in the last moments of the message. The summons was often implicit in the development of the whole sermon, but made explicit in the closing call. The late Alan Flavelle, listening to James Philip's address at a Portstewart Convention meeting in Northern Ireland, remarked to me that the application at the end of the message was the logical and inevitable climax of the progressive development of the theme in the sermon.

During the short period in the sermon when the application to the individual was made there was a certain electric atmosphere in the building. This was the listening-for-pins-dropping time. People were on the edges of their seats, sometimes literally, as the great issues of heaven and hell, sin and salvation, faith and repentance were pressed home with urgency and love. The consciousness of God's near presence was very evident to the believers in the congregation – and sometimes to the unbelievers as well! I recall taking a colleague from the Gas Board on several occasions to evening services and he would scuttle away out the door at the end and freely admit that the preacher had 'got under his skin' and 'frightened the living daylights out of him'.

I remember in the late 1960s and early 1970s the tremendous sense of expectation that built up, particularly in connection with the evening series at Holyrood Abbey Church. In this period the Commonwealth Games were held in the adjacent stadium in Meadowbank, and before, during and after the games increased numbers attended the church services. The balcony used to be packed with the high side galleries filled. Those who attended over these years will never forget the awesome sense of God's reality in the preaching and particularly in the application part of the sermon.

This, then, was the weightiness of content in James Philip's ministry of the Word. There are some clear lessons to be learned for present and future generations of preachers. In the present Christian scene, what was once objective in God's being, what once stood over against the sinner, is either being lost or transformed into something to be discovered first and foremost in ourselves. It seems that often in contemporary public ministry, there is an over-emphasis on God's immanence and a diminished emphasis on his transcendence. The preaching ethos in today's church has often resulted in the proclamation of a God with whom we are on easy terms and whose reality is little different from our own. We who are in the pulpit today have so often been guilty of transforming the God of mercy into a God who is at our mercy. But a God who is merely there to satisfy our needs has no real authority to compel and will soon bore us. Human beings, made in God's image, are fundamentally moral beings, not consumers. The satisfaction of our psychological needs pales into insignificance compared with the enduring value of doing what is right.

Jim Philip's Holyrood pulpit ministry over forty years highlighted the transcendence of God and the accountability of humans. Present preaching must recover the worth of these weighty dimensions. David F. Wells has famously coined the phrase 'the weightlessness of God' to describe much of current church life and contemporary Christian preaching.

> It is one of the defining marks of our time that God is now weightless. I do not mean by this that he is ethereal but rather that he has become unimportant. Those who assure the pollsters of their belief in God's existence may nonetheless consider him less interesting than television, his commands less authoritative than their appetites for affluence and influence, his judgement no more awe-inspiring than the evening news,

and his truth less compelling than the advertisers' sweet joy of flattery and lies. That is weightlessness. [2]

James Philip would fully share that view.

Of course it would be true to say that the cultural context of the first years of the twenty-first century is somewhat different from that of the major part of Jim Philip's ministry. We are told repeatedly that we have moved from a modern to a post-modern culture. If we take our present context seriously, then we will attempt, responsibly, to communicate unchanging truths and timeless principles in a package that will be appropriate and meaningful to post-modern people.

Thus there are some things about the Holyrood preaching of these forty years that we could not or would not imitate, in the same way as we would not with Spurgeon's sermons which belong to a Victorian culture. In our age we have, I believe, to win the attention of hearers from the outset of the sermon. We do not have the luxury of having the time to build up our argument and show the relevance of what we are teaching towards the end of the sermon. We also have to adapt to the story-telling milieu and imaginatively retell the text in modern garb. In addition, there is, I would hold, a greater need for the use of vivid, graphic, contemporary illustrations – what used to be known as notes, quotes and anecdotes. Application of biblical truth should be the key element in our preaching today, and thus we should make strenuous efforts in preparation to focus upon this aspect of the sermon. Here there can be no greater ideal to follow than that of the eighteenth-century theologian, Jonathan Edwards. It was said of him that 'all his doctrine was application and all his application was doctrine'. We need a huge amount of wisdom to follow that principle in preaching to post-modern people.

I would contend that the weightiness of James Philip's style could be seen and summarised in the one word, seriousness.

2. David F. Wells, *God in the Wasteland* (Grand Rapids, 1994), **88**.

The serious demeanour was evident in the call to worship, the selection of the opening item of praise (rarely any concession to modern hymnology at Holyrood) and the first public prayer. The worshipper in the pew was left in no doubt but that approach to God in prayer was a serious business. Great stress was made on the majesty of God in the opening words and the congregation was invariably reminded, from the outset, of the enormous privilege of access to a holy God through Christ by the grace of the gospel. The Bible reading was often lengthy and solemn and while light relief was provided in the children's talk, there was an undeniable air of gravitas throughout the whole service.

However, it was in the preaching of the sermon that the weighty seriousness was most obvious. It has been said that casual visitors and young people who listened to many of James Philip's sermons may not have understood much of what was being said. However, all would affirm that here was someone who was intensely serious about what he was saying. The seriousness of the preacher and thus the ultimate seriousness of the subject matter must have made a substantial impact upon large numbers of untaught and unlearned folks over the years. His seriousness, of course, is not something we can imitate. That would be folly. Jim Philip's seriousness was sourced, as he once said, from early impressions made upon his soul concerning the ineffable holiness of God. Consequently the Scripture text, 'Thou God seest me', impacted on him profoundly throughout his life. Allied to that was the strong sense of call to the ministry and being set apart as the 'Lord's anointed' within the congregation. This inevitably resulted in strong commitment of time and energy to the work of ministry and an overwhelming sense of responsibility for all aspects of the Sunday church services. The serious business of being a preacher and pastor led to a prodigious work output that left many of us exhausted just thinking about it. The essential seriousness of the preaching style allowed for a delightful droll touch of humour on occasions. Jim Philip has a lovely quick wit, as all his friends would say. Nor did this seriousness mean that there was any dearth of warmth. It was the very opposite! The warmth of his care, concern and compassion for the hearers was very evident and the strong emotional presentation at times tended to underline the seriousness of the issues involved.

The preacher today often feels pressured to be something of an entertainer in order to attract listeners. Therefore, we have much to learn from Jim Philip concerning the essential seriousness of being a servant of the Word of God. Obviously different personalities will express that seriousness in different ways. Also the varied cultures and subcultures within a range of localities and congregations will necessitate an adaptation of style. For some there will be authentic humour in the pulpit or a lighter feel to services or wider participation in worship in the context of team and lay ministries. None of this need contradict the weighty seriousness that is part of the legacy of James Philip's ministry.

'A man of wecht', indeed! Thomas Chalmers, the author of this descriptive phrase, was once preaching in a remote border church around 1820. The writer, John 'Rab' Brown, describes that day from his childhood, as recorded by Professor Alec Cheyne.

It was with the sermon – that climactic moment in every Evangelical Sabbath – and its eloquent meditation on the subject, 'Death reigns', that the worshippers were brought to confront dimensions of existence barely glimpsed in their ordinary, weekday lives. 'We all had insensibly been drawn out of our seats, and were converging towards the wonderful speaker. And when he sat down, after warning each one of us to remember who it was, and what it was, that followed death on his pale horse (Revelation 6: 8), and how alone we could escape, – we all sunk back into our seats. How beautiful to our eyes did the thunderer look – exhausted – but sweet and pure! How he poured out his soul before his God in giving thanks for sending the Abolisher of Death! Then, a short psalm, and all was ended. We went home quieter than we came; we did not recount the foals with their long legs, and roguish eyes, and their sedate mothers; we did not speculate upon whose dog that was, and whether that was a crow or a man in the dim moor, – we thought of other things. That voice, that face; those great, simple, living thoughts; those floods of resistless eloquence; that piercing, shattering voice, – "That tremendous necessity".[3]

The closing phrase, it seems to me, could be appropriately used by all those who had the privilege of listening to James Philip and who owe so much to that 'man of weight' and servant of the Word.

---

3. A.C. Cheyne, *The Transforming of the Kirk* (Edinburgh, 1983), 33, quoting John Brown, *Horae Subsecivae*, 3 vols (London,1900), II, 145-6.

The Glory of God and the Congregational Prayer Meeting

Douglas Kelly

For upwards of forty years now, both here in Holyrood and earlier in my first charge, I have met for prayer with God's people, and I am in no doubt that it is this that has definitively shaped and fashioned my pulpit ministry. Its value for me is simply inestimable. [1]

How often in Scripture do we see the Church in distress and perplexity, crying to God to make bare His holy arm, and following this, God coming to them with rich promises of grace and help, and finally the fulfilment of this promise and a wonderful manifestation of His divine power. And does not this reflect our own situation in Scotland today? It is not too much to say that the men of God in our land who are bound together in the bonds of prayer are in fact founded upon this conviction, and have been maintained by it for over a quarter of a century that God is faithful to His promises and that we do not hope in vain. One day – one great glad day – Psalm 76 will be our experience, and we shall say, 'Lo, this is our God; we have waited for Him. . . .' (Isa. 25:9).[2]

Authentic Christianity has always been deeply marked by a vision of and passion for the glory of God. Everything else in its thought and practice is a mere servant to that. The high priestly prayer of our Lord in John 17 anchors the church and

---

1. J. Philip, *Holyrood Abbey Church of Scotland Congregational Record and Daily Bible Readings*, October 1990, 5. Hereafter the title will be shortened to *Record*. Unless otherwise stated the author is always James Philip.
2. *Record*, Oct. 1987, 17.

its eternal purpose in a time-bound, decaying world in the Son's giving her the glory he received from the Father (v. 22), and in his asking the Father, 'I want those you have given me, to be with me where I am, and to see my glory, the glory you have given me because you loved me before the creation of the world' (v. 24). It is only in this context of the mediation of the heavenly Father's glory through the body of his beloved Son, the church, into a dark, shameful and sin-cursed world that we can understand the significance of the Holyrood Abbey Church of Scotland prayer meeting over the forty years of James Philip's ministry.

The Holyrood congregational prayer meeting is for me no merely academic subject (although I am an academic), for since 1968, when I first became part of it, the glory of the Lord has frequently brightened my own life and ministry through the weekly intercession of the people of God in Holyrood. Although I was blessed to have been brought up in a true Calvinist home and church, I did not become part of Holyrood until I was twenty-five years old, at which time I was caught up in a clearer, stronger and happier vision of God's own glory coming down and making everything right through the channel of the weekly congregational prayer meeting. The sheer beauty and thrill of the calling to align ourselves with the intercession of Christ for the glory of the Father to break upon our desperate generation so took hold of me that it profoundly shaped a parish ministry of some ten years, as well as the last eighteen years of theological training of the ministry.

In order to press forward and onward this vision of God's glory descending through the congregational prayer meeting to a needy world, what could be better than to draw from the writings of James Philip himself to grasp the heart and soul of the matter? It has long been noted that much of the finest theology in both Scottish Calvinism and in the Southern Presbyterian tradition of the USA has come from the pens of parish ministers. One thinks of preachers such as John Knox, Robert Bruce, Samuel Rutherford, the Erskines, Thomas Boston and Thomas Chalmers in Scotland, and of men like Benjamin Palmer, John Girardeau and Robert Dabney in the old South. Well-equipped and diligent pastor-scholars, if they are men of prayer, can often join the ranks of the best theologians because of the necessity of their wrestling with exegesis of Holy Scripture three times a week, their knowledge of their people's and their own hearts through pastoral work, and because they are lifted up by the piety of corporate worship and by the wings of intercessory prayer on their behalf. That has been the story of James Philip, and it is my hope in writing this piece that many another will join him from all across the world as the vision of glory takes shape before them.

In a memorial to an elderly saint, Mrs A. Murray, James Philip noted that 'She had a long association with Holyrood, and was one of a small group of praying ladies who lifted hands and hearts to God during the last vacancy, and whose faithful intercessions were instrumental in bringing about the present ministry.'[3] This young minister who was 'prayed in' to Holyrood knew what he was about even before he arrived there. Referring to Joshua 15:18-20 (where Achsah asked a further blessing of her father, Caleb), he once stated that he turned these very words into prayer as he came south to Edinburgh from Gardenstown: 'Give me a blessing; for thou hast given me a southland; give me also springs of water. And he gave her the upper springs and the nether springs.'[4]

The Vision

'Where there is no vision, the people perish' (Prov. 29:18), but when the people catch a glimpse of God's glory, dry bones are raised into a living army by divine power through Word and Spirit (cf. Ezek. 37). In discussing Joel's picture of coming peace and prosperity (3:18-20), James Philip finds

---

3. *Record,* Apr. 1997, 6.
4. *Record*, June 1985, 13.

echoes of other Scriptures. We think of Ezekiel's vision (47:1-12) of the waters issuing from under the threshold of the house of the Lord (compare also Zechariah 14:8 and also Revelation 22:1ff, which for very beauty and longing make us cry out, 'Even so, come Lord Jesus') . . . The establishment of the kingdom of God in its fullness will bring unimagined glories in all realms, the material, the natural, the cosmic, as well as the moral and spiritual . . . the restoration of material prosperity signified the renewal of fellowship between God and His people, and this is the heart of it all – the Lord dwelleth in Zion (20). John brings the same thought out in Rev. 22:3,4 where the ultimate beatitude is described with elemental simplicity – 'They shall see His face'. Ah, in the light of this, we may well hold on grimly as the day of doom approaches, knowing that the noise of battle, and the fierce agony of the wounds sustained in the fight of faith will one day yield to the victor's song and the glowing welcome and glad consummation when we shall see Him as He is (1 John 3:2). It will be infinitely worth all the trials and tears and the taking up of the cross, to have that Face turned to us in love and commendation. God help us, how should we have ever thought otherwise?[5]

It is clear that this glory of God from eternity to eternity is centred for us in the person of the Lord Jesus Christ, for he is 'the brightness of his glory and the express image of his person' (Heb. 1:3). The greatest need of this world and the only hope for transforming it is to see that glory, as both prophets and apostles have taught us. The divine glory has made itself known in transforming power in many of the nations of the West, not least Scotland, in both Reformation and revival. Vast numbers experienced the reality of 2 Corinthians 3:18, 'But we all, with open face beholding as in a glass the glory of the Lord, are changed into the same image from glory to glory, even as by the Spirit of the Lord.' In a moving contrast between the tragic secularism of the modern nation and its once faithful and happy status, Mr Philip comments:

---

5. *Record,* Sept. 1977, 19-20.

The Gospel of our forefathers, the Reformers and the Covenanters, was obscured and well-nigh lost in the early years of the twentieth century, largely under the influence of theological liberalism and modernism ... Now sufficient time has elapsed for us to examine all this in relation to the fruit it has produced. Well, what do we see? We see a shortage of ministers for the parishes of Scotland; we have seen the dwindling of missionary strength to half what it was in the immediate pre-war years; we see a shortage of money everywhere; we see dwindling congregations and attendances; we see disappearing evening services and the emergence of the Lord's 'half-day'; we see ... throughout the land an abysmal ignorance of the Scriptures, with great tracts of it pagan, with children who have never heard the name of Christ or God except as swear-words. This is the Scotland of John Knox! By their fruits shall ye know them. This is the fruit of wrong doctrine, of false teaching, of the obscuring of the doctrine of justification by faith. And – be it noted – this is the kind of darkness that was upon Scotland before the Reformation. But when the central truth of the Gospel, justification by faith, was recovered and began to be preached, what happened? In a generation, the whole nation was transformed and a great new vitality surged through its veins. A foundation was laid which made Scotland great and Scotland's sons known throughout the world for their sheer moral and spiritual worth.[6]

The same transforming gospel glory manifested itself after the Reformation through anointed preaching in answer to valiant intercession in various times of revival. For example, James Philip writes:

In this regard, it will not be out of place to refer to the events that led up to the great awakening and spiritual quickening of 1859, in a Scotland in which the three dominant branches of Presbyterianism constituted 70% of the population of approximately 3 million people in the land, and in which [all

---

6. *Record,* May 1991, 15-16.

three churches] acknowledged the 'great and blessed fact' of the revival as bringing untold blessing to the whole nation.

He then quotes J. Edwin Orr to show that something like one fourth of this large membership had been involved in weekly prayer meetings for revival throughout Scotland.[7] In both Reformation and revival, people saw who Jesus was, and then grasped the hideousness of their sins, 'the love of his atonement', and – by virtue of their union to Christ in his death and resurrection – thought new thoughts, spoke new words, and lived new lives empowered by the purity and beauty of the indwelling Holy Spirit. John the Baptist's stating that Christ would baptise with the Holy Ghost and fire (Matt. 3:11,12) gives the clue to what takes place when people see the glory of Christ:

> Christ plunges us into this fire . . .[as in] Romans 6, where Paul speaks of being baptised into Christ's death and resurrection . . . The fire, then indicates the nature of what Christ seeks to do for us and in us. It represents 'divine energy' working in grace towards men . . . This is what happens when the grace of God lays hold of one dead in trespasses and sins. Christ kindles a fire on the cold hearths of men's hearts and sets them aflame with love for God and man. . . . And when the love of God is kindled in our hearts it burns all the impurities out of our system.[8]

Much as he has longed and prayed for revival, James Philip has maintained a healthy approach to the whole matter. He uttered wise words in saying that we must never put revival above Christ!

> We do well to remember that the object of our faith and hope must not be revival, but God Himself. Some people are so concerned with revival that they tend to lose sight of Christ Himself . . . No, it is joy in God that is our truest fulfilment. It

---

7. *Record*, Aug. 1992, 4.
8. *Record,* Feb. 1991, 28.

is what we were made for, as it is also the beginning of all straight thinking, about revival or anything else. Our first priority is to be right with Him, to glorify Him and enjoy Him forever; only thus do we learn to allow Him to do His own work in His own way and in His own time.[9]

Although holding the highest aspirations for whatever spiritual blessings God deigns to send, it is always the church's task to delight herself in the ordinary means of grace (the Word, the sacraments and prayer), which are the places where she meets her Lord and to which she must bring those who do not yet know him. Indeed, one of the founding professors of Princeton Seminary, Archibald Alexander (who was converted in the Second Great Awakening in Virginia in the 1780s), points out in his *Thoughts on Religious Experience* that revival is essentially the unusual 'speeding up' of the effectiveness of the ordinary means of grace, and not something qualitatively different or superior to the daily life of the church. So then, sound thinking will show that whether God works rather slowly (as he seems to most ordinarily) or very quickly (as on occasion in times of Reformation and revival), what matters long term in transforming the world is fidelity in the basic means of grace.

Trustingly plodding on week by week in preaching the Word, dispensing the sacraments, and fervently covering it all in prayer is surely the truest reflection of the inspired answer of David to the command of a gracious God: 'When thou saidst, Seek ye my face; my heart said unto thee, Thy face, Lord, will I seek' (Psalm 27: 8). This seems to have been a major motivation of the great Christian statesman and theologian of the Netherlands, Abraham Kuyper, who poured out the energies of his long and fruitful life 'in order that the ordinances of the Lord might once again be restored in the home, the church, the state and the school' (to paraphrase one biographer).[10]

---

9. *Record*, Oct. 1977, 33-34.
10. Biographical introduction by John H. de Vries to Abraham Kuyper's *Lectures on Calvinism* (Grand Rapids, 1898), iii.

James Philip realistically took into account how undramatic and tiresome it can all seem, and regularly reminded his people of the importance of the 'ordinariness' of the means of grace:

> What I am certain of is this: a great many of the problems and difficulties that beset young Christians' lives, and the not-so-young as well – temptations, pressures, mixed-up-ness, loneliness, depression, discouragement, or whatever – would be well on the way to solution if only they would at last submit themselves to the 'ordinariness' of the means of grace, and applied some discipline to themselves in terms of getting themselves under the word of ministry on a regular, as opposed to a spasmodic basis. . . . God is faithful, and He says, 'Them that honour Me I will honour.'[11]

The Divine Strategy

The means of grace given by God to his church as the channel of his transforming glory through her to the world are the key to the divine strategy to defeat Satan, restore the sin-devastated creation and gather from every tribe and tongue all his elect into union and communion with himself through Christ in the Holy Spirit. The vision of James Philip to offer his ministry as a channel through which the glory of God in Christ might reach his generation was certainly shaped by the time-honoured insight of John Calvin and his followers in Scotland and elsewhere that Word and Spirit must always be held together if the resurrection life of Christ is actually to spring forth through the church's proclamation of the divinely inspired Holy Scriptures and her administration of the sacraments.[12] And from the church being the church comes the gradual transformation of the culture around her.[13]

---

11. *Record*, Feb. 1977, 3-4.
12. See for instance John Calvin, *Institutes of the Christian Religion*, 1:7: 3,4,5 and 3:1:1.
13. James Philip's emphasis was in line with that of Calvin and other Reformers and their Puritan and later evangelical successors, upon men and women in vital union with Christ pushing out into a sinful

For James Philip and his honoured mentor, the late Revd William Still, and a host of others now in active ministry in Scotland and across the world, the divine strategy could, in a sense, be expressed in the original motto of Glasgow: 'Let Glasgow flourish by the preaching of the Word and the praising of His Name.' The preaching of the Word, and the administration of the sacraments as well, will fall lifeless to the ground without being empowered by the largely unseen, but mighty spiritual weapon of congregational prayer. That was understood by Calvin, the Scottish Reformers, the Puritans and later Evangelicals, and was re-emphasised in the most concrete way by William Still, James Philip and others of their generation.[14] Far from being passé, if I am not mistaken, it is just beginning to do its leavening work amongst hundreds of ministries across the globe. These good men will see no more than a very small percentage of the effects of their testimony and practice in this regard 'until the day break and the shadows flee away', and undoubtedly they are happy enough with that!

Preaching the Word

For the purposes of this chapter, I can only make the briefest reference to preaching the Word in order to concentrate on the prayer meeting which empowers that preaching (and to this end of brevity, I must regretfully neglect discussing the sacraments, which in no sense were neglected by James Philip). Mr Philip writes:

> We need all the truth of God for our balanced growth, not merely this or that doctrine, this emphasis or that. Christ is made unto us wisdom, righteousness, sanctification and redemption, and to get a whole Christ we need the whole Word.[15]

---

world order with the transforming justice and mercy of God to change its structures in a holy direction, expressive of the divine love.
14. See Calvin, *Institutes*,3:2:33, 'accordingly, without the illumination of the Holy Spirit, the Word can do nothing.'
15. J. Philip, *The Church - God's New Society* (1974), 57.

In an extended article, 'The Ministry of the Word', he lucidly explains why and how getting the whole Christ across to the people is best done by expository preaching three times a week, with the sequential working through text after text of the various books of the Bible.[16] A companion volume would be William Still's *The Work of the Pastor*. Both of these men followed prophets, apostles and Reformers in expecting the letting loose of the Word of God through anointed preaching to do wonders in church and society. James Philip frequently lifts up our eyes to this vision:

> And if there is anything calculated to encourage . . . the church . . . of our time, it is the steady recovery of the Word in power and authority in more and more churches and gatherings . . . God laid His hand on the young Samuel. And presently it began to be noised abroad that the Word of the Lord was with him; and in quarter of a century – it took all of that time – the whole national situation was transformed. . . . It is when God and His Word are in the midst of the Church that it moves forward like a mighty army.[17]

But as John Calvin made clear, the ministry of Word and sacrament will remain lifeless without the vital working of the Holy Spirit. Although the third Person of the Holy Trinity is always sovereign and mysterious in his ineffable person and work, yet Christ (upon whom the Spirit delights to 'turn the spotlight' - cf. John 16: 13,14) tells us that this blessed Person is given in answer to prayer (Luke 11: 13). This has been the urgent rationale behind the call to the weekly congregational prayer meeting in churches such as Holyrood from the late 1950s and Gilcomston since the mid-1940s.

---

16. *Journal of Christian Reconstruction* 9 (1982-83), 24-58.
17. *Record,* Feb. 1980, 22.

The Congregational Prayer Meeting

St Paul asked for prayer for his ministry to be effective (Eph. 6: 19), as have all true servants of the Word of God. Paul asked to be given 'utterance'. James Philip comments:

> 'Utterance' is something more than eloquence . . . [It is] burning words fraught with spiritual power to change lives. This, he indicates, comes through prayer, and a battle has to be fought with the powers of darkness before such an unction can be bestowed upon a preacher. Nor is it his battle alone . . . it is also the congregation's . . . It lies in their hands and in their prayers for him to put the sharp cutting edge on his ministry. Who can doubt that this is the greatest need in the proclamation of the gospel today? It is prayer – intelligent, focussed, concentrated, persistent prayer – that turns orthodox truth into Spirit-charged, life-giving dynamic.[18]

> It is prayer that releases the authority and the compassion of God upon the lives of men. Do we long for the compassionate touch of the Saviour's hand upon the broken lives around us? Then we must be much in prayer to God, for in no other way will this be. . . . A prayerless church is a church that is dead.[19]

The sin-blinded nations of the world will not pray for themselves in any meaningful way; the church must therefore do so. Much of the professing church will not pray; therefore, a remnant must do so, and their relative smallness does not in the slightest diminish the stupendous power they have in accomplishing the pre-determined purposes of God for the whole created order. Since God has 'chosen the weak and foolish things of this world to confound the mighty' (cf. 1 Cor. 1: 27), obviously he likes to take humble and 'low-prestige' congregational prayer meetings to make supernatural glories break forth in the land.

Mr Philip illustrates this principle by Hannah, mother of the

18. *Record,* June 1977, 20-21.
19. *Record,* Jan. 1976, 19.

prophet Samuel: 'The burden of 1 Samuel 2 is the apostasy under Eli and his renegade sons – a dark and terrible picture, indeed – but over against that, here is a praying woman!'[20] And from Daniel's intercession a similar lesson is drawn:

> A whole nation will never cry to God for mercy; this is the task that the faithful in the land must take upon itself. God generally works through minorities, and when He finds a minority who in their own heart take and feel the sin of the whole nation, then there is the prospect of a way out and of blessing.[21]

Inspired by Professor T. F. Torrance's sermons on Revelation, *The Apocalypse Today* (especially on chapter 8), James Philip speaks of 'the incense' of the intercessions of Christ being sprinkled upon the prayers of his church, so that when the saints pray on earth and have their requests perfumed by the risen Christ in glory, then as a result, fire is cast into the earth! He adds:

> Well! If the prayers of the saints can really do this, then this is the answer that the agony and the urgency of our situation needs today, above all else. If it is through prayer that the Spirit of God comes upon the Church in tongues of fire, and that Satan falls as lightning to the ground, then prayer must be the unquestioned and unassailable first priority in our lives and in our fellowship.[22]

The Cost and the Glory

For Holyrood, this priority has meant something over a solid hour of intercessory congregational prayer every Saturday night since James Philip arrived there in 1958. To say the least, this is not always a convenient time in view of the social

---

20. *Record,* Sept. 1995, 15.
21. *Record,* Dec. 1989, 13.
22. *Record,* Aug. 1992, 5.

engagements people tend to have on that night of the week. He has given a reasoned discussion of this less-than-convenient time more than once over the years. Basically, it comes down to what our chief priorities are.

> Doubtless the many who have been faithful over the years could very profitably use their Saturday evenings in a variety of different and constructive ways; but to believe that corporate prayer is far and away the most important task facing the Church is to give it an absolute priority in one's Christian life.[23]

He has never hidden the cost factor in valid Christian experience:

> As D. M. McIntyre says, 'Prevailing prayer draws its virtue from a disposition that has been brought into conformity with the mind of Christ' (cf. John 15: 7, 1 John 3: 22, 5: 14). But a filial relationship of fellowship with God is not something that is natural to men, nor is its continuing existence a natural, automatic thing. It costs, to maintain a close fellowship with Christ.[24]

> To follow Him is to commit oneself to His enterprises, to stand by Him in the battle, to stand with Him in the battle, till the building is done and the battle won. It is therefore the quality of the disciples rather than their quantity, that is important. This is why He did not hesitate to thin out their ranks with His heart-bruising ministry [referring to Luke 14: 28-33].[25]

'A spiritual life that costs nothing is worth nothing and will get us nowhere.'[26] On the contrary, in terms of the torch-light shining through Gideon's broken jars (interpreted by Matthew Henry in connection with 2 Corinthians 4:7 – 'But we have this

---

23. *Record*, Oct. 1990, 5.
24. *Record*, Aug. 1978, 17.
25. *Record*, Oct. 1978, 13.
26. *Record*, Jan. 1982, 21.

treasure in earthen vessels . . .'), James Philip draws this gladdening conclusion:

> And Paul speaks of how he bears about in his body the dying of the Lord Jesus, that the life also of Jesus might be manifest in him. The vessel has to be broken to let the light out to men . . . The 'weakness' of the believer's crucifixion, the breaking of the vessel which is his life, is the way God gets through to men, the channel by which blessing comes.[27]

The believer's identification with Christ in his death inevitably leads to the glory (for himself and a needy church and world) of many resurrections with him (cf. Rom. 6 and Gal. 2: 20). Nothing less than that is the motivation and fruition of the faithful and costly congregational prayer meeting. It is a God-ordained channel of the divine glory, which is the greatest treasure of heaven and the most desperately needed reality on earth.

Those believers who faithfully and self-forgetfully join 'the Lord's remembrancers' (cf. Isa. 64: 5), even in the humblest congregational prayer meeting, in some small but real way have the eternal honour of reflecting here below the pure, compassionate heart and victorious supplications of our Great High Priest above (cf. Heb. 4: 15 and John 17), 'the man in the glory' (cf. Psalm 8 and Heb. 2: 6-18). He sends down from the throne his Holy Spirit to re-echo within true seekers his own heavenly intercessions (cf. Rom. 8: 26-27). His Father always hears him (John 11: 42). That is why when the church's prayers increase, it is a sign that great glory is sooner or later on the way!

---

27. *Record,* Oct. 1991, 6.

'Blood-Earnest'
Experimental Preaching

Ian Hamilton

During my two spells of theological studies at New College, Edinburgh University, I was privileged to sit under James Philip's ministry in Holyrood Abbey. After a week of arid theological reflection, coming to Holyrood on the Lord's day was the greatest of delights. I knew, come what may, that I would be exposed to authentic, pulse-quickening, God-centred, Christ-glorifying preaching. In truth, the whole service was the greatest joy. The singing of God's praise and Jim's prayers were not so much preludes to the main event as God's means to prepare us to listen attentively and expectantly to his Word. It was Sundays at Holyrood that kept my heart and mind firmly rooted in the Spirit-inspired truth of God's living Word (and exposed much of what I was being taught at New College for the folly it was).

Early on in my studies, one of my lecturers was trying to tell my pastoral theology class that ten minutes was about the length of sermon the modern churchgoer would accept. When I mentioned that the minister at the church I attended preached morning and evening for around forty minutes, he simply replied, 'You must go to Holyrood Abbey.' It was not that James Philip was trying to be different. He was persuaded that he was dealing with holy and eternal things. The destinies of men and women depended on their relationship to Jesus Christ and ten brief minutes would not suffice to explain and apply God's saving truth.

Two incidents in those days of theological training remain etched in my mind. After I preached my first sermon as a student attachment, one of the congregation said to me, 'You preach just like James Philip.' His comment was intended as a barb, but to me it was the greatest of encouragements. My sermon had been on the centrality of the cross of Christ, and it was the theme of the sermon, rather than the effectiveness of the preacher, that drew the comparison with James Philip. Little did the person know that my heart soared at the thought that in any way my preaching could be likened to that of a man whose ministry had so profoundly affected me. The second incident was deeply personal. For some time I had questioned my call to the preaching, pastoral ministry, and wondered, perhaps, if I might not be better suited to some area of theological teaching. During this unsettling time, I was overwhelmed by a sermon preached one Sunday evening by Mr Philip. I do not remember what the text or passage was, but I remember walking back to my lodgings that night and praying, 'Lord, if you ever call me to preach the gospel of your Son, I want to preach like that man.' I did not mean that I wanted to sound like him. What gripped me was the 'blood-earnestness' of God's servant. Those words, used of Thomas Chalmers by John Mitchell Mason,[1] epitomised for me the appeal of Jim's preaching. He was a rigorous exegete. No one I have heard more helpfully set the biblical context of the passage he was preaching on. His biblical expositions were always insightful, and his theology was experimentally Calvinistic. But it was Jim's 'blood-earnestness', more than anything else, that made such an indelible impression on me. Week by week, I felt myself in the presence of unimpeachable, Spirit-anointed, 'blood-earnestness'.

In these present frivolous times, it is this note that needs to characterise true gospel preachers. David Wells, probably more than any other living theologian, has analysed the present state of Evangelicalism. He writes:

1.Quoted by James W. Alexander, *Thoughts on Preaching* (Edinburgh, 1864), 264.

> The fundamental problem in the Evangelical world today is not inadequate technique, insufficient organisation, or antiquated music, and those who want to squander the church's resources bandaging those scratches will do nothing to staunch the flow of blood that is spilling from its true wounds. The fundamental problem in the Evangelical world today is that God rests too inconsequentially upon the church. His truth is too distant, his grace is too ordinary, his judgement is too benign, his gospel is too easy, and his Christ is too common.[2]

For all our energy and enterprise, it can hardly be doubted that evangelical Christianity is increasingly theologically weightless and morally effete. Wells is not saying we should turn the clock back, but he is highlighting the pressing need for Evangelicals to return to their theological roots. Jim's preaching was rooted in the mature theology of the Westminster Standards and was always weighty, never shallow. I do not mean that it projected and commended a long-past era; on the contrary, for me at least, his preaching highlighted the abiding contemporaneity of biblical truth.

One unfailing consequence of preaching becoming freshly rooted in pristine evangelical theology will be this quality which I have called 'blood-earnestness'. This is in contrast to the often frivolous nature of much that passes for evangelical preaching today. It would seem that many preachers today believe that 'jokes, quotes and anecdotes' are the best ways to win the attention of their hearers. Sermons become platforms for preachers to parade their verbal skills, not opportunities to expound the Scriptures with gracious gravity. James Denney (whom Jim loved to quote more than any other biblical exegete – at least it felt like that!) said, 'No man can give the impression that he himself is clever and that Christ is mighty to save.' James Philip never gave the impression from the pulpit that he was clever. He was too gripped by the gravity of his calling to engage

---

2. *God in the Wasteland* (Grand Rapids, 1994), 30.

in self-promotion. Paul's words in 2 Corinthians 2:15-17 reflect the weight of responsibility Jim felt when he stood to proclaim 'the unsearchable riches of Christ': 'For we are to God the aroma of Christ among those who are being saved and those who are perishing. To the one we are the smell of death; to the other the fragrance of life. And who is equal to such a task?' If evangelical preaching is not suffused with this holy gravity, whatever else it is, it is not evangelical preaching!

More than ever, I am persuaded, our manner in preaching must tell our hearers that to us, if to no-one else, we are handling the most urgent and serious of all messages. It is sadly only too common to find evangelical preachers today accommodating the message of the cross to the ethos of the age, and all in the worthy pursuit of relevance. Preaching has in many places been replaced by drama and dance, or peripheralised into a ten-minute homily. Many have been seduced by the mantra that the visual must take precedence over the verbal. We need to hear all over again Paul's apologia for preaching. Writing to the church in Corinth Paul declared, 'Therefore, since through God's mercy we have received this ministry, we do not lose heart. Rather, we have renounced secret and shameful ways; we do not use deception, nor do we distort the word of God. On the contrary, by setting forth the truth plainly, we commend ourselves to every man's conscience in the sight of God' (2 Cor.4:1-2). These words remind me of what it was like to sit under Jim's preaching ministry. It was gimmick-free. He had such unbounded confidence both in the inherent truthfulness and power of the gospel, and in preaching as God's principal ordained means for calling sinners into saving union with Christ.

There are fundamentally two sides to this 'blood-earnestness'. Negatively, it is characterised by the avoidance of all levity (not humour). Listen to Richard Baxter:

Of all the preaching in the world . . . .I hate that preaching which tends to make the hearers laugh, or to move their minds with tickling levity, and affect them as stage-plays used to, instead of affecting them with a holy reverence for the name of God. Jerome says, 'Teach in thy church, not to get the applause of the people, but to set in motion the groan; the tears of thy hearers are thy praises.'[3]

Baxter is not claiming that sermons should always be free of humour – though it should at least give us cause for thought that while there is humour in scriptural examples of preaching, it is almost always muted! There was nothing trivial or affected about James Philip's preaching, no attempt to 'tickle the emotions'. I do not mean that Jim could not lighten a sermon with a touch of humour; but he never used humour lightly or casually. Occasionally Jim's humour was unintended. I remember one occasion when he began an address to the church children with this question: 'Children, what's wrong with Britain today?' When no answer, not surprisingly, was forthcoming, Jim replied, 'Moral and spiritual declension'! I am not quite sure the children had the remotest idea what he was talking about, and a number of us sat with broad grins.

There almost seems to be an aversion to seriousness in the pulpit today. And yet, surely the Christian preacher, more than any other, should be characterised by the deepest seriousness (not moroseness) when he stands to preach the Word. Destinies are in the balance. When Lot pleaded with his sons-in-law to flee from Sodom because the Lord was about to destroy it, they 'thought he was joking' (Gen.19:14). There can be few greater indictments of a man's ministry than to have his congregation react to his preaching as Lot's sons-in-law reacted. No one who sat under James Philip's ministry could for one moment have thought he was joking when he spoke about the righteous judgement of God.

More positively, such preaching will mean manifesting earnest sincerity in all we say, in Baxter's devastating words, 'as a dying man to dying men'. Listen again to Baxter:

---

3. *The Reformed Pastor*, II. ii. xi, ed. W. Brown, 5th edit. (London,1862), 118-19.

> O sirs, how plainly, how closely, how earnestly, should we deliver a message of such moment as ours . . . In the name of God, brethren, labour to awaken your own hearts, before you go into the pulpit, that you may be fit to awaken the hearts of sinners . . .Remember, they must be awakened or damned, and a sleepy preacher will hardly awaken drowsy sinners . . .Though you give the holy things of God the highest praise in words, yet, if you do it coldly, you will seem by your manner to unsay what you have said in the matter. Speak to your people as to men that must be awakened either here or in hell.[4]

This earnestness has nothing to do with loudness, or even with much physical animation. Jim was never histrionic, and he rarely shouted. There was, however, a palpable intensity in his often quiet, always 'throaty' voice. Earnestness is a quality that suffuses our preaching because we ourselves have felt the power, the grace and the urgency of God's truth. It is the very thing Paul speaks about in 2 Corinthians 2:17: 'But as from sincerity, but as from God, before God, in Christ we speak' (literal translation).

Here I think we touch the heart of the matter. What gave Jim's preaching its Spirit-wrought 'blood-earnestness' was what he was as a man. The kind of preaching that God uses for his glory is not the performance of an hour, but the overflow of a life (E.M.Bounds). This is what Paul, at least in part, is highlighting in 1 Thessalonians 2:4: 'we speak as men approved by God to be entrusted with the gospel.' Whatever else Paul is telling us here, he is surely telling us that 'the man makes the preacher'. No-one has better stated this fundamental truth than E.M.Bounds:

> The preacher is more than the sermon . . . all the preacher says is tinctured, impregnated by what the preacher is . . . the sermon is forceful because the man is forceful. The sermon is holy because the man is holy. The sermon is full of divine unction because the man is full of divine unction. . . The sermon cannot

---

4. *Ibid.*, III.i.ii.2, 159-60.

rise in its life-giving forces above the man . . . Everything depends on the spiritual character of the preacher.[5]

All that E.M.Bounds wrote I saw manifested in Jim's life. I have no doubt that the key to the power and effectiveness of Jim's preaching was who he himself was. Edward Payson's words express what I believe to be true of James Philip:

> I was never fit to say a word to a sinner except when I had a broken heart myself, when I was subdued and melted into tenderness, and felt as though I had just received pardon to my own soul, and when my heart was full of tenderness and pity.[6]

There was a palpable tenderness in Jim's preaching. He showed me as a young divinity student that 'blood-earnestness' and tenderness are not mutually exclusive, but rather, inseparable partners in the work of the ministry.

What Baxter pleaded for was echoed by John Owen: 'a man preacheth that sermon only well to others, which preacheth itself in his own soul. . . . If the Word do not dwell with power in us, it will not pass with power from us.'[7] For me, James Philip exemplified a preacher to whom the Word of God had come in soul-convicting, character-transforming power. He was only commending to others the 'glorious gospel of the blessed God' that had so gripped and captivated his own soul.

It should be said at this point that, although he was an intellectually gifted man, James Philip's preaching was never merely cerebral. There was an intensely human quality about Jim both as man and as a preacher. He was never ashamed to show emotion in the pulpit. He was dealing with high and holy themes, with the truth of the living God, with the great issues of eternity, and his whole being was engaged in all he spoke. This

---

5. *Power Through Prayer* (London, n.d.), 11-12.
6. Quoted by Charles Bridges, *The Christian Ministry* (1830; repr. London, 1967), 335 n. 10.
7. *The Works of John Owen* (London, 1968), vol.16, 76.

was especially true of his preaching of 'Christ and him crucified'. Nothing more expanded Jim's affections than the message of the cross.

But where does such 'blood-earnestness' come from? Some words from Robert Dabney's *Sacred Rhetoric* highlight the source of this gracious quality:

> We are required to spend a life in the iteration of the same truths, until all the charm of novelty is gone. The most brilliant mind would fail to retain the attention of a charge, during a whole ministry by the mere force of mental interest.... Without a sacred weight of character, the most splendid rhetoric will win only a short-lived applause ... Eloquence may dazzle and please; holiness of life convinces.[8]

There are no techniques that can produce such palpable spiritual earnestness in a preacher. Such a gracious quality is wrought in the depths of our souls as the Holy Spirit conforms us, often through painful experience, to the likeness of Christ. The quality and impact of our preaching will be in direct correspondence to the spiritual character of our lives. 'Blood-earnestness' is not a technique to cultivate, it is the overflow of a life that has felt the grace and power of the gospel and the surpassing glory of the Lord Jesus Christ. It will be (sadly) a surprise to many Christians that the power in preaching does not lie in the preacher's eloquence or powers of persuasion. We are constantly being told that if only we get the atmosphere right, and target the right socially-profiled group of people, and make our worship services 'user-friendly', the gospel will prevail. The New Testament had a different conviction! Richard Baxter captures the essence of this conviction:

> Our whole work must be carried on under a deep sense of our own insufficiency, and of our entire dependence on Christ. We must go for light, and life, and strength to Him who sends us on the work ... he preacheth not heartily to his people that

8. *Sacred Rhetoric* (New York, 1870), 262-3.

prayeth not earnestly for them. If we prevail not with God to give them faith and repentance, we shall never prevail with them to believe and repent.[9]

This conviction was engraved on Jim's heart. The connection between Sundays at Holyrood and Saturday evenings, when we gathered for prayer, was theologically and spiritually inextricable. John Bunyan's dictum, 'You can do more than pray after you have prayed, but you cannot do more than pray until you have prayed', was the pulse-beat of Jim's whole ministry. I have little doubt that the effectiveness of Jim's 'blood-earnest' preaching drew its life-giving sap, not only from his personal devotions, but from the corporate prayers of the saints. It is a surpassing tragedy, at least in my own estimation, that Evangelicals will almost do anything other than engage together in serious, God-centred prayer. It may not be what the modern Evangelical thinks is a priority; but to God it is the *sine qua non* of spiritual usefulness.

For me, it was the greatest privilege to sit for five years under a ministry that so manifestly commended the grace of our Lord Jesus Christ. Jim was a 'bright and shining light', a flesh-and-blood example of preaching that commanded the blessing of God. Jonathan Edwards was described by Thomas Prince as 'a preacher of a low and moderate voice, a natural way of delivery, and without any agitation of body, or anything else in the manner to excite attention; except his habitual and great solemnity, looking and speaking as in the presence of God.'[10] This was James Philip. His preaching was 'blood-earnest', because as a Christian he was in 'blood-earnest'. Like his greatest theological mentor, John Calvin, he lived *coram Deo*, 'in the presence of God'. This, above all else, is what Evangelicalism needs so desperately to rediscover in these confused times.

---

9. Baxter, *Reformed Pastor*, II.ii.xiv, 122-3.
10. Quoted in John Piper, *The Supremacy of God in Preaching* (Grand Rapids, 1990), 102.

The Last Word: Expounding
the Book of Revelation

Jeremy Middleton

Thirty years later the memories are as fresh as ever. The number 5 bus across town. The damp darkness of a winter night. The intoxicating fragrance of expectancy which filled the church hall. The sense of eternity bursting like a spring flower through the hard ground of everyday life.

The midweek Bible studies at Holyrood were always a source of theological stimulus and spiritual nourishment. But high as the standard of teaching consistently was, one series of studies stands out as being quite exceptional. For one young student at any rate, the studies on the book of Revelation were little less than a revolution.

The impact of those studies is hard adequately to express. I recall to this day, as though it were but a moment ago, the experience itself, a potent cocktail of all that runs deep in the spiritual life, the like of which I had never known before. It is with no less clarity that I recall too the actual instruction we received. The substance and indeed the detail of these studies have survived the test of time. The truth was somehow driven deep into the very fibre of our beings, impressed upon our souls with such compelling force that over time it grew to be ingrained across our minds.

Yet even that but barely gives a hint of what those studies came to mean to me. They were more than just a reference point. They came to be in many ways a real defining moment in my life. This single series of studies, more than any other, brought into sharp focus the very essence of what it is to teach the Word of God. For all the main components of a godly, fruitful Bible-teaching ministry were here, crystallising out as Spirit-given

79

qualities to which the budding teacher should aspire, seven basic principles which underpin the ministry of all who would be fruitful in their teaching of God's Word.

1. Good Bible Teaching Resonates with Authority

This must be the first and primary characteristic of any good teaching of the Word of God. It is not an easy thing to define, of course, that strange, compelling, drawing power which cannot be explained in terms of either logic or emotion, something at once both frightening and enthralling. It lent real substance to what was being taught – something altogether different from the superficial platitudes which so often are the sum of popular preaching. It gave a sense of overwhelming 'size', a sense of the greatness and vastness of God. And it breathed a huge significance through all that was being taught, ensuring that it was somehow an encounter rather than merely information which was imparted to our hearts. And it was this, authority, which distinguished the ministry of Jesus: 'When Jesus had finished saying these things, the crowds were amazed at his teaching, because he taught as one who had authority, and not as their teachers of the law' (Matt. 7: 28-9).

Good Bible teaching resonates with authority. And those studies on Revelation were no exception. It was compelling stuff. But what lies behind that authority? How is it cultivated? Few issues are more important for the teachers of the Word of God to grasp if they would teach the Scriptures well. Authority is clearly a matter neither of learning nor of oratory – though not entirely unrelated to both, for the good teacher will always be an eager, avid learner and will always speak his well-considered words with a ringing, warm conviction. But this authority is something more than any mere amalgam of intellect and voice. Like a blazing fire, it flows from the union of two necessary components – the fuel of the teacher's preparation and the flame of the Spirit's anointing. The one involves hard graft, the other involves sheer grace: the mystery of the lightning in the sky, the drama of the spark which erupts from flint on flint. I sat at that blazing fire through those far off Wednesday nights. And I learned how authority works.

The Fuel: The Teacher's Preparation

Put most simply, James Philip was the master of his material. I was profoundly impressed by the order with which the issues were rehearsed, the thoroughness with which the issues were researched and the clarity with which the issues were relayed. That only comes through the graft of mind and heart, through the mental sweat of one who has laboured with all his might in the field of theological study. But the toil was never in vain. For these three constant qualities bequeathed to all who heard a confidence, not only in the man but also in the message which he brought. And that, in turn, becomes the sort of fuel which the Spirit then ignites.

I learned at that time, if I had not learned before, that the teacher must study hard and long. There are no easy short-cuts which the teacher can pursue, no substitute at all for long and weary hours in which both mind and heart alike are stretched and strained to quarry out the treasures of God's truth. The teacher's preparation is as vital to authority as fuel is to fire.

The Flame: The Spirit's Anointing

But the flame is as needful as fuel. The flame of the Spirit can ignite all that fuel and create once again the wonder of fire from on high. Something akin to the drama which Carmel once saw is what happened on each of those Wednesday nights. The fire of God fell as we gathered there, constraining in our hearts that same, instinctive cry, 'The Lord, he is God!' (1 Kings 18:39).

How does that happen? What happened on Carmel is instructive for us today. The prophet prayed (1 Kings 18:37-8). The flame of the Spirit's anointing is released by the prophet at prayer. But that is not the teacher's task alone. His people, too, must pray. And when they do, as people did with such unfailing faithfulness at Holyrood, then something in the heart of God is stirred and he who at the start said 'Let there now be light'

(Gen. 1:3) is moved to speak again a word which issues forth in fire.

2. Good Bible Teaching Starts with the Big Picture

The book of Revelation was a no-go area so far as I was concerned, a confusing maze of interwoven avenues of thought within whose shadowy alleyways there seemed to lurk a multitude of strange, disfigured, terrorising beasts, a disturbing book, to say the least.

Those studies on a Wednesday night effected for me a change which was like a programme of urban renewal. What once had been the shadowlands of truth from which a man would shy away in fear – these ghettos full of terrifying sights became instead great gardens filled with vista after vista which quite took the breath away, parks through which a man might gladly stroll and savour time and time again the beauty of the Lord. Such is the change a teacher of the Scriptures may effect.

The Spirit of God is the one who illumines our minds. But that being said, the Spirit uses means. He leads us into all the truth by giving us a teacher, whose task is so to guide his people over new and hard terrain that as they travel week by week they find that they are guided into truth (cf. John 16:13). The analogy is simple and its lessons are clear. For, in essence, Mr Philip simply gave us first a 'map', and he then walked with us over the land. Step by step, mile by weekly mile, we trekked across these wild and rugged heights of heaven's truth, our minds informed at every step as all that might be seen and known was pointed out by one who knew the way.

The key to it all was the map, for with that in our hands these chapters became not a walk in the dark but a sight-seeing tour for the soul. By the map I simply mean the overview, that mapping out the structure of the book which helped us see the way it holds together as a piece. He did not claim this structure was original to him. But original or not, the overview he gave was as fresh as a bright summer's morning, sufficient in itself to stir within our hearts a sense of newly-birthed expectancy.

With one deft touch, his simple, clear analysis untied the knot which all along had made this part of Scripture such a closed and complicated book.

This map, by which the structure of the book was made so clear, was the doorway into truth: so obvious when it is pointed out, so liberating to see. This is the 'big picture' with which good Bible teaching starts. For as the book of Revelation was for me, so the Scriptures themselves are for most today – largely inaccessible. The books of the Bible can often seem dauntingly large, the language and imagery strange. And when that is the case, to start by working through the details of the text will rarely be as helpful as a gentler and more general approach.

To concentrate the message of a book and crystallise it out in such a simple, single-sentence form that all can see its meaning and its relevance to them – that surely is the wisest place to start. And thus the teacher's task is first of all just this, to recognise the unifying theme which runs throughout the book, and having first articulated that, the structure of the book (by which the different sections of the book cohere around its central theme) must then be taught. The big picture is where it must start: only then do the details make much sense.

3. Good Bible Teaching Develops a Biblical Perspective

Scripture is today a foreign country for the people of our land, as remote and unknown as Nepal or Tibet and their towering, awe-inspiring Himalayan heights. Its language and its culture are a million miles away from what we are accustomed to – and therefore seem both hard to understand and well-nigh inaccessible.

And just as two-week package tours will never be enough to give the western tourist any more than glimpses of a culture so distinct from all we know, just so a superficial teaching of the Bible will never be sufficient to impart a living knowledge of the message which the book of Revelation brings. The traveller in the world of grace will look for something more than just a tourist guide to show him round. He needs a guide who lives there all the time and knows his way around: someone who will help him do far more than merely view it from afar, someone who will help him get beneath the country's skin and feel the people's heart-beat from within. This, I came to understand, must ever be a skill which those who would be teachers of the Word of God will cultivate and prize – the Spirit-given grace to open up a door through time and space and lead a people back into a world of long ago.

Those studies in the book of Revelation were a classic illustration of the processes involved in making us familiar with God's Word. First, we were taught the content of Scripture. Revelation simply teems with Old Testament life. Allusions abound to the stories and symbols, the numbers and colours and half-concealed codes which only initiates know. There are horses and trumpets and censers and scrolls, dragons and demons and all sorts of beasts, so bizarre and obscure and horrific in form that Stephen King is made to seem as tame as Mills and Boon. James Philip led us through this strange and frightening gallery of ancient art, explaining all the pictures as we slowly worked our way from room to room. He taught us what each picture meant and what the background was. He took us back to Scripture texts which lesser Bible teachers rarely dare to reach. He helped us see the truths they taught by working through the symbols which were used, expounding their significance by reference to the context and the genre.

We found our minds enlightened and our grasp of truth transformed: we understood the story and the symbols now made sense: the soaring peaks of this climactic book were climbed and from those Himalayan heights, the whole expansive world of Bible truth was at our feet. And thereby, too, we were taught the perspective of Scripture as well. We were given to understand not just the meaning of the text, but the 'mindset' of the Lord himself, the author of all truth. Our vision was transformed. We were helped to see the world no longer simply from our all-too-narrow, earthly point of view, but through the eyes of God himself. We learned to think biblically.

The teacher of the Word of God will always be aspiring to this goal. Our people do not merely wish to see this other world of which the Bible speaks: they surely wish to live there for themselves. And so the teacher strives with all his strength to make that far-off world a warm, familiar place where those who seek a country in the higher realms of faith may put down roots and live.

4. Good Bible Teaching Focuses on the Person of Jesus

A Bible-teaching ministry must never be an academic exercise. It has an essentially relational, rather than merely intellectual, thrust. The teaching of the Word of God will lead us to the Son of God. Revelation lends itself to that. This classic of apocalyptic literature is nonetheless, like all the Bible's books, a meeting-place where Jesus may be met and known; its opening words make that quite clear – 'the revelation of Jesus Christ' (Rev.1:1).

James Philip sought in all he taught us those Wednesday nights to cultivate in each and every heart, not least his own, a satisfying relationship with Christ. It all came back and down to him. We met the living Lord. He helped us catch a glimpse of who this Jesus is and why it is he captivates the heart. It was heady and memorable stuff. For over the weeks, no matter what the passage was in view, two grand, exalted themes were constantly impressed upon our hearts. They left, to this day, an indelible impression on my life.

First, there was the awe-inspiring greatness of our Lord. We were glad to be dwarfed by the sheer, exhilarating magnitude of Jesus Christ as in study after study these rich, climactic chapters of the Bible were expounded by a master at his best. To this day I recall the sensation there was in encountering such glory in Christ. I remember my breath being quite taken away, how my heart seemed to race with the pulse of excitement and thrill as we worked through the pictures which built up the vision of Christ. I had never experienced the like. Verse by verse John's strange, poetic language was explained as Mr Philip painted out the meaning of the text. More and more our spirits soared as that which hitherto had been at best but cryptic clues became so clear and threw a glorious spotlight on our Lord.

But alongside that we also learned the lordship of our Saviour Jesus Christ. Some pictures run right through the book of Revelation, and none perhaps is found to be more central to the message of the book than the picture of the throne. It is the teacher's gift to take these pictures out and paint them once again upon his hearers' hearts. There is today tattooed upon my inmost soul that picture of the throne. Jesus Christ is Lord. We knew it then: I know it to this day.

Such was the teaching impressed upon our hearts. And that, I came to see, is what good Bible teaching always seeks to do. It brings us back to Christ. He is the constant focus of the Scriptures, their all-pervasive theme, no matter where we look. He is himself the Word of God, the truth, and thus to teach the Word of God is in the end to introduce our hearers to the person of God's Son and nurture in their hearts an ever-deepening knowledge of the Lord.

5. Good Bible Teaching Carries an Incisive Prophetic Thrust

The Bible is the Word of God. The phrase slips off the tongue with such ease that we sometimes miss its startling, thrilling import for ourselves. We use the term to recognise that Scripture has been authored by no less than God himself, and rightly so, of course. But what we do not always grasp so well is simply this, that he who in the framing of that Word once spoke still speaks thereby today. And not by any means the least part of the skill the gifted teacher of the Scriptures will display is that old charismatic grace whereby he helps his people hear not just the Word, but more, the very voice of God, the God who speaks to us today.

It was, without doubt, this immediacy in the teaching of the Word of God which made those nights so alive. The hour simply rippled with the live and dancing currents of the great Creator's voice: it was a dangerous place to be! It was as if the Lord himself came down and made pronouncements there and then about the world in which we lived. That surely is the essence of the keen, prophetic thrust for which all those who teach the Word of God will strive. And strive they must! For this prophetic element will never be an easy thing for anyone to cultivate. The teacher's task in this regard is clear: if we aspire to have our people hear the voice of God, our aim must ever be to build a bridge between two very different realms. We bridge the gulf which stretches from God's heaven to our earth and thus allow the traffic of God's truth to pour across and travel through the highways of our broken, needy hearts.

The teacher of the Word of God will always be the builder of a bridge which spans the gap between the world of Bible texts and our contemporary world. The builder must work at both ends of the gulf, digging deep at each end to construct for this link the foundations a bridge will require. Mr Philip dug deep. He had read and reflected, pondered and probed, until he knew not just what the Bible taught, but also what it meant. This is where all Bible-teaching ministry begins – the spadework of this digging in the soil of Bible texts. There are no short-cuts here, no substitutes at all: just solid, patient digging with the muscles of our minds.

But there is a second sort of digging to be done, a digging on the other side – the study of the world in which we live and minister today. That is no less a task, as taxing on our time, as stretching and demanding on our minds, as all our constant study of the Bible texts will be. But this is how the teaching of the Word of God becomes for those who hear a rich, prophetic ministry of grace. James Philip earthed that ancient message in our troubled, modern world – a world he clearly knew, a world which he had studied long and hard. It was deeply impressive. Even as I sat and learned, I knew that such incisive ministry would only be forthcoming from myself if I in turn resolved to do this digging in the headlands of our modern world.

6. Good Bible Teaching Breathes a Pastoral Heart

God is the living Lord who speaks to us today. I had not really grasped that truth before those studies on a Wednesday night. But when I came to ponder why it was they left their mark in such a way upon my life, I came to understand that, as the Word of God is taught, God means to speak not simply to our world but also to our hearts. That pastoral dimension was a feature of the teaching from the start.

All Scripture has a context, and that context is the loom on which the weaving of the tapestries of truth takes place. To teach that truth must ever thus involve an understanding of the local situation into which the Spirit of the Lord first spoke and wove that living Word of God. Mr Philip took great care to teach and explain just where and for whom that message of the Bible's final book was first declared. He made for us a window on their world which helped us see the poignancy and aptness of the message of this book.

Yet that at best explains but part of how the teaching of the Word of God was woven through and through with pastoral threads. There is not just the context of the text, but the context of the taught as well. And this the teacher of the Word of God must recognise and strive to understand. Each study on those Wednesday nights was far from being a lecture or a talk. It was far more a ministry of grace through which the Lord himself, who long ago had spoken to his people in their need, now spoke to us as well. That Word first given there and then in ancient times is taught both here and now for us – and that by one who therefore must ensure he has a pastor's heart. This was a great distinctive of James Philip's teaching gift: he was before all else a pastor of the people whom he taught. And thus he knew them well. The teaching was so powerful precisely, so I saw, because it was so pastoral.

Such ministry requires the careful, constant exercise of three important, Spirit-given attributes which all who would be pastors surely prize. First, there is the grace of godly wisdom: that is, a wise, astute discernment of our human state, which understands the complex inner workings of the human heart. Then, tied to that, there is that finely tuned and gracious sensitivity of spirit, a listening ear which hears what cannot be heard – the whispers of the Spirit's voice, the groanings in the human heart, the language of a person's eyes and face. And then there is that free, expansive travelling of the mind which in a word we call imagination, the wonderful ability to dream of other worlds, to take the wings of mental flight and see all life through others' eyes.

Such are the basic attributes the pastor will display, the tools he will require to exercise his trade. And this – those studies taught me well – this is what the teacher of the Word of God will be: he is, and always must aspire to be, a pastor of the people who are taught. Nothing less will do.

7. Good Bible Teaching Generates a Spirit of Worship

Something special happened as the Word of God was taught, something which went far beyond the realms of reasoned thought and somehow touched those hallowed, fragile places in our hearts which nothing else can reach, releasing in our inmost souls a mighty stream of praise. That series of studies on a Wednesday night was both moving and truly alive. It was akin, I suppose, to the power which music can be – a surging, vocal dancing of the wellsprings of eternity, played out upon the frayed and flailing threads of troubled hearts. Scripture was the score, the music in the mind of God transcribed upon the pages of his Word. And like a good conductor with his orchestra to lead, the teacher of that Word of God will lead his people through the score and generate in each not just a grasp of all the notes, but music such that God himself is known.

Nothing is a substitute for this. Bible-teaching ministry will fail – for all that it excels in every other part – if worship is not kindled in the hearts of those who hear. It is therefore here that the teacher of the Word of God is challenged most of all. Is worship what I kindle in their hearts? Is music what emerges in their lives? Is God himself the One they learn to praise?

It is, of course, the Spirit who alone can take the tangled fibres of our souls and turn them into instruments of praise. Worship is his work within our hearts which no-one else can ever really replicate at all. That much is clear, as John himself suggests in setting out the context of the vision he received. 'I was in the Spirit', John declared, and so it always is. The Spirit breathes upon the embers of a long-forgotten song within our hearts and stirs them into flames of holy praise.

And yet, for all that that is true, the work of the Spirit is never a magical thing, as if it were but conjured up at the snap of the finger of God. There are conditions which favour the kindling of fires, and contexts conducive to music being made. It has something to do with the heart of the teacher himself. Here in Mr Philip was a man who long before he ever came to us had worshipped at the throne of God and therefore brought the fragrance of that sacred place, the haunting, whispered echoes of that music which reverberates through heaven's realms. If Bible-teaching ministry will issue in such worship on the part of those who hear, that worship first must fill the teacher's heart.

It has something to do with the method the teacher employs. I do not mean technique, but rather, the settled recognition that the way we have been made requires a thorough-going engagement with our minds if all the best emotions deep within are truly to be reached, aroused and channelled into praise. Bible-teaching ministry must ever be directed to the mind. The notes must first be learned before they can be played.

Last, but by no means least, this also must be said. That moving of the Spirit in our hearts has something to do with the substance of what is taught. The Spirit is given to glorify Christ: there is nothing he loves to do more. And when the teacher takes the score of Scripture and teaches Jesus Christ, the Spirit of the living God comes down and turns that score to symphonies of elevated, soaring adoration in our souls. James Philip did no more than open up that score and give a glimpse of God. Bar by vibrant bar he simply taught the glory of our risen, living Lord

– the Lord who was the Lamb, the King who was once crucified, the Son who made us children of the great eternal God. The Spirit did the rest. Our lives would never be the same again. The music had begun. A song would now be sung within our hearts for evermore.

And I resolved that I would strive with all my might and down through all my days to teach the Word of God like that.

Grateful Memories
of a Hungarian Pastor

Peter Balla

There is a long history of relationships between the Church of Scotland and the Hungarian Reformed Church. I stand gratefully in the line of those who had the privilege to study in Scotland with a scholarship from the Kirk. The origins of this scholarship go back to the 1840s. John Duncan, the minister of the then newly-founded Scottish Mission Church in Budapest, was well known as a scholar of Hebrew language and literature. When at the Disruption in 1843 the Old Testament professor in Edinburgh University decided to stay in the Established Church, the Free Church invited John Duncan to be the first Old Testament Professor at New College. So he returned from Budapest in 1843, and soon started to invite Hungarian pastors to study there. This was continued also after the united Church of Scotland came into being in 1929. The Church of Scotland regularly invites Hungarian pastors for a year's bursary, organised by the Board of World Mission. Until now about 160 pastors have studied in Scotland on this basis.

I have had the immense privilege of studying at New College twice: first, for one year in 1987-88 for the degree of Master of Theology, and then for three years in 1991-94 for a PhD. My family and I have experienced great love and help from the congregation at Holyrood Abbey Church. As an ever-grateful 'member' of that congregation, I recall some memories of my visits to Scotland. In doing so I would like to express my gratitude to the Revd James Philip personally and also to those members of the congregation who have helped us in so many ways. Both minister and members remain deeply in our hearts and in our prayers.

My connection with Holyrood Abbey Church began in 1984 when I was a student of theology in Budapest, and with some friends planned to go on a round trip of the British Isles. As poor students we asked advice from Hungarian pastors as to whom we might turn as hosts during our visit. The Revd Miklós Szarka recommended that we should contact Mr Philip in Edinburgh. To our letter he promptly replied saying that we could stay as guests at Rutherford House during our days in Edinburgh. What is more, when we actually arrived, there was a letter on the door of our room from two members of Holyrood Abbey, inviting us for a meal. So much help and care from people who had not even known us personally! This love and care have been poured on us ever since.

After those few days it was natural that when years later I arrived in Edinburgh on my first scholarship I should go to Holyrood Abbey Church to worship. I well remember my very first visit to that church. I arrived in Edinburgh on a Saturday, so the following day I went to church there. In Hungary, in most congregations worship begins at 10 a.m. I had not phoned to check whether it was true in Scotland; I simply went to church by 10 o'clock. The church was open, but there was only one man in the building – I was a little surprised. I asked him about the worship, and – to be honest – could not understand every word of his answer, but from his reassuring smile I understood enough to stay for the worship at 11. A little later I learned that the friendly man was none other than the church officer, who was just opening the doors and making the final touches so that one hour later the service could start in a beautiful and well-ordered church building. (He and his wife have hosted us many times; I now know that I am not alone in having difficulties in understanding his marvellous Scottish accent!)

May I mention a few more memories from that year? I shall never forget how many students attended and sang the hymns so beautifully at the evening services. Mr Philip was not only a preacher but also a teacher of the Word, and we went to the services both for spiritual nourishment and for a thorough Bible study. Mr Philip paid special attention to the theological students who attended his congregation: he also invited us as a group to his home for informal discussions. I hope many pastors follow his example in looking after students of theology in such a caring way.

During my first scholarship it happened that the renovation of the apartment the Church of Scotland rented for another student and me was not finished. When one couple from Holyrood learned about the difficulty, they immediately offered me lodgings with them. So the first month – which is naturally a difficult period with homesickness – was easy for me, because I felt I was a member of a family. The deep fellowship between many members of the congregation at Holyrood and me could be seen in the great honour shown to us when three members of the congregation came to our wedding in July 1989 in Budapest.

As a most lasting memory of that year I have to mention my second great experience with Rutherford House. My father-in-law (now a bishop, but then a *persona non grata* in the Hungarian monolithic system prior to the democratic changes) had written a manuscript in English as a synthesis of twentieth-century systematic theology. In those days there was no chance that it would be published in Hungary, and of course he himself did not have enough money to place it with a Western publisher. I brought the manuscript to Dr Nigel Cameron, then Warden of Rutherford House, who had a great understanding of our situation and accepted it for publication. This is the first book of my father-in-law, Dr Loránt Hegedüs, published abroad. Of course, publication takes time, so that when it eventually came out, the Revd Loránt Hegedüs had been elected as the new bishop right after the democratic changes. Professor John C. O'Neill, who wrote a very appreciative Preface, had to revise his text, so that it not only recalled the life story of an undeservedly neglected pastor, but also referred to the then fresh historic changes.

But before I turn to the period after the changes, another event has to be mentioned that proved essential for the rest of my life. My teacher and mentor at New College, Professor O'Neill, came to give lectures in Budapest in February 1990. He very kindly offered that I could study with him for a PhD and was willing to speak about this matter to my church authorities. He visited the deputy bishop, the Right Revd Dr Tibor Nagy, and asked him to give me leave for three years. Dr Nagy helpfully agreed, since he had the vision that this would not only help one person, but that the whole Hungarian church would be enriched if one of her members had a PhD from Scotland. Professor O'Neill also approached the Church of Scotland as well as the Hope Trust for support, and as a result a dream came true: I returned to Scotland for three years, this time with my family.

It is difficult to decide which memories I should mention from those three years; after all, it is a reasonably long period of one's life. We stayed in a missionary furlough house of the Kirk, some distance from Holyrood. We arrived with a little boy, Zsolt, seven months old, and two more boys were born there, Gergely and Csanád. It was natural that with little children we often went to the morning service just 'down the road' to our local congregation, St Stephen's Comely Bank, but we also attended Holyrood as often as possible. We had great help in that Holyrood members offered to take us by car to Holyrood Abbey. My wife, Gyöngyi, or I alone could also attend the evening services often with such help. Several members would often knock at our door offering a lift. So we could keep in touch with the congregation also during this second long stay in Edinburgh. As we were less mobile, people came to visit us. We will never forget, for example, that one member visited us every week, and even helped my study by providing us with a computer.

During these years I had the privilege of preaching at Holyrood and also of showing slides on the Reformed Church in Hungary to the midweek Bible study on Wednesday evenings. I will never forget how moving it was when I first saw our photo on the prayer board in the church hall. It was and still is a strength to us that the congregation at Holyrood continues to pray for us although it is many years since we have lived in Scotland.

Finally, I should like to add that the faithful work of a minister of the Word can be seen also in the life of his congregation. I remember happily how much it meant for me to see at Holyrood so many people of so many different backgrounds united in their love for the Word of God. As I am now a lecturer at the Theological Faculty at the Károli Gáspár Reformed University in Budapest, I mention gratefully the good example of one of the lecturers of Church History at New College (one of the editors of this volume) who sat there humbly in the pew week by week as a congregational member (and who was also ready to preach when need arose). Scholarship and devotion were not separated in his life. I should like to be a pastor and a teacher in my home country in such a way that all the enriching examples I saw in Scotland become part of my life for the benefit of those whom I have the privilege to serve.

May the Lord bless the pastor, Mr James Philip, now in his retirement, and the congregation which brings forth many fruits from his ministry. My family and I, and through us the Hungarian Reformed Church, express our gratitude for so much dear hospitality, and physical and spritiual nourishment, to the pastor, congregation, and the whole great Kirk of Scotland!

Part 3

The Wider Mission

The Northern Ireland Dimension

David Temple

Many a little boy has had the experience of throwing a stone into the middle of a smooth pond and watching the ripples radiate outwards and come right back to the shore side. Of course the deepest impact is where the stone lands but gentle ripples reveal the ongoing influence of the initial impact. Certainly when one looks at the ministry of James Philip it is like that of a stone being thrown into a pool. The strong impact was in Gardenstown and Holyrood Abbey in Edinburgh. However, the God-given gifts of this man were to have far-reaching effects, not least in Northern Ireland.

When James Philip began his ministry in Gardenstown in north-east Scotland, the evangelical faith in Northern Ireland was on the wane, after the impact of the Nicholson campaigns of the 1920s. In the largest of the Protestant denominations, the Presbyterian Church in Ireland, liberalism and neo-orthodoxy had been undermining a rich biblical inheritance and blunting the sharp edge of the gospel. Some might argue that the teaching of Barthian views in the Presbyterian Church's theological colleges was the beginning of a return to a more evangelical viewpoint, but certainly in that Church's ministry, evangelical ministers were thin on the ground and often their views were ignored in the courts of the Church.

Spiritual Drought and the Moving of the Holy Spirit

The work of the Spirit of God is fascinating when viewed on a national scale because at the time of the outpouring of the Spirit through James Philip's ministry in Gardenstown there was also a movement of the Spirit at congregational level in Ireland. This was seen specifically in a number of ministries in different parts of the Province of Ulster. In the little village of Ahoghill, near Ballymena, there were reports of many conversions in both Brookside and Trinity Presbyterian Churches under the ministry of the late Dr William Fleming and Dr Jim Matthews, both of whom later became Moderators of the General Assembly. In north Belfast the ministry of Dr James Dunlop in Oldpark was having a striking influence. South of Belfast, in the provincial towns of Lurgan and Portadown, there was significant evidence of the Spirit's outpouring in the ministry of the Revd Len Heaney (Hill Street, Lurgan) and Dr William Craig (First Portadown), and Alan Flavelle's ministry in Mourne Kilkeel was attracting a congregation of almost 1000 each Sunday.

Combined with this were increasing numbers of evangelical young men offering themselves for ministry, but the fear was that their evangelical zeal would be blunted by liberal and neo-orthodox theology. It was at this level that the ministry of James Philip was to have an extraordinary influence. There have always been close ties between the Church of Scotland and the Presbyterian Church in Ireland. Many students for the ministry in Ireland were attracted to New College, Edinburgh, particularly to the teaching of Professor James S. Stewart in the New Testament Department. Whilst living in Edinburgh many of these students found their way to Holyrood Abbey, where not only did they find a warm, welcoming congregation, but also a minister true to God's Word and aware of the theological problems with which evangelical students were grappling.

James Philip clearly had a great love and concern for those preparing for the Christian ministry. He gave much time to helping those students and introduced a monthly At Home in the manse on a Friday evening where students could discuss their spiritual and theological problems and receive sound advice in preparing for their ministry. I suspect these meetings were akin to Luther's table-talk and probably had the informality of Elijah's schools of the prophets. All who attended were impressed at the wide theological reading and grasp of the issues evident in James Philip's helpful and always gracious discussions. Indeed it was one Irish student, Drew Moore, who affectionately named James Philip 'the Prophet'. Having himself benefited from the ministry in Holyrood, he encouraged, nay implored, Irish students going to Edinburgh to make the Prophet's church their spiritual home. None of us ever regretted that decision. Indeed many of us, looking back to those days, realised that God was shaping us through James Philip's ministry. One student who came back to Belfast for the summer break after two years' worshipping in Holyrood was preaching in a congregation for summer supply. After the service the deaconess, Mary Angus, approached him and thanked him. She then turned to him and said, in so many words, 'You know when I was training as a deaconess at St Colm's College in the 1960s I worshipped in Holyrood Abbey, and I have never heard anyone handle the Word of God the way you did today since I sat listening to James Philip – do you happen to worship there when you are studying in Edinburgh?' This particular student had been paid his greatest compliment ever and realised, just as many others have done, how much he owed, under God, to the ministry of James Philip. Few of us had ever heard the gospel preached with such passion. The motivating factor in his life and ministry was once summed up in his own words when he said, 'The gospel that lifts the burden of sin from our hearts lays upon us another burden – the burden of a lost world.'

The Portstewart Connection

In times of spiritual drought, God has his own way of bringing sustenance to his people. For Elijah he provided the brook Cherith and the food supply of the ravens. In Northern Ireland, God supplied the ministry of the Portstewart Convention. This is the North of Ireland Keswick Convention which takes place on the last week of June each year. As J.T. Carson says in his history of the Convention,

> These unique gatherings were held in a large marquee over which floated the text 'All One in Christ Jesus' with its

attendant flags, 'faith', 'hope', 'love', 'joy' and 'peace'. The intention was not to provide a seaside holiday, with a few religious gatherings thrown in; it was a search for a deeper life of communion with Christ, and the experience of a life that in character was Christ-like, in Christian warfare was victorious and in Christian service was empowered by the Holy Spirit of God. [1]

The Convention had since its inception valued the ministry of Scottish ministers with visits by such well-known names as Duncan Campbell, G. B. Duncan, R. A. Finlayson, William Fitch, Duncan Leitch, William Still, J.G.S.S. Thomson, Alexander Fraser and John MacBeath. James Philip's first visit was in June 1957. Mr James McDonald, the honorary secretary of the Convention during 1944-94, first met James Philip in the manse of Springburn Hill Church, Glasgow, when he was assisting Dr William Fitch. In 1947 William Still was one of the Convention speakers and no doubt in the Convention House Party when talk of future speakers was being aired the name of James Philip was to the fore. His visits increased throughout the seventies, eighties and nineties and from 1981 onwards he assumed responsibility for the Bible Readings which were a major highlight of the Convention week. Dr William Craig, chairman of the Convention, and himself a popular convention speaker at both Strathpeffer and Keswick, in a personal interview, remembered James Philip's contribution in the following comments:

He was at his best in the preaching situation where he brought a great awareness of the holiness of God. In his preaching there was a great sense of awe at the presence of God. He was a charming member of the House Party and always had a twinkle in his eye. But James Philip also had an interest in the small details, such as a man's family, and he never forgot a name, so that one was left with the impression that they were clearly on

---

1. *The River of God is Full – The Portstewart Convention Through Seventy-Five Years (1914-1988)* (Portstewart, 1989), 3.

James Philip's prayer list. He was also keen to use all of the gifts God had given him and it was not uncommon to find in him a willingness to play the piano at the early morning convention prayer meetings. His humanity shines forth and whenever he came to the convention he was never thought of as a minister from afar, for he was much beloved by everyone privileged to sit under his ministry of God's Word.

However, James Philip's ministry at Portstewart was not confined solely to the preaching. Early on, the Convention treasurer and Presbyterian elder, the late T.S. Mooney, would gather together students for the ministry to meet James Philip informally, often over ice-cream and coffee, at the famous Morelli's Café on the seafront. There students found, not an eminent, aloof preacher, but a warm Christian man interested in their problems and ever available to give wise counsel, no matter how much that might have infringed upon his personal time.

The ministry in the Bible Readings was varied. Not only did James Philip guide people through books of the Bible such as Philippians in expositions which were later published, but he also taught some of the great themes of the Scriptures. Anyone who has come to know James Philip will realise the impression the writings of James Denney made upon him, especially on the theme of the cross of Christ. So it was that on the last of his visits to Portstewart he took as his theme for the Bible Readings 'The Cross of Christ'. He did not enter upon this lightly and indeed consulted with the secretary James McDonald, trawling upon his encyclopaedic memory. He was surprised to learn that the last occasion on which anyone had spoken directly on the cross in the Bible Readings had been some forty-one years previously. Then, Professor R. A. Finlayson presented a series of Bible Readings based on Isaiah 53:5, 'But he was wounded for our transgressions; he was bruised for our iniquities; the chastisement of our peace was upon him, and with his stripes we are healed.' James Philip's were memorable, because seldom would any congregation of God's people have been given such an in-depth grasp of the marvellous grace of God revealed in the death of his dear Son. Here was a series of Bible Readings that were intellectually stretching, devotionally challenging and inspirationally stimulating. Many are unlikely ever again to listen to such a thorough presentation of the cross of Christ.

Wise Churchmanship

During the period from the mid-sixties to the early eighties various trends within the ecumenical movement and the World Council of Churches (WCC) were causing deep disquiet within the Presbyterian Church in Ireland. This led to the decision of the 1980 General Assembly to cancel its membership of the WCC on the grounds that the gospel espoused by the WCC was not consistent with the Presbyterian Church's understanding of the gospel as presented in the New Testament.

Prior to this satisfactory outcome many younger evangelical ministers had been questioning whether or not they could stay within the ministry of the Presbyterian Church in Ireland. Over those years of debate various fellowships had been formed to galvanise Evangelicals in their Reformed faith and also to organise concerted action against continuing WCC membership at Presbytery and General Assembly levels. One of James Philip's great contributions was to provide a steadying influence to many of these ministers who may otherwise have been tempted to leave the Presbyterian Church. Dr William Craig recalls how on one occasion James Philip was addressing a group of Irish Presbyterian ministers on the issues causing so much disquiet. In answer to a question from the floor he said, 'I cannot foresee any situation in which I would leave the Church of Scotland.' This kind of stickability in faithfulness to the gospel, in the midst of a mixed denomination, made a deep impression on those present and his urging of men not to secede from their denomination did not fall on deaf ears. The subsequent years and changes in the Presbyterian Church in Ireland have proved the wisdom of James Philip's advice.

In 1997 the Moderator of the General Assembly, Dr Samuel Hutchinson, invited James Philip to conduct the worship at the General Assembly. Unlike the Scottish General Assembly, all the Irish Church's ministers and representative elders can attend every year. Those lunchtime worship sessions were well attended. Many could have given testimony to the help they had received over the years from James Philip in their own ministry. The one enduring comment that came from many lips hearing him pray and preach in the hushed silence of the Assembly was 'vintage Philip'.

Conclusion

Dr J.T. Carson paid this tribute to James Philip in the seventy-fifth anniversary book of the Portstewart Convention:

> James Philip came to our Convention in 1957[2] when he was minister at Gardenstown in Banffshire. Later he moved to Holyrood Abbey Parish in Edinburgh and there he exercised a ministry of power and ever-expanding usefulness for over 30 years. Greatly loved by his own people, he is also highly esteemed in the city. Christian students of the university and other colleges in Edinburgh are drawn like filings to a magnet to Holyrood and welded to the gospel and to Christ in a significant way. His links with so many missionaries, often forged in their student days, are maintained in an unbelievably faithful manner, in prayer, correspondence and love. He is no more on the platform than what he is in life, a man of God who is devoted to his Lord and his work.[3]

Speaking at the Portstewart Convention, Paul S. Rees once said:

> You can have power that seems to sway a multitude, power to prepare and deliver impressive sermons, power of eloquence, but have you power in your own home, and with your own children, with your own officers in the church? Have you power

2. Dr Carson's book has the year incorrectly, as 1959 (Ed).
3. *The River of God is Full*, 49.

to be Christ-like in your mood, manner and spirit? The power of the Holy Spirit is a power for Christlikeness before ever it is power to go out and do things that produce headlines in the newspapers.[4]

We shall be ever thankful to God that in James Philip we have witnessed such Christ-like power.

---

4. *Ibid.,* 42.

A Ministry that Spanned
a Missionary's Career

Marion Conacher

It cannot have happened very often that the same minister who presided over a missionary's valedictory service was still there to welcome her back after thirty years of service overseas. It was my privilege to have had that experience under the ministry of the Revd James Philip.

The congregation of Holyrood Abbey Church has played a large part in my life. I was not yet a month old when I was carried into the Church by my parents to be baptised by the Revd John Gilmour. I grew up in the midst of a caring congregation, nurtured through Sunday School, Bible Class and Youth Fellowship, initially under the ministry of John Gilmour, to be followed by the Revd Archibald Russell, both well-loved and respected ministers. Throughout those years I had always had a keen missionary interest. Unknown to me, this had been fanned by the prayers of one of my Sunday School teachers. When I came into church membership in 1952 I had already come to faith as a young teenager and knew that God was calling me to serve him overseas. My early attempts to enter nurse training were frustrated on health grounds but no experience is ever wasted in God's service. The years I spent in a legal office, followed by a year in America, were all to contribute to my preparation for service overseas. In 1957 I was at last accepted for nurse training and entered the Royal Infirmary, Edinburgh, a year before the Revd James Philip was inducted as minister of Holyrood Abbey Church.

I had never heard of expository preaching, but soon after Mr Philip arrived I knew that this was the teaching I had been looking for and sat enthralled as he opened up the Scriptures week by week. In those student days I did not want to miss a single opportunity to be present, knowing how little time remained for me to sit under such a ministry. For the next three years I was for ever trying to negotiate my off-duty to enable me to be present as often as possible, whether for the Bible Study on Wednesday evenings, the Prayer Meetings on Saturdays or at least once on Sundays, when I was usually accompanied by other student nurses.

In those days we would crowd into the north transept of the church, now the library, for the Bible Study and Prayer Meeting, until eventually we spilled over into the centre of the church, and finally into the church hall where we still meet today. My early memories are especially of studies in Genesis and Romans, but as the years passed, book by book, and sometimes more than once, the whole Bible was to be opened up for us.

After a year in Glasgow for midwifery, during which time God's call to missionary service was confirmed, I returned to Edinburgh to spend a year at St Colm's College under the auspices of the Church of Scotland, prior to sailing for India. Our various college assignments left us free only on Sunday evenings to be present at services of our own choice. So it was that each Sunday evening a large group of students, mostly preparing to go overseas, could be seen making their way from St. Colm's to Holyrood Abbey. Over and over again at the end of a service one would hear the remark, 'Oh, if only he would go on preaching for the rest of the evening!' We were all hungry for the Word that Mr Philip was so ably opening up for us.

By now the tape ministry and the Daily Bible Readings had been established and so began another aspect of Mr. Philip's ministry that was to mean so much to so many, but especially to those of us overseas, and so I soon realised that I was not to be cut off from Mr Philip's ministry after all. As I set sail for India in 1963 the fellowship presented me with a tape recorder. How grateful I was to be for that in the coming days! It was unpacked almost as soon as I arrived in India and used first of all in language school, as I along with other missionaries, who were equally grateful to have such a ministry available to them, gathered in the language lab on Sunday afternoons.

It had been decided that I should begin by studying Hindi, since that was the language used in the hospital to which I was going, but all church services were conducted in the local tribal language. It was to be three years before I had an opportunity to begin the study of that language also. And so for me, and other missionaries in similar or isolated situations, this ministry of the Word coming to us by means of the tapes and the Daily Bible Readings was a blessing beyond measure and made us realise even more so how privileged we were to be the recipients of such a ministry.

In my first place of service at Bamdah, Bihar, electricity cuts, lasting for hours, would often be a source of disappointment as we gathered, usually on Sunday evenings, to listen to the most recent tape to arrive from home. After four years I was transferred to a more isolated location, Pokhuria, a place with no electricity supply at all, and how grateful I was for the gift from a member of the congregation of a battery-run tape recorder to enable me to continue to have access to the tape ministry. This machine served me well over the next eight years.

The last eighteen years of service were spent at Tilda, Madhya Pradesh, and here the original tape recorder came into use once more. In Tilda there were more people with an understanding of English who could share the tape ministry and we were often joined by the young people who came to us through the Church of Scotland's Youth Share programme, or medical students doing their electives.

Throughout these thirty years of service overseas, through these varied means, I was able to continue to 'sit' under Mr Philip's ministry. What a privilege that has been. The Daily Bible Readings, faithfully produced each month, was a mammoth task in itself for Mr Philip, but greatly appreciated and in such great demand as evidenced by the hundreds of copies dispatched each month to every corner of the world. In India, rural pastors do not have the means to acquire a library of commentaries, nor are such easily accessible, and so the Daily Bible Readings met such a need for some of our local pastors.

On more than one occasion during my years in India in these different postings, the Daily Bible Readings provided a verse that assured me of God's protecting hand for that particular day. Many years ago, when I was still in Pokhuria in Bihar, I set out one day with our pastor and two other passengers in the Land Rover which I was driving to another of our mission stations. This involved travelling for some distance along the Grand Trunk Road which stretches across North India. That morning the Daily Reading had directed my thoughts to Psalm 138, in which David praises God for the truth of his Word. It was not until that evening that the full import of the latter part of verse 7 came home to me –'You stretch out your hand against the anger of my foes, with your right hand you save me.'

As we approached a village that straddled the road, I had automatically slowed down. Coming in the opposite direction was a heavy lorry. At that moment a little girl ran across the road in front of us, quickly followed by her small sister. The only direction for me to go was to steer off the road and as I came to a halt the little girl ran into the side of my vehicle. A crowd quickly gathered and I got down to check that the girl was all right. Amazingly the lorry had stopped and the driver came back to see that all was well. Having satisfied ourselves that there was no injury and she had just had a bad fright, he returned to his lorry and I prepared to drive off. At that moment a brick was thrown through my windscreen, the door wrenched open and some of the villagers attempted to drag me out of the vehicle while my passengers grimly held on to me. My watch and shoes quickly disappeared! But the miracle was that having realised what was happening the lorry driver once more returned to remonstrate with the crowd, and to tell me they needed to be given money! This I did, one of my passengers took over and we drove off to a safe distance where we could stop, to give thanks to God for our safe delivery and for me to take over the driving once more. 'You stretch out your hand against the anger of my foes, with your right hand you save me.'

Some years later I had been transferred to Tilda in Madhya Pradesh and there, with a School of Nursing affiliated to the mission hospital, I became involved with nurse education. One day I set out by train from Bilaspur to travel to Indore to attend a meeting of the executive committee of the Mid-India Board of Examiners, a journey that could take up to twenty-four hours. Late that same night we passed an express train travelling in the opposite direction. Only after my arrival at Indore I learned that soon after passing us it had been involved in a dreadful accident. Four or five days later, our work completed, we prepared to set out on our respective return journeys. That morning the Daily Bible Readings led us to Psalm 91 and as a result over breakfast we had been focused particularly on verse 11 – 'For he will command his angels concerning you, to guard you in all your ways.' All of us regularly travelled widely over long distances and were very conscious of the truth contained in this verse as was expressed in the various experiences related.

I alone was travelling back to Bilaspur. At 2 p.m. I was seen off at the station by the Board Secretary. There was nothing to indicate that this train would not reach its destination. The ticket collector checked my ticket as I entered the platform, and again in the course of the day it was checked at least twice, but no one ventured to say that the line was still blocked from the accident and this train would not be able to reach Bilaspur. Only in the course of the next morning when a group of policemen entered the carriage and enquired where I was going did I learn the extent of the accident. By then it was too late to get off at Jabalpur and they advised that I should stay with the train as far as it would go and then return with it to this same junction to take an alternative route. This I did and, after various delays, late that night I finally arrived back at Jabalpur and spent that night in the waiting room. Over and over again as the hours passed the words of verse 11 rang in my ears – 'For he will command his angels concerning you, to guard you in all your ways.'

Early next morning I joined a train on a narrow gauge railway, about which I had no previous knowledge, travelled through the most beautiful countryside, and finally reached Gondia in the south, from where I could set out once more for Tilda. When I finally arrived there I was a day and a half late.

Soon after Mr Philip's arrival amongst us the first of many valedictory services that would take place during his ministry had been held. By then at the Prayer Meeting we were conscious of his world-wide concern for those serving overseas as he introduced us to the needs of some of those already known to him. Over the years how much it has meant to each one of us to know that we had gone forth from a praying fellowship, that Saturday by Saturday the needs of the work and the people to whom we had gone would be upheld. This was especially so when we were faced with difficulties and we knew that, having shared these difficulties with Mr Philip, they would be placed before the Prayer Meeting that Saturday evening.

At my own valedictory service Mr Philip spoke first of all from Acts 13:3, 'And when they had fasted and prayed, and laid their hands on them, they sent them away', then from Acts 14:27, 'And when they were come, and had gathered the Church together, they rehearsed all that God had done with them.' During forty years of ministry in Holyrood Abbey Church Mr Philip had the privilege of 'sending away' some twenty-five or more missionaries, and the 'rehearsing' by each one, on his or her return, of what God had done in so many different places throughout Africa, Asia and South America, has been very much a part of the life of Holyrood Abbey during these past years.

Somehow in the midst of such a demanding ministry, as he ministered to the congregation in Holyrood Abbey, both through the preaching of the Word and in pastoral care, prepared the Daily Bible Readings and other publications and fulfilled so many other preaching engagements including participation in conventions, he still found time to maintain a regular correspondence with each one of us overseas, providing wise counsel and advice when we turned to him for guidance. Not only that, but he gave so generously of his time to meet with each one of us while we were at home on furloughs. How blessed we all have been.

The cost to Mr Philip of such a ministry, to so many, throughout all of those forty years and more, will never be known in earthly terms. One day the story will be told when many will rise up to call him blessed.

Serving by Going:
The Missionary Call Then and Now

Kenneth Ross

The Word of God and the Call to Mission

A landmark in the history of service of the Word of God was the publication in 1792 of William Carey's *An Enquiry Into the Obligation of Christians to use Means for the Conversion of the Heathens*. From that moment it became ever more apparent to the church at large that it was under an obligation to take the good news about Jesus Christ to every community around the world. So much so that it became difficult to understand how the church, during its many centuries of being concentrated on the continent of Europe, had largely failed to apprehend, and act upon, the 'great commission'. Circumstances, of course, played a significant part but when the industrial revolution and the expansion of trade opened up practicable possibilities for spreading the gospel to those in distant parts who had never heard the name of Christ, thoughtful Christians began to be gripped by the church's missionary mandate. The last words of Jesus, as recorded in Matthew's Gospel, made plain the extent of the church's responsibility in the proclamation of the gospel: 'Therefore go and make disciples of *all nations*, baptising them in the name of the Father and of the Son and of the Holy Spirit, and teaching them to obey everything I have commanded you.'[1] Carey, and others like him, felt themselves to be direct heirs of the Pentecostal promise of the book of Acts: 'But you will receive power when the Holy Spirit comes on you; and you will be my witnesses in Jerusalem, and in all Judea and Samaria, and to the ends of the earth.'[2] The setting apart of Barnabas and

---

1. Matt. 28:19-20.
2. Acts 1:8.

Paul by the church at Antioch and their subsequent missionary journeys provided a paradigm within which modern Christians might form and express a sense of missionary vocation.[3] The drive which impelled Paul to think of going ever westward, even hoping to reach Spain, transmitted to many others in the course of the nineteenth and twentieth centuries an impulsion to go in Christ's name to new situations.[4]

Fresh reflection on such biblical texts led to a renewed appreciation of the inherence of missionary endeavour in the gospel itself. If God had uniquely and decisively entered human life and history in the person of Jesus Christ, then this must be made known to all people everywhere. This evangelical logic gripped many who felt 'constrained by the love of Christ'[5] to engage in the emerging missionary movement. As time went on, and as the gospel took root in new situations, it became ever more apparent that not only did the gospel have a transforming effect on many of the communities in which it was preached, but also their fresh interpretation of the biblical message shed new light on its meaning. There was a rediscovery of the reality that it is in the crossing of cultural frontiers that the Christian faith comes into its own. How much of the New Testament revolves around the journey of Christian faith from the Jewish into the Greek culture! How often in history a fresh and compelling expression of Christian faith has been coined not in the heartlands but out on the frontiers where the gospel is being received in a new context and culture. New questions are asked, new answers are mined from the Scriptures and new light is shed on the wonder that Christ the Saviour has come. The rediscovery of this dynamic reality fired the imagination of many and lent a vitality to the missionary movement, which has made Christianity what it is today.

---

3. See Acts 13:1-3.
4. See Rom. 15:23-4.
5. 2 Cor. 5:14.

The Emergence of the Modern Missionary Movement

At first, when the missionary movement began to get underway in the early nineteenth century, the missionaries were widely regarded as fanatics or subversives. Little by little, however, their heroism, endeavour and evangelical obedience began to gain popular approval, with David Livingstone's funeral in 1873 perhaps marking a turning point. Nevertheless, even the Blantyre Mission, set up as a memorial to the pioneering missionary-explorer, struggled in its early years to find suitable candidates for service.[6] Yet the historical judgement of Andrew Walls is secure: 'When Livingstone and [Henry] Venn died, a new missionary period was dawning in which a tidal wave of eager young people and a host of new agencies would seek the evangelisation of the world.'[7] Under the impetus of the movement associated with the ministry of D.L. Moody, the Student Volunteer Missionary Movement was formed in 1886.[8] Every student who joined had to sign a declaration which read: 'I am willing and desirous, God permitting, to become a foreign missionary.'[9] It was in this period that large numbers of graduates, clergy and other professionals began to feature in the missionary movement.[10] By the time of the Edinburgh 1910

6. See A.C. Ross, *Blantyre Mission and the Making of Modern Malawi* (Blantyre, 1996), 18-19.
7. A.F. Walls, 'David Livingstone 1813-1873: Awakening the Western World to Africa', in G.H. Anderson, R.T. Coote, N.A. Horner and J.M. Phillips, eds., *Mission Legacies: Biographical Studies of Leaders of the Modern Missionary Movement* (New York, 1994), 140.
8. See C.H. Hopkins, *John R. Mott 1865-1955: A Biography* (Grand Rapids, 1979), 26-9, 60-61.
9. Later changed to 'It is my purpose, if God permit, to become a foreign missionary.' See T.J. Thompson, *Christianity in Northern Malawi: Donald Fraser's Missionary Methods and Ngoni Culture* (Leiden, 1995), 75.
10. See Adrian Hastings, *The Church in Africa 1450-1950* (Oxford, 1994), 264-70.

World Missionary Conference there was a great army of missionaries in the field with an inspiring sense of confidence that the world could indeed be evangelised within a generation.[11] Though their confidence and enthusiasm were tempered by the carnage of World War I, great dynamism remained and in the course of the twentieth century this was passed on to many of the emerging indigenous churches with whom the future of Christianity is increasingly seen to lie.

Though patient of analysis from many angles of interpretation, it is important to recognise that the modern missionary movement at its roots was a matter of theological commitment. At its heart lay the conviction that the gospel of Christ mattered and that it was of the utmost importance that the good news about Jesus Christ should be proclaimed and received in every part of the world. For this to occur it was necessary for men and women to go to communities where Christ was not yet known. Since the Christian faith had come to be largely concentrated in Europe and America, the missionary project was focussed on the vast territories of Asia and Africa. It found expression in the decisions of thousands of young people to dedicate their lives to this task and to journey across the world to establish themselves in a new community – with language, culture and customs quite different from anything they had known before. The physical dangers of tropical conditions and sometimes hostile receptions were real and all new missionaries were aware that an early grave might await them. Should they survive, a life of hardship, privation and insecurity would be guaranteed. Yet a sense of call gripped people and sent them on their way as part of a movement which was to transform world Christianity and to introduce marked changes to the religious demography of humankind.

---

11. See D.J. Bosch, *Transforming Mission: Paradigm Shifts in Theology of Mission* (New York, 1991), 334-9.

The Missionary Call
Central to the impetus of the modern missionary movement
was the decision taken by thousands of young people to devote
their lives to serving Christ overseas in this way. This became
known as 'the missionary call', which has been defined as:

> a special and unique call to full-time ministry . . . the command
> of God and the setting apart by the Holy Spirit of an individual
> Christian to serve God in a culture, a geographical location,
> and, very likely, in a language different than the missionary's
> own. The personal recognition of this call comes with a growing
> conviction that God has set the recipient apart for this service.
> The result of this conviction is an intense desire to obey and to
> go wherever God leads.[12]

You touch the heart of the modern missionary movement when
you enter this sphere. For while it is a movement which has
many dimensions and is capable of being considered from many
different angles, it was with this sense of call that every
missionary career began and it was this inner momentum which
lent a distinctive quality to missionary service. Like all religious
experience, the missionary call does not lend itself to
comprehensive definition. Yet it is a matter of well-attested
historical fact that countless missionaries spoke of it as the
mainspring of their life and service. Often they could look back
on a decisive moment, as James Matthews did when he recalled
an evening when

> the church was crowded, for the preacher was Bishop Azariah
> of Dornakal Diocese in South India. . . . I do not know how it
> was with others present that night, but I know how it was with
> me. It seemed to me that once again Jesus stood behind that

---

12. T.L. Austin, 'Missionary Call, The', in A.S. Moreau, ed.,
Evangelical Dictionary of World Missions (Grand Rapids, 2000),
645-6.

preacher, his hand on the preacher's shoulder and the source of Azariah's power. Though not ordinarily much given to this sort of thing, I knew then and there that I must become a missionary to India.[13]

It was with such a sense of conviction that thousands of young people were gripped, particularly at the high point of missionary enthusiasm in the late nineteenth and early twentieth century.

James Philip, Holyrood Abbey and Missionary Vocation

The high noon of the modern missionary movement was already past by the mid-twentieth century but its later years were not without fruitfulness. Among the congregations where the tradition of missionary call and missionary service found continuing expression was Holyrood Abbey during the ministry of James Philip from 1958 to 1998. The foundation was the overwhelming sense of the seriousness of the issues at stake in the proclamation of the gospel, which gripped generations of students and young people who crowded the galleries of Holyrood. Once it was established that the gospel *mattered* supremely, there emerged the environment in which the missionary call was a possibility. A more explicit challenge often arose from expository sermons, particularly in Sunday evening messages ending with a stirring summons for those present to consider what the Lord was saying to them about the purpose and direction of their lives. A key resource in answering that question was the Saturday evening prayer meeting where week by week members joined in prayer not only for congregational and national concerns but always also for missionary work in different parts of the world. Engaging in earnest prayer for overseas missionaries and their work did much to create a frame of mind in which there could develop a

13. J.K. Matthews, 'My Pilgrimage in Mission', *International Bulletin of Missionary Research* 23/1 (January 1999), 19.

sensitivity to the possibility of a missionary call. Individual missionaries who wrote regularly to the minister and periodically made visits to Holyrood acted as role models and there was always missionary literature available.

Quietly, unpretentiously but steadily and consistently, the point was thus made that the worldwide missionary task was at the heart of the church's purpose and responsibility. For those whose hearts were burning with the desire to serve Christ, one question they had to answer was whether or not God was calling them to the 'mission field'. Steadily, year by year, there were those who found that the answer was 'yes'. As they heard and obeyed the call, the whole congregation was called to identify with it and to commit themselves to ceaseless prayer as another missionary vocation took effect. In all this there was a cumulative effect. The sense of awe which marked Holyrood services was formed, at least in part, by the consciousness that in the event of the worship, and particularly in the preaching of the Word, people might well be gripped by the missionary call which would be the determinative turning-point of their lives, sending them to the ends of the earth. 'Serving by going' bore testimony, more eloquently than any words could, to the impact of the living Word in the lives of the listeners.

Trends Affecting Missionary Service in the Twenty-First Century

In retrospect it is possible to appreciate that we have now entered what Andrew Walls has called the 'old age of the missionary movement'.[14] This is for the very good reason that the missionary movement has been, to a remarkable degree, successful in its stated objective of spreading the gospel and planting the church in societies where it had not been known before. It has become commonplace to observe that the strength of the church increasingly lies in the former mission fields of

14. A.F. Walls, *The Missionary Movement in Christian History* (New York, 1996), 255-61.

the 'south' – Africa, Latin America and parts of Asia. A product of this success is that the missionary task is no longer a matter of going out from Christendom to 'heathen lands across the sea'. Having worked for several generations within that paradigm of missionary endeavour, it can be uncomfortable for Western Christians to adapt to the new situation. Having been for centuries the repository of Christian faith and its authoritative expositor, the Western church has to undergo a mental revolution if it is to recognise that Christianity's centre of gravity has shifted to the south. David Smith has commented that:

> The perplexity experienced by many European churches today is related to the struggle to come to terms with the fact that the real centres of Christian life and growth are now located in the non-Western world. Long established habits of thought and practice based on the assumption that the churches of the West occupy centre-stage in the purposes of God must be abandoned in the light of this new reality. We find ourselves standing in the wings, witnessing others take the lead in God's still unfolding drama of redemption.[15]

This recognition is a big step for Western Christians to take. Ultimately, however, they have no choice. Having encouraged and enabled others to receive the gospel on their own terms, Western missionaries must be prepared for the faith to find a new form and idiom. The cat is out of the bag. As Lamin Sanneh comments: 'When one translates [the gospel], it is like pulling the trigger of a loaded gun: the translator cannot recall the hurtling bullet.... The centre of the religion shifted to the particular culture that was being addressed.'[16] Having offered the faith to others, Western Christians must be prepared to live

---

15. D. Smith, 'Junction or Terminus? Christianity in the West at the Dawn of the Third Millennium', in T. Yates, ed., *Mission – An Invitation to God's Future* (Calver, 2000), 92.

16. L. Sanneh, *Translating the Message: The Missionary Impact on Culture* (New York, 1989), 53, 69.

with the consequences of these others' passionate engagement with it, and with the reality that the outcome has often proved to be quite different from that which was anticipated. As Dana Robert has remarked: 'Ultimately, the most interesting lessons from the missionary outreach during the Western colonial era is what happened to Christianity when the missionaries weren't looking, and after the colonisers withdrew.'[17]

The outcome, on a global scale, is that both the nature of the church and the structure of its mission have undergone an irreversible change. As Andrew Walls observes:

> Christian faith is now more diffused than at any previous time in its history; not only in the sense that it is more geographically, ethnically and culturally widespread than ever before, but in the sense that is diffused within more communities. The territorial 'from-to' idea that underlay the older missionary movement has to give way to a concept much more like that of Christians within the Roman Empire in the second and third centuries: parallel presences in different circles and at different levels, each seeking to penetrate within and beyond its circle.[18]

Another sea-change is the vast increase in travel and communication which brings Christians into contact with others in many different parts of the world. Last year 47 million people took flights out of the UK and this number is currently increasing by 5% per year. Even if a modest proportion of these travellers include an awareness of Christian mission in their experience, this would be a significant expression of mission in our time. Furthermore, the arrival of the internet has vastly increased the contact which people have with distant parts of the world. Though many internet-users remain within a limited sphere and relate largely to commercially-driven material, there are wider possibilities to be explored. If, of the 400,000 emails sent every

---

17. D. Robert, 'Shifting Southward: Global Christianity since 1945', *International Bulletin of Missionary Research* 24/2 (April 2000), 57.
18. Walls, *The Missionary Movement in Christian History*, 258-9.

second, only a tiny proportion contained material of missional significance, this would constitute an important missionary movement of our time. We may not easily recognise it because it has none of the regimented, well-oiled machinery of the modern missionary movement of the nineteenth and twentieth centuries. There is no head office, no organising committee, no command structure, and no comprehensive strategic direction. It is a post-modern movement of individuals making their own connections, developing their own perspectives and functioning within networks which they themselves have constructed. Paul Pierson reflects on this change when, as a member of the older generation, he contrasts his experience with that of young people today:

> We were loyal to the concept of missions, we trusted institutions, including mission organisations, and of course we were interested in specific missionaries. The younger generation today wants to know and experience everything almost immediately and is generally impatient and distrustful of institutions of all kinds. An additional factor is a general suspicion and fear of long-term commitments, which affects attitudes toward traditional institutions, including mission agencies.[19]

To those shaped by a classical Enlightenment approach to the construction of knowledge and the organisation of society, this diffuse, individualised, networking world is a confusing one. Yet it holds possibilities for a new form of missionary engagement fitted to the global culture emerging in our time.

New Patterns of Missionary Service

If church overseas mission boards and independent missionary societies are to be effective in this new context, they have to

---

19. P.E. Pierson, 'Local Churches in Mission: What's Behind the Impatience with Traditional Mission Agencies?', *International Bulletin of Missionary Research* 22/4 (October 1998), 148.

pass through a considerable paradigm shift. Stanley Green indicates what this has involved for North American Mennonites over the past few years:

> We needed to be willing to adapt our self-identity from that of a centralised bureaucracy that 'owned' the mission (we designed the initiatives, recruited the workers, deployed the personnel, and then courted and cajoled congregations to support our program) to a more decentralised, networking entity focused on developing synergistic partnerships with regional . . . conferences, congregations, and international partners.[20]

Perhaps the most marked feature of this paradigm shift is that the missionary enterprise ceases to be the project of a tightly-knit core of dedicated professionals who make a career of it, and becomes an open-ended venture in which large numbers of people can enjoy direct participation for longer and shorter periods.

Gap years, career breaks, post-retirement appointments, even creative use of vacations – such forms of short-term involvement in the work of mission open the door to an ever wider range of people. It would be easy to dismiss their efforts as little more than tourism with a religious flavour and to contrast this with the life-long commitment of missionaries of earlier years. But Ted Ward offers wise counsel when he writes that:

> Although in the case of some of these people, at least in the short run, such experiences may be a waste of time and resources of the mission agency, for many of these Western adventurers such overseas junkets are the spark that ignites mission consciousness and awakens a concern for more effective forms of missionary presence. For slow-minded mission agencies the short-term phenomenon will be an

---

20. Stanley W. Green, 'How Mennonites Repositioned a Traditional Mission', *International Bulletin of Missionary Research* 23/4 (October 1999), 162.

increasing nuisance. But for creative agencies, ways are already being found to encourage and support these activities as additional species and types of Christian relationship and development.[21]

Not least of the reasons for undertaking such adaptation is the fact that exposure to the youthful vigour of Christian movements elsewhere may be the spark that ignites a renewed experience of faith for a new generation of Westerners.

A significant feature of this new framework is that the 'call' is set in the context of the discipleship which marks the life of every Christian. In contrast to the past when 'missionary' was a category of service quite distinct from that of the ordinary church member, we have entered a period in which there is the possibility for many Christians of giving some part of their life to 'missionary service'. It is an open, dynamic and fast-moving field where getting the right person in the right place at the right time, even for a short period, may be of great strategic significance.

In this context, the life-long career is no longer the normative pattern of missionary service. As Andrew Walls wryly remarks: 'The missionary no longer answers a lifetime call, and certainly does not get a visa for it.'[22] However, this is not to conclude that there is no longer any need for dedicated, full-time mission practitioners. Far from it! Without in any way undervaluing short-term mission involvement, there remains a pressing need for those who will give their best years to the work of sharing the gospel of Christ in a context and culture overseas where such ministry is desperately needed. The business of learning another language, entering into another culture, sharing your life at a deep level with another people – this is not something

21. Ted Ward, 'Repositioning Mission Agencies for the Twenty-first Century', *International Bulletin of Missionary Research* 23/4 (October 1999), 150.
22. Walls, *The Missionary Movement in Christian History*, 260.

which can be realistically attempted on a short-term trip, however valuable that may be in other respects. It remains a necessity for effective mission that there should be those who invest the prime of their lives in the great enterprise of taking the gospel of Christ across new frontiers.

One area where the salience of the missionary call comes particularly into prominence today is in relation to the globalisation which is rapidly increasing the gap between the affluent and the impoverished in the world community. The United Nations Development Programme speaks of 'parallel worlds': security, affluence, power in the one, violence, poverty and disintegration in the other.[23] What a wide gulf between the two and what a demanding journey to cross it. The pioneering missionaries of the nineteenth century had to make journeys that were physically arduous and hazardous. But socially the gulf was often not particularly great. The social conditions in rural France and rural Uganda were not so very different. The economic conditions which David Livingstone found in southern Africa were not so very strange to him because of all that he knew of the life of his grandparents who had lived in the Highlands of Scotland.[24] Today, when a plane takes you across the world in a day and an email connects you worldwide in seconds, ironically the gulf between the rich and the poor is becoming much greater and it is ever more demanding to cross. Those who take the gospel of Christ to the refugees, sex-workers, street-children, HIV/AIDS sufferers and others who are on the losing side of the globalisation process will require all the conviction and momentum which comes from a sense of missionary calling. It may be no longer a territorial 'from-to' movement but the need is greater than ever for those who will sacrifice affluence, comfort and security in order to follow Christ

---

23. United Nations Development Programme, *Human Development Report* (New York and Oxford, 1999), 6.
24. D. Livingstone, *Missionary Travels and Researches in South Africa* (New York, 1858), 2.

to situations of violence and deprivation. So far as Western churches are concerned it might be the 'old age of the missionary movement' but if the church is alert to its identity and calling, it will continue to give some of the best of its members to the mission of Christ in other parts of the world.

Before they are ready to go, however, they will be overwhelmed by a sense of the seriousness of the issues at stake, informed about what is involved in missionary service in today's world, and convinced that God is calling them quite specifically to offer themselves and to go to a new context to witness there to Christ's love. While the territorial 'from-to' pattern of mission is an historical episode from a time now passed, the missionary call which lay at its heart has continuing validity in a new context. The world is waiting for those who will set forth with the conviction that God has called them to play their part in advancing Christ's purposes today by making the gospel known in new situations which have opened up in our time. James Philip's ministry across the second half of the twentieth century was marked by a profound appreciation of the seriousness of the issues at stake in the proclamation of the gospel and carried a lively sense of the possibility that anyone hearing the biblical message might be called quite specifically to missionary service. While forms of service may change, this will remain the foundation of pioneering Christian witness in the twenty-first century. 'Serving by going' will remain an active option for those who are gripped by the majesty of the gospel, and a passion to make it known and to see it take effect 'even to the ends of the earth'. The missionary call may take different forms, but it will remain the beating heart of effective outreach in Christ's name.

By Tape to Zambia and Swaziland: James Philip in Africa

Bill Fraser

The place and the importance of our friend Jim Philip's tape ministry in the work and service of a medical missionary in Southern Africa will no doubt come to be fully known only on the 'accounting day', when the God we serve dispenses his awards to those servants who prepare the seed of his Word as well as those who reap its fruits.

For nearly thirty years, we have been privileged to receive the tapes of the morning and evening services from Holyrood Abbey Church. What a thrill it was to receive that first tape! We had just arrived in Zambia to take up the post of medical officer in the hospitals of the copper mines in Luanshya, the garden city of the Copperbelt (incidentally, we never did find out who gave our name and address to the tape folks at Holyrood Abbey, but they must have been guided by the Lord and we surely are grateful to them). Not only was my life enriched by listening to the tape as I travelled by car between the Luanshya and Roan Hospitals in the course of a day's work, but I went into theatre knowing the peace of God and his power experimentally from the tape dealing with Philippians 4. What warm-hearted exhortations unfolded from this little cassette, assuring us that our work was not in vain in the Lord!

As I think back to those days, I call to mind the numerous occasions when the timing of the delivery of the tape was truly ordered of the Lord. My responsibility extended outside the realm of medicine and surgery as an elder in the local fellowship known as Luanshya Chapel. The building itself had once served as the Jewish Synagogue, but as the Jewish community in Luanshya dwindled, we were able to buy 'for a song' the facility as well as its most comfortable chairs. Quite a miracle! After listening to one of Jim's tapes, our Zambian brothers and sisters at our weekly Bible studies held at the Chapel were greatly blessed and inspired. An added bonus for us expatriate Scots was to hear Jim's rich Scottish voice. His tapes reached to the far corners of Zambia and were a great blessing to all who heard them. At weekends, as chairman of the medical sub-committee of Mission Medic-Air – this was before the days of the Zambian Flying Doctor Service – we were called upon to fly in our single-engine Cessna aircraft to rural hospitals and mission stations, to treat difficult cases and, where necessary, to airlift patients to Luanshya hospitals. Often these flights would be to the Luapula Province where the mission hospitals just happened to be manned by dedicated nursing staff from Scotland, some of whom knew of Jim's ministry at Holyrood Abbey Church and some who had been commended to the work by Brethren assemblies in Edinburgh and other parts of Scotland and were serving under the banner of Christian Missions in Many Lands (CMML). Just as eagerly as the medical expertise was awaited, so was the most recent tape from Holyrood Abbey and the staff savoured the rich teaching contained therein.

Another aspect of our work in Zambia was more of a pastoral nature, in time spent with miners from Malawi and other surrounding countries, away from home for long stretches and anxious about their families left behind. So often, the most recent tape would be especially appropriate to their need, assuring them of the safe-keeping of the Good Shepherd of John 10. Many of these men were believers who were pursuing the Emmaus Bible Courses. My wife, Mary, was kept very busy marking and correcting their exam scripts. What a wonderful adjunct to this ministry the tapes proved to be, and again, always arriving at just the right time. I am reminded of a particular topic – our position 'in Christ' from Ephesians 2. To handle material in which one has confidence is a great blessing, not only on the mission field but elsewhere. Jim's exposition of the Word of God had our fullest confidence as we listened and examined the various truths contained in the tapes. Dr Livingstone did not have this amazing resource.

The fall in the price of copper (Zambia's main export) on world markets had a grave effect on the exchange rate of the kwacha. It became increasingly difficult for us to externalise enough money to pay for our children's education at George Watson's College, Edinburgh. We took this as an indication from the Lord that we should move elsewhere. There were no suitable schools in Zambia for our four children and we looked to him for guidance as to our future sphere of service. In so many ways, it was confirmed to us that we should move to Swaziland – a country of which we had never heard until this time. In 1976, together with our elder son, Alistair, we took a step of faith and moved south to this tiny kingdom. God was in the move as subsequent events proved. On the very day on which I arrived at the 450-bed Mission Hospital in the town of Manzini looking for employment, the superintendent of that hospital had a perforated peptic ulcer. This was a great tragedy since the medical and surgical staff at the hospital was already greatly depleted. I had 'dropped from heaven'. Accommodation was provided and the rest of the family was able to join us. Alistair completed his A levels at Waterford/Kamhlaba, a United World College in the capital city of Swaziland, Mbabane. Kirsty, our elder daughter, remained at St Denis School in Edinburgh to finish her secondary schooling while our two younger children, Keith and Emma, were enrolled at a fine local school in Manzini. It also transpired that the Teacher Training College attached to the mission was desperately in need of lecturers and my wife was able to meet that need. I am so glad to report that this transition period and change of address did not interrupt the regular flow of tapes from Holyrood. We were not starved of the Living Bread.

The superintendent of the mission hospital, Dr Samuel Hynd, another expatriate Scot, made a good recovery and went on to become the Minister of Health for Swaziland. As far as my work was concerned, again we saw God's hand in this. Dr Hynd was able to identify a vacant post at the government Hospital in Mbabane that could be funded by a medical aid programme from Britain and required the all-round experience that I possessed. So we all moved to Mbabane to a house provided by the Swazi government. There were also new opportunities for ministering God's Word through the Hospital Christian Fellowship with regular meetings with the nursing staff and students at the Nurses' Training College. Here again Jim's tapes proved so helpful, with his outreach emphasis of the morning services and the emphasis on the up-building of the Christian in the evening services. The nurses had no difficulty understanding him either, because they were quite used to hearing Scottish voices around the hospital.

During this time in the capital, as a family we sought a fellowship of the Lord's people and found one that was, or at least had been, meeting in a school hall. However, the pastor of this group was leaving to take up a pastorate in Australia and there was a need for someone to fill the role of senior elder so that the work could continue. As a family and after much prayer, we felt that we should continue there and as our fellowship grew in numbers into a true local church, it was considered necessary that we should have a name. So began Mbabane Chapel, a non-denominational fellowship with regular worship services, gospel outreach services, Sunday School, Bible Studies and prayer meetings. For a time we felt a bit like the children of Israel, wandering in the wilderness, as we moved from one school hall to another. At one time we even shared a church building with another church fellowship, with Mbabane Chapel holding our morning service at 9 a.m. to allow them to have their service at the usual time of 10.30 a.m.

This was all very unsatisfactory and after a great deal of prayer and much sacrificial giving on the part of our church fellowship, we were able to purchase land from the City Council and build our very own church premises on this prime site within the city boundaries. At this very time my wife, Mary, had been appointed by the Prime Minister to serve as a City Councillor, in which capacity she became aware that this particular plot of land was for sale. This land on which Mbabane Chapel now stands is just next to the international school called Sifundzani (siSwati for 'What are we learning?') which the Swazi government asked my wife to start and of which she has been the Principal for the past twenty-one years. Sifundzani is a Christian school with four hundred pupils drawn from forty different countries and it offers, we believe, a quality of education second to none. Yet again, this was confirmation that the Lord wanted us here in Swaziland. As before in Zambia, so here in Swaziland the tapes from Holyrood Abbey provide a wonderfully rich resource for our Bible Study groups and other fellowship meetings. We sometimes wonder what we would ever do without them.

On a personal note, our elder daughter, Kirsty, her husband and daughter, aged five, are in Johannesburg in the Republic of South Africa. That is approximately 370 kilometres from our house here in Mbabane and like all doting grandparents, we often want to visit our granddaughter (if not her Mum and Dad!). The journey by car there and back is never complete without two tapes from Holyrood Abbey – one to hear on the way to Johannesburg and one for the way home. It is amazing how much shorter the journey seems when we can listen to both the morning and evening services and hear those tremendous expositions, not to mention the powerful singing. Often too, on these journeys, we have been asked to give someone a lift and we are happy to do this, provided they realise that we will be listening to Jim's tapes, as is our wont. They are certainly wonderful as idle-gossip stoppers and we pray that perhaps some of those who are not believers will listen attentively and as a result will be born again. The occasion of writing this chapter has served to remind me of that well-worn but very apt saying, 'One sows, another reaps, but God gives the increase.' If that be so, then what shall we say of him who prepares the seed for the sowing? Surely his reward will be great when 'the books are opened'. On a much lower level, it is difficult to express our gratitude to our friend, Jim Philip, for all that we have enjoyed of his ministry on tape over these past thirty years. 'Well done, good and faithful servant' (Matt. 25:21).

Teaching Expository Preaching in Korea

Willie Black

They read from the book of the Law of God, making it clear and giving the meaning so that the people could understand what was being read (Nehemiah 8:8).

This is as good a definition of expository preaching as you will find in the Bible. Clearly the written Word of God was seen to be central to the teaching the people needed to hear. Its meaning was carefully explained and applied to their lives. The aim was very much that everyone who was listening could understand. This is the essence of expository preaching. All the teaching in a sermon should be seen to come out of the passage being preached and its contents carefully and practically applied to the lives of those who listen.

I had been converted to Christ at the age of sixteen but had little opportunity to hear biblical preaching until I went to university, although there was one memorable weekend, perhaps a year after I became a Christian, when I visited my brother who was at university in Edinburgh. We attended morning service at Charlotte Chapel and the evening service at Holyrood Abbey. It was just manna to my soul and created a hunger for biblical teaching and spiritual truth which did not begin to be met until I went university myself and worshipped in churches where God's Word was taught. When I studied at New College the opportunity to attend Holyrood on a regular basis came about and I increasingly found that the most satisfying preaching was of a systematic expository style. A group of theological students attended each week. We talked avidly of what we had heard that night and eagerly anticipated what would be taught on next week's passage. Bit by bit the whole of the Bible would be taught; difficult sections had to be dealt with – for uncomfortable subject-matter could not be ignored.

What I heard in those informative years in Holyrood and in other situations determined me from the beginning of my own ministry to attempt a similar preaching style. It was a case of trial and error. I still remember taking three and a half years to cover the Gospel of John in Kinlochbervie. A glance at the notes of these early sermons shows a far too heavy reliance on commentaries, but the freedom from the difficulty of what to preach each week, the ready listening of a people who had a real desire for the Word of God and the effects (as with Nehemiah) of repentance, faith, obedience and joy in the lives of God's people were sufficient spur to keep on.

It was not without opposition. On one occasion I was accosted at the end of an evening service by one of our members seriously upset by the slow progress through 1 John and the constant demands on him to love his brothers in Christ. He told me in no uncertain terms that this kind of preaching could result only in people being driven away. A visit to his home to talk over the problem only made the matter worse. Both he and his wife reaffirmed his opinion in strong terms. It was not easy the next Sunday to get up and preach the next section of 1 John. After that evening service another member took me aside and asked me if something had happened during the week, because one evening she had felt strangely constrained to pray for me and had only been able to receive one word of guidance from the Lord, 'Pray that Willie will guard the Word of God' – and so she had prayed that. Needless to say tears followed as I shared with her what had happened that week. The person who had protested turned up a few weeks later in tears himself and acknowledged that he had a lot to learn yet about loving his brothers and sisters in Christ. These were formative years – years of learning the art of preaching, and fortunately in the providence of God with a people who were generally encouraging and hungry for God's Word. I little suspected the next step God had in mind.

The Call to Korea

God is full of surprises. An OMF representative came every year to our church in Kinlochbervie and Durness. In 1981 it was the turn of Durness to host the meeting. Dick Dowsett spoke that night on the needs of the world in terms of mission from Isaiah 42. I found myself virtually sitting at his feet on a small child's seat and as he spoke sensed myself increasingly pounded by the Word of God and the needs of the world. A deep conviction set in. As people left, Dick casually made the remark that OMF needed Presbyterian ministers to go to Korea to teach expository preaching. A chance remark became God's Word for the moment. Of course it had to be tested. Emotion is never a great basis for a call. And anyway the whole thought was so terrifying it seemed best to me to find a way out. My simple prayer the next day was that, if that had been the voice of God, then if someone else mentioned Korea that day I would follow it up. I presumed I would be safe since we intended to drive to Glasgow that day, but that night, while sharing the gist of the sermon with my friend, the Revd Iain Laing, he simply asked if God was calling me to Korea.. Suffice to say, the Lord confirmed his leading two weeks later at a Christian conference in Largs when the preacher on the last night said two significant things, 'Someone tonight must leave a work he really loves and begin a new work' and 'Someone here tonight must go thousands of miles in the will of God – he must do it'. It was a clear and unmistakeable call – a call to Korea and a call to work in expository preaching. In January 1982 our family left for Singapore and in April arrived in Korea.

The Church in Korea

The history of the church in Korea is a remarkable one. Right from the start it was firmly based on the Word of God. The story is now well known of Robert Thomas who went to Korea with the Gospel of Luke in Chinese. He was martyred right away but the Gospels were kept, read and used by the Spirit of God to draw people to faith, so that when the first missionaries entered Korea they discovered believers already there. Another interesting influence was that of two Scottish missionaries to Manchuria, John Ross and John MacIntyre, who found themselves ministering to Koreans on the border and eventually produced a translation of the New Testament from the Chinese into Korean. The main influence however came with an influx of American Presbyterian missionaries in the north and Australian Presbyterians and Methodists in the south. Revival in North Korea in 1907 saw many brought to Christ. The Korean war caused many of the Christians in the north to flee south to give a significant boost to the church in the south. From then on the growth of the Korean church has been remarkable. In a very short time it has grown to embrace 25% of the population with some of the largest congregations in the world meeting in Seoul and churches in every town and on every street corner.

There are many reasons for this growth: the sovereign grace of God working in a downtrodden nation, the great emphasis on prayer that from the early days has been part of the Korean church, aggressive evangelism on the streets, generous giving, a weak form of Buddhism, involvement of the church in the independence movement, etc. The result has been a church which is strongly Presbyterian in government and largely Reformed and conservative in its theology. In a country with a strong Confucian background, the more formal nature of Presbyterian government and the authoritarian nature of its teaching, with pastors revered and unquestioned, appeals to the Korean mind.

With most pastors having to preach ten times per week – each day at the dawn prayer meeting, twice on Sundays and once midweek – a systematic expository approach to preaching would be an extremely helpful one. The tradition, however, in most churches was one of topical preaching. It was into this situation that in April 1982 we arrived, looking to the Lord to guide us in setting up a ministry in this area but not really knowing if it was wanted or indeed how to do it.

The Ministry Begins

In the midst of language study I was asked to preach once a month at the OMF prayer meeting in Seoul. About sixty people attended. Practising what I had come to preach, with an excellent interpreter, I worked my way through the book of Jonah. In the midst of that series a group of pastors asked me to begin an expository preaching Bible study. They had liked what they had heard. When we began it was difficult, for they had little English and I had little Korean, but we persevered. When I asked them one day why they persevered when it had to be of little benefit to them, we discovered a remarkable fact. In 1981 they had attended an expository preaching seminar given by Dennis Lane and had been so blessed that they had begun to pray for someone to come and teach them. As they prayed, God began to speak to us in Kinlochbervie. As we shared these facts we wept together as we came to a deep realisation of this God who is not beyond answering prayers half way round the world. It was a learning experience for me as I began to get to grips with their weaknesses and their needs in the area of preaching.

A year later saw our formal language study come to an end and we learned that our designation was to be Pusan, a huge city on the south coast. We were appointed to a church of about 400 people which belonged to the Koshin denomination, an old, very respected denomination similar to the Free Church of Scotland. On an introductory visit six months before we moved, I spoke briefly before the church of our plans and our vision to teach expository preaching. At the end of the service I met a young pastor who happened to be visiting the church that day. He also had attended Dennis Lane's seminars. He assured me that as soon as I could get there he would have a group ready and waiting. In fact he even offered to fly me down each week till we could move.

The day after we moved into our house some Bible students came to the house. They had heard of our arrival and wanted me to begin a group for Bible students. It was soon apparent that God was way ahead of us. Getting a ministry up and running would not be the problem. And so it was over the years that requests came in steadily. Organisations like Scripture Union and Tyrannus (committed to teaching the Quiet Time and expository preaching) began organising weekly groups in various nearby cities and three-day seminars all over Korea in the school holidays. Opportunities to preach in churches and conferences soon followed. I made sure I only practised what I had come to preach, always teaching in a systematic and expository manner. Having a ministry was never the problem, but how best to help these men in their own preaching was something which had to be learned.

The Development of a Teaching Method

It soon became apparent that two main problems needed to be addressed if pastors were to learn an expository preaching method. First there was the problem of gleaning the preachable truth from the passage of the Bible under consideration. Secondly there was the problem of applying the truth in a practical and communicating manner.

Drawing the Truth from the Bible. At first I tried the method used by Dennis Lane in his seminars. This was a simple method of dividing each verse into phrases and writing down opposite each phrase what could be taught from it. Let me illustrate from Titus 1:1.

> *Paul, a servant of God* – Paul first of all saw himself as a servant of God – a slave – it was a title much revered in the Old Testament – it meant he had no personal rights.
> *and an apostle of Jesus Christ* – Paul was chosen by Jesus – appointed to a special task by Jesus – given a high position in the church – was 'sent out' by Jesus.
> *for the faith of God's elect* – Paul's responsibility was to bring those chosen by God to faith – to help them develop their faith. God has chosen some to be saved – they will be brought to faith in due course.
> *and the knowledge of the truth* – It is important for every

Christian to have a personal knowledge of Jesus and also to know the Bible; it is the job of the pastor to help with this. *that leads to godliness* – God wants us all to be like him – we need faith – we need to know him – we need to know the truth if we are going to be like him.

However, since most pastors did not have the heritage of a daily Quiet Time which most of us in the West have, they found this to be very difficult. So to help them I asked them to look at each verse, to ask what it was about and make a question to which several answers could be found in the text. For example, in Titus 1:1, what do we learn about Paul?

a) He was a servant of God; b) he was an apostle of Jesus Christ; c) he had a responsibility to lead people to faith and to grow in their faith; d) he had a responsibility to help people know Jesus and the Bible; e) he had a responsibility to help people become godly.

Obviously each of these answers would be expanded with some of the thoughts in the example under Dennis Lane's method.

After a little practice this method seemed helpful. It did of course have the danger of making the pastor focus too much on just that one verse, and so care had to be taken to see the verse in context and the links between verses. Generally, however, it seemed helpful and pastors got excited to discover that even without the aid of commentaries it was possible to find a great deal to say from the text. I encouraged pastors to do this before looking at commentaries because it meant that much of the teaching in the sermon came from their own discoveries. This helped make the sermons more relevant and powerful. Sermons that are too dependent on truths gleaned just from commentaries are prone to be very ponderous.

Applying the Truth of the Bible. The second problem was to take the truth thus gleaned and apply it during the sermon to the people who were listening. This was much more difficult. Over the years I developed several methods to help people think in more applicatory ways.

'Divide your people into groups' method. In this method I simply asked the pastors to think of the different groups of people who make up every congregation. Always there are the basic believer and unbeliever groups. But of course even in these two basic groups there are further distinctions. In the unbeliever group some know nothing of the gospel, some are resistant to the gospel, some are very close to committing to Christ, etc. In the believers group some are new believers, still untaught, some are lukewarm in their faith and some are mature and keen to go on with the Lord, etc. But then there are also other groupings: men and women, young and old, married, divorced, single and widowed, clever and stupid, etc. If application is to be relevant we need to think who in our congregations need to hear a particular truth and apply it to them.

'**Scripture Union' method**. One method for the Quiet Time taught by Scripture Union helpfully tells us that we need to look at the passage and see if there is a) a command to obey, b) a promise to believe, c) a warning to heed, d) an example to follow.

'Arrow questions' method. At various points throughout the sermon we need to stop and apply the truth in simple questions aimed at the hearts of the congregation. For example on a passage on prayer we might ask 'How often do you pray? How long do you pray for? Do you attend the church prayer meeting?' etc. I always urged that application be made throughout the whole sermon and not left to the end.

'**Correcting wrong thoughts' method**. This and the following method I gleaned from Martyn Lloyd-Jones's book *Preaching and Preachers*. After looking at what truths could be taught from the passage, you would ask yourself what wrong thoughts these truths might be used to correct. The wrong thoughts would be introduced at the start of the sermon or section of the sermon and then the truths expounded by way of an answer.

'Solving problems' method. Similarly to the above method the preacher would ask himself what problems could be solved by the particular truths in the passage. The problems would be stated and then the truths expounded by way of an answer.

Bit by bit by practising the above methods a more practical approach to preaching could be learned and sermons could become more relevant. No one finds application easy but it needs to be prepared and thought out in advance, although of course we all recognise that it is ultimately the job of the Holy Spirit to apply the truth to the heart.

The years spent in Korea were amazing. I got to spend most of my time doing what I liked best – studying God's Word and seeking to share and help others in that work. Seeds were sown years before in Holyrood, and now hundreds of pastors seek systematically to expound God's Word. The monthly *Congregational Records* from Holyrood, Gilcomston and Sandyford were spotted in my study and were duly photocopied and occupy a helpful place in many pastors' studies in Korea today.

'They read from the Book of the Law, making it clear and giving the meaning so that the people could understand what was being read' (Nehemiah 8:8). That is what it is all about!

The Minister and Overseas Mission

Warren Beattie

This article seeks to consider the role that James Philip played within his congregation in relation to cross-cultural mission. It is written by a member of his congregation who has become a minister and then gone to work overseas with the church in missionary training and theological education. What follows will focus on three areas where I gained insight into the work of missions, and the encouragement of mission, in the ministry of James Philip. I want to highlight them as they go beyond a direct pastoral input, although that is a component of a minister's involvement in mission from within a congregation and will also be discussed below.

Encouraging Missions through Preaching

Biblical teaching will do at least three things: a) it will create interest in and awareness of mission; b) it will allow members to develop a sense of commitment to mission and in some cases encourage them to sense their own call to involvement in God's mission in the world; and c) it will help with the development of a biblical perspective about God's world.

a) Creating Interest and Awareness in Mission

It is not surprising that a minister who took seriously the task of teaching and preaching the whole of the Scriptures should have dealt with themes such as God's concern for the nations; Jesus Christ as a Saviour for the world; the church's task in witness and evangelism and its responsibility for sharing the good news of Christ to the world. James Philip's teaching from the Old Testament, using books such as Genesis and Deuteronomy and the prophetic literature, allowed an understanding of God's view of the world and the nations, and God's motivation and concern for reaching out to his world. A God-centred theology helps us avoid superficial or human-centred understandings of mission.[1] At the same time, James Philip's sermons from the Gospels and Acts, with their stress on the evangel, showed the emerging church's response to the coming of Jesus and the practical results of people who wanted to share the good news with others. Studies in the New Testament epistles dealt with the human and psychological dimension of spreading the gospel as well as the doctrinal nuances of the message itself. Throughout the preaching, examples were given which related to the struggles that Christians working cross-culturally encounter. This systematic teaching of Old and New Testament led to a greater awareness of the church's responsibility for mission – an awareness no doubt backed up by meeting and hearing missionaries themselves.

b) Fostering a Sense of Commitment and Call

Through both the teaching and the example of members of the congregation, I was drawn to take initial steps into ministry. Activities with young people and students in Scotland led to a short-term experience in Europe working with both students and later the local church. Returning to Scotland, I remember attending a series of midweek services on Genesis. A sermon on the life of Abraham and his awareness of God's call from Ur made a significant impression on me, so much so that I remember speaking to James Philip afterwards – not something I did very often at that time. It made me realise that the God of Abraham, Isaac and Jacob still wants to direct the lives of those

---

1. See Bosch's description of four key missionary motifs in Scripture, which include God's mission, God's compassion, and God's connection to history with his people. Even the fourth category, *martyria,* has an implicit God-ward dimension. David Bosch, 'Reflections on Biblical Models of Mission' in J. Philips and R. Coote (ed.), *Toward the 21st Century in Christian Mission* (Grand Rapids, 1993), 180-87.

who trust in him. Having just returned from two years of cross-cultural ministry, I was uncertain where my future lay, but I was reminded that God calls people to serve him and has a concern for the nations of the world. Preaching through Genesis is not necessarily the place where pastors would think of starting to shape missionary, or indeed other, vocations within their congregation, but God speaks through the whole counsel of the Scriptures, which James Philip always recognised.

c) Developing a Biblical Perspective on the World

This third category may seem less directly relevant to the preparation of missionary candidates, but it was suggested to me by a comment made by Dr David Tai-Woong Lee, a Korean who is responsible for an influential missionary training centre in Seoul in South Korea.[2] In an essay on two-thirds world perspectives on mission, David Lee comments on the importance for missionaries of being able to connect the Bible to their context when they are working cross-culturally. He feels, however, that it is a quality which often needs to be more developed than it actually is.[3]

Like David Lee, I am currently involved in trying to help those who work cross-culturally and to prepare them to teach and preach the Bible in other contexts. Two things are important if one is to teach the Bible cross-culturally. One factor is an awareness of the dynamics of functioning and communicating in cross-cultural situations, including an ability to use the language and understand the ethos of any particular context. The other is the ability to make sense of the Bible and its teaching

2. He has been the Director of the Global Missionary Training Centre in Seoul, and is chairperson of the World Evangelical Fellowship Missions Commission.
3. David Tai-Woong Lee, 'A Two-Thirds-World Evaluation of Contemporary Evangelical Missiology', in William Taylor (ed.), *Global Missiology for the 21st Century: the Iguassu Dialogue* (Grand Rapids, 2000), 143-4.

in one's own context. It is only to the extent that we have done this, that we will be able to apply its content to other cultures. I am grateful for the way in which James Philip's teaching at Holyrood Abbey made sense of the Bible and applied it to the context of Scotland in the 1980s and 1990s. I think Christians who have shared in such ministry will find it easier to apply the biblical teaching both to their own context and to other cultures, if they move into cross-cultural ministry.

As I have had the opportunity during my theological education and ministry in Scotland, and later in South Korea and Singapore, to put theory into practice, I am aware that it is no easy task and that it does not depend, in any sense, upon techniques. In Singapore, my colleagues and I teach homiletics to Asian students. We are conscious that communicating skills of how to organise material and how to speak in public are reasonably attainable tasks. It would be necessary to add, however, that this process itself is complicated by the need to encourage the students to pay attention to their own culture's different styles of thinking and rhetorical structure, rather than simply adapting or importing western formats.[4] That said, helping prospective teachers and preachers to make sense of biblical passages, theologically, and to make them relevant to their hearers, in their own cultural setting, is a more complex task.[5]

---

4. Examples of the kind of reflection done on culture and preaching for Chinese peoples include the following. On thinking, see H. Nakamura, *Ways of Thinking of Eastern Peoples* (Hawaii, 1964), and P. Chang, 'Steak, Potatoes, Peas and Chopsuey: Linear and Non-linear Thinking in Theological Education', *Evangelical Review of Theology* 5(1981), 279-86. On rhetorical structures and preaching, see J. Tai, 'Preaching in the Church in China', *Chinese Theological Review* 11:1 (1996), 21-30.
5. For theological engagement with Chinese hearers see, for example, G. Oblau, 'Protestant Sermons in China – Harbingers of an Evolving Contextual Theology', *China Study Journal* 11:1 (1996), 16-28, and S. H. Chao, 'Confucian Chinese and the Gospel: Methodological

I have read articles on theological and cross-cultural themes, to gain insight into the dimensions of preaching which are involved when sharing in a cross-cultural context. However, it is against the background of hearing a minister engaging in the task of communicating not just the Bible, but the Bible's perspective, week in and week out to his congregation in my own culture, that I have reflected on this process myself. James Philip's example has been formative, not just in preaching through books of the Bible, but even in the series of messages he prepared for the Christmas seasons. He would try, in the space of five or six sermons, to make sense of the biblical message, not just as regards its teaching of the good news made manifest in the incarnation of Christ, but how this should affect his hearers that very Christmas. In other words, the biblical message was to inform how we view the world and how we respond to God's acts of grace in the here and now.

James Philip's commitment to making the whole Bible relevant to his congregation has given a model which is an inspiration, though I have never felt constrained to follow exactly either his style or his format. If he has one technique as such it has escaped me. Although we have very occasionally discussed the content of sermons he or I have preached, he has never suggested to me that any particularity of his own approach is of special value. That is an example, and a freedom, I have been very happy to pass on to theological students in Asia!

Encouraging Missions through Relationships
Another area where I have noticed a commitment to mission is in the way in which he fostered relationships which encouraged his own and the congregation's participation in mission.

Considerations', *Asian Journal of Theology* 1:1 (1987), 17-40. I am grateful to Lynette Teagle, a DTC alumnus, for giving insight into the relationship between the mindset of Chinese people and preaching.

a) A Commitment to Long-Term Missionaries

It was clear from Sunday services, midweek meetings or weekly prayer meetings that Holyrood Abbey was connected to those involved in mission. Missionaries were mentioned and prayed for in Sunday services; they would lead worship from time to time on Sundays and midweek and news would be shared and many missionaries prayed for at the prayer meeting. In all of this, there was never a sense that these people were either strangers to or devout emissaries of the Scottish church, to be treated gingerly, if respectfully, as examples of a rarefied spirituality that the church preferred to have in someone else's country rather than its own. Rather they were friends and colleagues, warmly welcomed back to the fold, so that we could hear what they had to say and to share and encourage them in their task.

b) A Commitment to Prayer

It does not really do justice to James Philip or the congregation simply to say that they prayed for missionaries. It is certainly true that during the Prayer Meeting, photos and names of missionaries were displayed, as an *aide-mémoire*, but communication was much fuller and more personal than that. News was shared from letters, often, but not always, read by James Philip, and read in such a way as to communicate the real situations of the missionaries and reflecting also his concerns, his happiness or possibly even his uncertainty as to what to make of things. You could not accuse James Philip of impartiality in mediating and sharing the ups and downs of missionary life. If some of the accounts ended with a shake of the head and a puzzled frown, many a story ended with a hearty, 'Well, well, well!' as a humorous anecdote was enjoyed. There was a close sense of connection and involvement.

c) Sharing those Long-Term Commitments with the Congregation

These long-term commitments fashioned the congregation's understanding of mission. Inasmuch as missionaries were part of the minister's life, they were part of the congregation's life. It became natural for me to hear of people like Willie and Katie Black (Korea) and Mary Alexander (Japan), who were part of OMF International, before I knew a great deal about OMF itself. I was aware that missionary life in Korea might involve keeping a close check on one's dentures on the subway, as well as learning an intricate language and relating to the hurly-burly of mega-church life.

Long before I considered going to Asia, or even South Korea, I was interested in the model of ministry exercised by the Revd Willie Black, as unusual and yet relating to my own interests and inclinations. A few years later, when shared ministry interests meant candidacy for the same organisation, and in fact work in the same country, we arranged to meet. At that point I felt that I was not meeting a stranger, but someone whose work I knew and whose personality had been communicated to me.

At a time when commitment to mission in the church is mixed and long-term commitments to mission are at a low ebb in some parts of the world, lessons could be learned from James Philip's style of ministry. Relationships have been foundational in his approach to mission, starting with those from within the congregation who have become involved in mission, and extending to others through contacts made over the years. Personal contact with these people, and continuing communication shared with the congregation provided opportunities for ongoing prayer and other kinds of support. These, and opportunities for missionaries to share about their work when back in Edinburgh, have contributed to a strongly relational model of mission which is shared by many in the congregation.

It is significant that many of the missionaries connected with Holyrood Abbey have been involved in long-term commitments, often serving for many years outside of western Europe, though not always in one place. It lies beyond the scope of this article to analyse why this should be so, but it seems that the dynamic between the minister, congregation and missionaries has fostered the growth of long-term commitment to mission. This speaks well of the selection of candidates and the quality of missionary support, both pastoral and in other ways.

A recent report was offered to OMF Singapore on mobilisation for mission. One of its observations was that a significant part of missionary recruitment comes through good relationships between missionaries and prospective candidates.[6] Relationships could well be a foundational element to which we should give more attention in Scotland, in improving understanding of the missionary vocation. It is an area that has been extensively and naturally developed at Holyrood Abbey over the years. Such an approach to ministry is facilitated by having a congregation in a capital city, with universities and theological colleges offering under-graduate and post-graduate courses to students from around the world. Many other ministers and congregations in Scotland maintain links with missionaries and meet with them and care for them when they are in the country. But the exceptional range and scope of the relationships that James Philip fostered over the years at Holyrood Abbey still serve as a reminder of their great importance in building good relationships with missionaries from a congregation.

Encouraging Missions through Personal Involvement
There are three final areas that I select for mention.

a) Involvement in Mission Structures within Scotland
Mention ought to be made of James Philip's involvement in the Scottish Council of OMF International. This was a concrete expression of his own commitment to share in the work of mission in one region of the world and one particular organisation's approach to mission. It allowed for a greater familiarity with some of the struggles of being involved in

6. Matthew Cobbett *et al.*, *Mobilisation in Singapore* (2001), 15.

mission from the individual's or the family's viewpoint. He also made a trip out to East Asia visiting Indonesia and other countries, to meet with missionaries and to do some teaching himself, a long time before such trips were as fashionable as they are today. Direct involvement in the work of a mission council allows ministers to see that the kind of issues they face in their congregation with missionaries and missionary candidates are by no means unique, and can help to give perspective when they deal with difficult situations.

b) Acceptance of the Wider Dimensions of the Church's Task

James Philip also showed an awareness of the wider dimensions of the church's task in the world. In addition to the more traditional church-planting ministries, he valued the role of support ministries such as teachers in Nepal, or medical support for missionaries in Japan and Singapore. When many in the United Kingdom baulked at any involvement in South Korea, he supported OMF's model (one shared by sectors of the Korean church) of limited international involvement, with two couples from Holyrood working there over a period of many years. At the prayer meeting, prayer for Europe, for ministries in countries like France and Hungary, and for a few colleagues in North America was shared along with concerns for Africa, Asia and more traditional 'missionary' areas. This, I think, gave an understanding of mission which was not based on purely geographical distinctions. The particular challenges and stresses of cross-cultural ministry in linguistically and socially different and distant contexts were acknowledged, but not in any way exaggerated.

c) Evident Concern for the Pastoral Care of Missionaries

Although this article has focussed on involvement beyond the pastoral role, it would be necessary to mention this as an area which found genuine expression in the ministry of James Philip. He maintained links with missionaries, particularly at times of transition or stress. We appreciated his input at crucial times in our own experience, for example during candidacy issues in Scotland, prior to our move to Korea and latterly following our move to Singapore. He showed interest, there was dialogue and, where appropriate, pastoral advice. He was not afraid to contact a sending agency directly if the situation really merited it, but he had a good sense of the fine line between involvement and interference in mission. This is still a challenge for many churches, particularly in the Asian context where the role between the church and missionary organisation as joint sending agencies is evolving and lines of responsibility are frequently blurred.[7]

Conclusion

Many ministers in Britain have been committed to the work of mission, and we can think of examples, both from the past such as Charles Simeon and in our own generation such as John Stott, of ministers in city or university charges who have been deeply involved in promoting mission and encouraging active participation from within their own congregations. In a similar way, the ministry of James Philip has shown that it is possible for someone whose focus of ministry is the local church and its life, to be significantly and naturally involved in the wider cross-cultural mission of the church. Such a commitment is not only compatible with an emphasis on biblically informed preaching, but flows from it as a consequence of the missiological aspects of the biblical message. It will not only see church members called to engage in mission but will help prepare them to function in cross-cultural contexts with a clear sense of a biblical perspective on the world. It can also result in an informed and constructive pastoral relationship with such members should they move beyond the local church's boundaries into overseas mission.

---

7. *Ibid.,* 10-13.

Part 4

Perspectives:
Biblical, Theological,
Church-Historical

'Let us Worship God'

Eric Alexander

It must be well over fifty years ago. I was a schoolboy, and one evening the new Assistant Minister at our church in Glasgow came to visit my family. He was the Revd James Philip from Aberdeen, who had just completed his university studies after service in the Royal Air Force. The conversation was very unusual, in my experience. This Minister had not come to discuss the weather, or how different Glasgow was from Aberdeen. He had come to speak about God, about the Bible, about faith in Jesus Christ, and all in a way that was neither forced nor unnatural. The striking thing to me was that he obviously believed deeply all that he said, and it was not surprising that before he left, he suggested we should pray.

I was not yet a Christian, but what happened next had a profound effect on me. This man led us right into the presence of God, whom he obviously knew personally and deeply. What I could only describe as a sense of awe dawned upon me. The whole experience was quite overwhelming, and, as we rose, I thought, 'God is here, and he must be very great and very wonderful. I wish I could know him like Mr Philip.'

That was a unique moment in the life of a teenage boy. But I have lost count of the people who have remarked to me over the years that one of the most memorable, moving and maturing things about sitting under James Philip's ministry was being led in worship by him. He began every service with the words, 'Let us worship God', and throughout the service there could be no doubt in anyone's mind that God was at the centre of everything we were engaged in. The immensity and glory of God in the Trinity of his Persons was the great distinctive of worship led by James Philip.

This understanding and experience of worship is becoming rare in the evangelical church worldwide. Indeed, in contemporary Evangelicalism, both in Britain and North America, the very concept of worship has been so distorted that the focus is on the worshipper and whether he or she finds it acceptable and enjoyable, rather than on God and whether he is pleased with it and finds it acceptable. We have forgotten that 'worship' is a transitive verb: that is, it is meaningless without an object and it is on the object that the verb focuses. The object of biblical worship is God and God alone, and the design of biblical worship is to focus our whole being on him that we may offer to him worship that is acceptable.

The importance of all this is that the highest activity of the church on earth, and the constant activity of the church in heaven, is worship. W. Nicholls describes it as 'The supreme and only indispensable activity of the church.'[1] Calvin broadens the significance of worship when he writes, 'The chief object of life is to acknowledge and worship God.'[2] It is therefore of paramount importance that we should find a biblical answer to the question, 'What is worship?'

There have, of course, been many very helpful definitions of worship, which are frequently quoted, from John Calvin, John Owen, Archbishop William Temple and many others. However, I hope it may be possible for us to work out our own definition of what worship is from the definitive teaching of Jesus in his conversation with the Samaritan woman in John 4:19-24. The remainder of this chapter will be devoted to that end. Such a definition will not give us an exhaustive account of the biblical teaching on worship, but it may give us a basic biblical framework within which we may think more fully. It is from the primary principles Jesus teaches that the secondary issues should be approached and reformed.

---

1. W. Nicholls, *Jacob's Ladder : The Meaning of Worship* (London, 1958), 9.
2. Calvin, *Comm.* on Isa. 44:9, Calvin Translation Society, vol. III (Edinburgh, 1852), 368.

A Definition of Worship from Jesus' Teaching in John 4: 19 – 24

The word 'worship', either in its noun or verbal form, occurs ten times within these verses. It should therefore be helpful, by way of preliminary, to enquire a little into matters of vocabulary. The English word 'worship' comes from an Anglo-Saxon root which lays the emphasis on the *worth* of something or someone. Its concentration is therefore on the object of worship which is *worthy* of adoration and honour and praise. It is therefore not surprising that both in the Old and New Testament the language of worship in our English translation frequently includes the word 'worthy'. Examples are in 1 Chronicles 16:25, 'Great is the Lord and most worthy of praise', and Revelation 5:12, 'Worthy is the Lamb, who was slain.'

The biblical words for worship, both in the Old and New Testaments, mean 'to prostrate oneself' or 'to bow or fall down before the object of worship'. The whole idea is contained in the thought of wanting to exalt the object of worship to the highest place, and to humble ourselves to the lowest place. Thus God is worshipped in Scripture when men bow down with their faces touching the ground as in Nehemiah 8:6. The posture is not prescriptive but illustrative, and it illustrates the idea that you cannot get lower than that.

Now we might legitimately draw from these matters of vocabulary the first sentence of our definition of worship:

> To worship God is to humble ourselves before his great majesty, and bring him the honour and praise which belong to him alone.

The woman with whom Jesus had been in close conversation at the well of Jacob raises with him in verse 19 one of these secondary issues about worship. The woman may well have been attempting to divert the conversation from the painful subject Jesus had raised in the previous two verses. However that may be, Jesus certainly does not dismiss the issue to which she has turned as though it was unimportant. Indeed the question of worship, if only she would realise it, was the central and fundamental issue of her life. The Father who is seeking her is seeking a worshipper.

Notice that she is drawing Jesus' attention for the second time to the gulf between the Jews and the Samaritans (cf. v. 9). The division between them was threefold: it was racial, spiritual and theological. Racially, the Samaritans were a mixture of Israelites and several Mesopotamian nations. Spiritually, they tried to combine the worship of other gods with the worship of Jehovah. 2 Kings 17:33 describes the result of all this in this way: 'They worshipped the Lord, but they also served their own gods in accordance with the customs of the nations from which they had been brought.' Theologically, they had rejected all of the Old Testament apart from the Pentateuch (the first five books of the Old Testament), and had thereby cut themselves off from the full revelation of himself which God had given.

Now at this time, the great issue between the Samaritans and the Jews was whether the temple should be at Gerizim or at Jerusalem, where God had authorised Solomon to build it. Jesus responds to her difficulty about where to worship by pointing her to the central truth of all Christian worship, namely that it finds its centre and focus not in a place but in a Person – that is, in Jesus Christ himself. The crucial phrase in verse 21, repeated in verse 23, is 'the hour is coming'. It is one of John's characteristic phrases, always pointing, as Don Carson says,

> to the hour of Jesus' cross, resurrection and exaltation or to events related to Jesus' passion and exaltation (as in 16:32), or to the situation introduced by Jesus' passion and exaltation.[3]

So Jesus is explaining to this woman that it is in Christ and chiefly in his death that true worship becomes possible. It is his

---

3. D. Carson, *The Gospel According to John* (London, 1991), 223.

saving work on the cross, which will make both Jerusalem and Gerizim obsolete as places of worship. And the reason is that the place where we meet God as Father is neither Jerusalem nor Gerizim but Calvary. There he opened a new and living way through the curtain, that is, his body, and we may now draw near to God with a sincere heart in full assurance of faith (Heb. 10:19-22). It is Jesus Christ who is the true temple. He is the only sacrifice and offering which atones for our sin, the great barrier between God and ourselves. He is our great High Priest who gains entry for us into the holy of holies. So the key issue of worship is not location but mediation, and the only mediator is Jesus Christ, crucified, risen, ascended and exalted to the right hand of God.

Thus our definition of worship must be expanded to add 'in and through Jesus Christ'. It would then read:

> To worship God is to humble ourselves before his great majesty, and bring to him, in and through Jesus Christ, the honour and praise which belong to him alone.

Now in verse 22, Jesus adds another vital truth to our definition, which could be summarised in the words of the Puritan Stephen Charnock:

> It is impossible to honour God as we ought, unless we know him as he is; and we could not know him as he is without divine revelation from himself.[4]

Jesus' words in verse 22 sound strange, even abrupt and almost racist to twenty-first-century ears: 'You Samaritans worship what you do not know: we worship what we do know, for salvation is from the Jews.' However, what Jesus is really saying is that knowing God is a matter of revelation, not of speculation.

---

4. S. Charnock, *The Existence and Attributes of God* (London, 1853), vol. I, 208-9.

The revelation of himself which God has given he gave through the Jewish nation, and we find it in the Old Testament Scriptures. Jesus' point is that the only means by which we can come to know God and therefore worship him is through the revelation he himself gives. Now the Jews stood inside the stream of revelation and the Samaritans had put themselves outside of it. This is why the Psalmist says in Psalm 76:1, 'In Judah is God known.'

The abiding principle we should deduce from this is that for us this revelation is in Holy Scripture. And the relation between the revelation of God in Scripture and the theme of worship cannot be over-emphasised. Dr James Boice of Philadelphia once put it like this:

> It is the reading and exposition of Scripture in worship which reveals to us the nature of God in his glory and grace. Our capacity to worship God truly and acceptably is measured by the place Scripture occupies in our life and in the ministry exercised in the place of worship.[5]

This of course is what makes it so foolish for people to say, 'I don't come to church to listen to a man, I come to worship God.' Now that sounds at first hearing very spiritual, but in fact it betrays a double delusion. It is a misunderstanding both of worship and of preaching. Worship is not a vague, mystical or sentimental exercise. It is pondering on the infinite glories of the character of the God who has revealed himself to us in Holy Scripture. On the other hand, sitting under a God-anointed ministry of the Word of God is not 'listening to a man'. It is actually listening to God as he speaks from his Word which is being expounded.

Thus our definition of worship is enlarged by this significant addition, 'according to Scripture'. It would now read:

---

5. J.M. Boice at a Seminar in Tenth Presbyterian Church, Philadelphia.

> To worship God is to humble ourselves before his great majesty, and bring to him, in and through Jesus Christ and according to Scripture, the honour and praise which are his alone.

Finally, in verses 23 and 24, there is this repeated emphasis from Jesus that true worship must be 'in spirit and in truth'. That is the kind of worship the Father seeks (v. 23b). In other words, this is the worship which pleases and satisfies him. Let me emphasise that this is what really matters in all our thinking about worship. It is a serious distortion of biblical teaching when the test of the acceptability of our worship is whether or not it pleases and satisfies *us*. George Swinnock wisely warns:

> When we believe that we should be satisfied in worship rather than that God should be glorified, we put God below ourselves, as though he had been made for us, rather than we for him.[6]

So biblical worship is never a means to an end of our own. Its only proper end is the glory and pleasure of God.

Now, if the worship which pleases and honours God is worship in spirit and in truth, we must enquire more fully what exactly that means. Notice first that Jesus describes the worshippers of whom he is speaking as 'true worshippers'. That is, there is such a thing as false worship and false worshippers. At the very least it is important to examine ourselves and ask whether what we are offering to God is true worship or false worship. The seriousness of this is illustrated in Leviticus 10 by the dreadful judgement that fell on the sons of Aaron when they went into the sanctuary and worshipped God in a way that was contrary to the commandment he had given.

Secondly, Jesus describes true worshippers as those who will worship the Father. That is highly significant, because it focuses the object of true worship as the God whom Jesus Christ

---

6. Quoted in an address given in Glasgow by Dr J.I. Packer.

exclusively revealed as the Father of his children. It also implies that true worship is only possible for a regenerate heart, which has received the Spirit of sonship by whom we cry 'Abba, Father'. It is that Holy Spirit who himself testifies with our spirit that we are God's children (cf. Rom. 8:15-16).

Thirdly, Jesus teaches us that true worshippers will worship the Father in spirit. You will notice that the word 'spirit' has a small 's'. Jesus is referring not to the Holy Spirit, directly, but to the human spirit. Spiritual worship is worship which is inward rather than merely outward and external. The nature of our worship must accord with the nature of the God we are worshipping. In this case it is the spiritual worship of a God who himself is spirit. Jesus applies the truth of this teaching to the Pharisees in Mark 7:6-7 when he says, 'Well did Isaiah prophesy of you hypocrites as it is written, "This people honour me with their lips but their heart is far from me"'. John Stott has written: 'In essence, the worship pleasing to God is inward not outward, the praise of the heart not the lips, spiritual not ceremonial.'[7] Stephen Charnock has this splendid comment:

> Spiritual worship is worship from a spiritual nature. The heart must be first cast into the mould of the gospel, before it can perform a worship required by the gospel.[8]

Fourthly, Jesus insists that true worship will be worship in truth. If worship in spirit means inward heart worship rather than outward formal worship, worship in truth means worship regulated by Holy Scripture rather than by our own preferences, and undergirded by the revelation of God in his Word. So, when we are seeking to discover how God is pleased to be worshipped and honoured by his people, we ought not to turn primarily to manuals or the examples of other people in different places to

---

7. J.R.W. Stott, *Christ the Controversialist* (London, 1970), 166.
8. S. Charnock, *The Existence and Attributes of God* (London, 1853), vol. I, 223.

find 'how they do it'. We ought to turn to the Scriptures and seek an obedient spirit that may enable us to conform our worship to God's own revealed will. Hence Calvin's shrewd comment, 'No one rightly worships God, except he who is taught by his Word.'[9] He underscores the seriousness of this position when he says in his commentary on Ezekiel, 'When men introduce their inventions, it immediately causes God to depart.'[10]

One of the implications of this emphasis on worshipping in spirit and in truth is that the truth of God feeds our worship of God. John Stott reminds us of

the first fundamental principle of Christian worship, namely that we must know God before we can worship him. It is true that Paul found an altar in Athens, which was inscribed 'To an unknown God'. But he recognised it as a contradiction in terms. It is impossible to worship an unknown God, since, if he is himself unknown, the kind of worship he desires will be equally unknown. That is why Paul said to the philosophers: 'What therefore you worship as unknown, this I proclaim to you.'[11]

This relationship between truth and worship inevitably touches not only upon the ministry of the Word, but upon the hymns and songs we sing as we worship God. We dare not avoid asking the question 'Do our hymns and songs contain substantial and biblical truth about God, Father, Son and Holy Spirit, which will enable us to glory in who he is and what he has done?' Or are they simply rather vacuous ditties which may have a catchy tune, but contain either minimal truth, or even positive error? Whatever generation or tradition the piece belongs to, these are the questions we must ask. The spiritual leader who feeds the

---

9. Calvin, *Comm.* on Zech. 14:19, Calvin Transl. Soc., *Minor Prophets*, vol. V (Edinburgh, 1849), 448.

10. Calvin, *Comm.* on Ezek. 8:6, Calvin Transl. Soc., vol. I (Edinburgh, 1849), 284.

11. J.R.W. Stott, *Christ the Controversialist* (London, 1970), 162-3.

souls of his flock on the latter kind of hymn or song is breeding something in the church which will put it in peril for generations to come.

Thus, our definition of biblical worship emerges likes this:

To worship God is to humble ourselves before his great majesty and, in spirit and truth, to bring him, in and through Jesus Christ and according to Scripture, the honour and praise which are his alone.

Now that is not a piece of elegant English, nor is it intended to be so. But it may encapsulate the central truths about biblical worship. Nowhere have these truths been more consistently exhibited than in the ministry of James Philip. I, and countless others now scattered all over the world, thank God with all our hearts for his influence and example.

'Great and marvellous are your deeds,
Lord God Almighty.
Just and true are your ways,
King of the ages.
Who will not fear you, O Lord,
and bring glory to your name?
For you alone are holy.
All nations will come
and worship before you,
for your righteous acts have been revealed.'

Revelation 15:3-4

The Imprecatory Psalms Today

David Searle

If one were to try and highlight some of the cardinal features of the ministry of James Philip – I mean aspects to his ministry which have been absolutely pivotal in all that God has been pleased to accomplish through him – there could be no denying that first and foremost would be Mr Philip's practice of declaring the whole counsel of God. The expository method of dealing consecutively with each book of the Bible invariably meant that in his preaching plan nothing of Scripture was omitted. No hard (or embarrassing) incidents or chapters were passed over. For example, his sermons faithfully expounded lessons arising from the failures and shame of God's people as well as those arising from their victories and godliness. There was never any avoidance of hard passages, never any skimming over thorny problems – of which there are undoubtedly many in the Bible.

It might seem rather an unusual tribute to James Philip's expository ministry, but I want to take up in this chapter one of those controversial areas of Psalms which are seldom heard expounded in the pulpit nowadays. While I could never match his skill and sureness of touch in unpacking such a biblical passage, my hope is that this brief exposition of an imprecatory Psalm will remind those who minister the Word of God that we may not select what we think will please our congregations, but must, like James Philip, be preachers of the whole Word, however unpalatable its message might seem to modern ears.

There are quite a number of imprecatory psalms. Some contain just a verse or two which are 'imprecatory'. A few examples would be: 69:22-28; 137:9; 139:19-22; 140:9-11; 143:12. Others are more full of imprecation. Psalm 109 is perhaps the most disturbing of these. It is truly awesome. A sense of total outrage that has come upon David seizes him – he cannot shake it off. So he expresses himself in these terrible words and this almost unbelievable prayer before God.

The Psalm begins with David explaining to us his burden. Those he has loved and to whom he has shown kindness have turned against him and are now accusing and hating him. They are using deceit and falsehood in their evil attempt to bring him down. He has prayed for them and entreated them, but they have responded by increasing their bitterness and venom towards him (vv. 1-5).

Now we can understand that. We know what it can be like to be hated for the sake of truth and purity and goodness. We can also endorse the conclusion of the psalm (vv. 30-31) and David's offering of thanksgiving and praise to God. But what about the main part of the psalm, where David calls down the most terrible curses upon his enemies? This central section makes our blood run cold.

Let us see if we can come to any understanding of why Psalm 109 (along with the other imprecatory psalms) is in the Bible at all, and also to enquire if there are any lessons here to help us in our daily Christian living.

1. Are we Today all That far Away from this Psalm?
One possible approach is to say, 'David lived in the stone-age. This is all you can expect of a semi-savage who knew nothing of modern civilisation and restraint.' But is that true? Middle-eastern manners for centuries have been far more ceremonious and courteous than anywhere else in the world. For those who lived in David's day, conventions of hospitality, even towards your enemy, were strong. Yet here we find resentment freely expressing itself, without restraint, disguise, shame, or self-consciousness. We are here face to face with what appears to be hatred in the raw, to use C. S. Lewis's phrase.

Yet 2000 years after Christ, is it not true that just the same sort of maledictions can be found in our hearts? Of course, we express our feelings more subtly. We might say, 'He'll live to get his just deserts—just wait and see', and we conceal that we are saying we hope he will live to meet his just deserts for the dreadful deeds he has done, though we carefully pretend that we deeply regret this might happen to him. In the final analysis, are we really all that much different from David?

Imagine three men have been imprisoned for fifteen years, but were totally innocent of any crime. How do you think the three men would feel towards the crooked policemen who on fabricated evidence put them behind bars for all those years? Might they not have feelings akin to David's in this Psalm? Who would not have some sympathy for them if while languishing in prison they hoped their accusers would one day meet their just deserts? Would not we understand their feelings and silently agree – at the very least?

2. The Consequences of Inflicting Evil on a Fellow Human Being

Consider the bitterness many Irish feel against the British who have wronged them down the centuries. The Irish have every cause to resent the centuries of British occupation and exploitation of their island. In the 1840s an estimated 3 million died of starvation during potato famines in Ireland, yet meanwhile English administrators of commerce were ordering the dumping of ship-loads of corn at sea to protect the business interests of English merchants. There is not much point in saying that today there is equality-of-opportunity and fair-employment legislation in Ireland. The wrongs have been done over many centuries, and the Irish have not forgotten. Many of them still carry deep resentments, but the greater sin is surely that which first caused them to hate!

Now that is another element of what we have here in Psalm 109. David's outpouring is the consequence of his being cruelly inflicted with injury by a fellow human being. Treat people badly and unjustly, or take away their dignity from them, and what else can we expect but a sense of outrage and bitterness on the part of the one who has been wronged. The one who has caused the resentment and suffering is far more in the wrong than the one who wrestles with the resentment.

3. We Have in this Psalm a Highly Developed Awareness of Evil

Some Bible commentators suggest that David's mood here should not be judged by New Testament standards. They point out that we stand on the near side of the cross, while David stood on the far side of it. While there is some weight in that argument, it is not as valid a point as might at first appear. It is not enough to say that we know as Christians that we should forgive those who hate us and spitefully use us. The Levitical law said the same:

> You shall not hate your brother in your heart... you shall not avenge nor bear any grudge against the children of your people, but you shall love your neighbour as yourself (Lev.19:17-18).

> If you see the ass of someone who hates you lying down under his burden, you shall help him with it. If you meet your enemy's ox going astray, you must bring it back to him (Ex.23:4-5).

> Do not rejoice when your enemy falls, do not be glad when he stumbles . . . If your enemy hungers, give him something to eat (Prov. 24:17; 25:21).

Therefore, although we undoubtedly do stand on the near side of the cross, we must realise that the grace of the God of the covenant is also present in the Old Testament. Christ is in the Old Testament also. It bears witness to him. He came not to abolish its teachings but to fulfil and affirm them.

If we argue that the believers of the Old Testament dispensation were not Christians as we understand that term, then we should expect their attitude to be much the same as that of other 'non-Christians'. We would expect them to have the same attitude towards their enemies as any other writers who had not come into the sunshine of Christ's smile and grace.

However, in pagan literature there is a complete absence of the sort of cursings which are so manifestly present here. Non-Christian literature certainly contains plenty of violence and brutal material; it also contains plenty of explicitly sexual sensuality and even sadism and other very unsavoury excesses. But we also find to our astonishment it does not contain the kind of imprecatory statements which are in Psalm 109. Is that not both significant and remarkable? In Holy Scripture alone are such curses uttered – uttered by members of a nation specially chosen by God to be the cradle for the incarnation of his own Son.

Let us consider this from a different angle for a moment. Think of the condition of many in our land today who seem to be growing up without any moral sense at all. In twenty-first-century Britain, we have children who can take iron bars and batter to death other children, and then go home and behave as if everything was quite normal, and when questioned by the police hold out for weeks, even months, without confessing. Is our society producing children as hardened to violent crime as that? So many in the younger generation have apparently little or no idea of what is right and wrong. They abuse their bodies with drugs; they take others with them into the very pit of hell, without apparently any qualms of conscience – for their consciences are lifeless, deaf to constraints and warnings from the Spirit of God. But here in the imprecatory psalms, we find the psalmists have the most highly developed consciences and an awareness of right and wrong which is so acute that any kind of sin causes them intense pain. The power of this disturbing Psalm actually lies in this: that David is enraged by deceit and falsehood, by naked wickedness, by the deliberate attempts of former friends to frame him and have him convicted of wrongs he never committed. But more: a key aspect of his maledictions is not that those who have done wrong have transgressed just against mere men, but have transgressed against God himself. His terrible prayer is to a God before whom he knows these men are guilty. Their sins are 'before the Lord'

173

(twice – vv.14, 15). And this Lord before whom their sins are exposed in the prayer is the righteous God and the offenders have acted in the face of his steadfast love of the covenant.

Now this is the significant fact we must realise, that David, whose God had said, 'Love your enemy', and who uncovers in his heart such a powerful intensity of hatred against the twisted deceitfulness of his accusers, David, whose prayer in this Psalm cannot be paralleled by anything in secular writing, is here showing a highly developed sense of right and wrong – an intense awareness of evil in the sight of God, a moral sensitivity that we do not find today.

4. The Psalmist is Committing his Cause to God

In pagan literature, whenever some wrong has been done to another, the theme that invariably unfolds is that of revenge. So we have the famous sagas based on blood feuds in which the family of the one who has been wronged pursues their enemy's brother or son for years until at last they wreak their revenge on his behalf.

But the imprecatory psalms never suggest any kind of action by the one who has been wronged. They are invariably committing the offender to the righteous judgement of God. The psalmist is never strapping on his sword and going out to avenge himself. Rather is he alone with God, unburdening his soul before his God, calling on God to act righteously and give the sinner his just deserts. 'May this be the Lord's payment to my accusers' (v.20), 'Help me, O Lord my God' (v.26), and, 'Let them know that it is your hand, that you, O Lord, have done it' (v.27). And this, is in spite of the fact that David's accusers have actually brought him to deepest distress. Their scheming against him at this point is being extremely effective. He is starving almost to death. He is outlawed and discredited. Yet he will not lift a finger himself against those persecuting him. For all the intensity of the maledictions, David is committing his cause to God. This is quite different from sheer anger.

5. The Psalmist Recognises that God is the Judge of All the Earth

There is an important point of difference we must note between the Old Testament and the New Testament. It is that there is no explicitly developed doctrine of eternal punishment in the Old Testament, certainly not as we have it in the New Testament. But nevertheless, the psalmists were acutely aware that God never compromises with wickedness. As we have already seen, the writers of the Old Testament had a moral sense far more highly developed than the general sense of moral awareness today.

David is here calling on God to vindicate his own holy standards and demonstrate to the world that he does no deal with sin. He is asking God to show his implacable hatred of all that is treacherous, despicable and twisted. He is revealing a heart which loves truth, purity and faithfulness, and, because of this, he cannot help but reveal a heart which hates all falsehood and evil. This is why some of the older commentators called these psalms not psalms of malediction or imprecatory psalms, but judicial psalms. They understood them as reminding the world that God who is of purer eyes than to look upon iniquity will certainly reward the evil doer for all his wrong-doing.

David is actually echoing Abraham's words as he stood on the mountain praying for the two cities of the plain far below him: 'Shall not the Judge of all the earth do right?' (Gen.18:25). David has the same confidence in God's ultimate justice even though his own personal circumstances would tempt the most robust and courageous soul to doubt that there ever could be final justice in this topsy-turvy, fallen world.

6. There is No Place for Complacency in a Believer's Heart

The maledictions are examples of the literary device known as hyperbole. Jeremiah called down terrible curses on the unfortunate and unsuspecting fellow who ran to let his father know his wife had borne a son:

> May that man be like the towns which the Lord overthrew
> without pity. May he hear wailing at morning, a battle cry at
> noon. For he did not kill me in the womb, with my mother as
> my grave, her womb enlarged forever (Jer. 20:16-17).

Did he really want the midwife's husband to be cursed like
that? Surely this is hyperbole. Jeremiah demands that we listen
to him. He is deliberately shocking us and riveting us into
attention. We have to listen. His words shake us out of any
complacency.

That is what we have here in Psalm 109. David's words
scream at us. They refuse to allow us to sit and engage in an
armchair discussion as many do about wickedness and
wrongdoing. They are telling us that when a man has come
face to face with evil, he is driven to God. Let me illustrate
what I mean.

The prison in São Paulo, Brazil, is a horrendous place. The
rations are so inadequate that when a prisoner starves to death
the other prisoners prop him up to make it look to the warder
who peers into the cell through a tiny window in the door that
there are still ten men in the cell, so that food for ten is still
passed through. They will endure the stench of a dead man for
days to try to obtain his daily rations. A few years ago, prisoners
in that dreadful place rioted but were mown down by machine-
guns without mercy. Over a hundred died, killed by the armed
guards.

Now if you visited that kind of place because you had a
brother or father or son wrongly imprisoned there, you would
ultimately end up screaming at people. You would use all the
powers of description and language you could summon to bring
home to others the horrors your loved one was enduring.

That is another aspect of this psalm. An innocent man is
undergoing the most intense suffering, which actually becomes
in Psalm 22 a foretelling of the suffering of Christ in his passion
on the cross. In the depths of his suffering, David uses this
hyperbole, this deliberate exaggeration to scream. I for one

cannot stand in judgement over him for that. I think if I were an outcast, starving to death, reduced to skin and bones, and all because a man I had loved and served faithfully had turned against me in jealousy and told a pack of lies about me in the attempt to have me executed, I would scream too.

What lessons are there for us here as we live in a secular world that does not know God, but is increasingly tolerant towards so much that is wrong? I limit my application to four brief points.

a) God does No Deal with Sin

This Psalm's main theme is the sinfulness of sin. When I am conducting church conferences on 'Change', I ask the participants to write down ways in which God never changes. Not once has anyone ever volunteered that God's attitude towards sin never changes. I am given answers which tell me God's love never changes – right! His faithfulness never changes, his promises never change, and so on. But I have yet to have someone say, 'Sin remains sin, evil remains evil, impurity remains impurity, God is still of purer eyes than to look on any kind of wrong-doing.' That disappoints me, but does not surprise me. That is the world we live in. Sin does not matter. Impurity is fair game for some jokes, some laughs. But these truly awesome and terrible imprecatory psalms (of which 109 is but one) remind us with an eternal solemnity that God does no deal with sin.

b) The Psalm Rebukes our Apathy

The imprecatory psalms say this to us: there is really no place in the Christian church for armchair discussions about morality. Christians are not arm-chair theologians. They have their say in the common rooms of fellows and students in many of our theological faculties. We are called to be soldiers of Jesus Christ, servants, bond-slaves of our wonderful Master. Our commission is to get out there, with jackets off and sleeves rolled up, to engage in the real world. I have yet to find an armchair theologian in Scripture. But I find plenty of men and women of God at the coal-face, toiling for their Lord, spending themselves and being spent in his royal service. A common theme of my teenage years in the 1950s was sacrifice. I was brought up on the saying of the great English missionary, C.T.Studd: 'If Jesus Christ be God and died for me, then no sacrifice can be too great for me to make for him.'

How can we be apathetic and complacent before a prayer like Psalm 109? While it may make our hair curl, and our hearts miss a beat, this man knows no apathy, for reasons I have tried to unfold. God preserve us then from being lukewarm, either towards sin, or towards God.

c) Ultimate Justice is Assured

We tend to turn from Psalm 109 to Psalm 110 with relief. Psalm 110 is much more to our liking. It is about King Jesus, his enthronement, his priesthood and his victory. But remember that it too contains the lines,

> He will crush kings on the day of his wrath.
> He will judge nations, heaping up the dead,
> and crushing the rulers of the whole earth (vv. 5-6).

I once was interviewed on the subject of hell. I completely muffed the first question, 'Are you in favour of hell?' I waffled about that being the wrong question. But it was the right question. And my answer should have been, 'No, I am not in favour of hell, and neither is God – he is not willing that any should perish, but that all should repent.'

But nevertheless, the question of ultimate justice remains: the paedophile murderers of so many little children, snatched and abused and then disposed of when the pervert has satisfied his evil lust; the perpetrators of so many wicked deeds – evil men who grow rich off the sale of heroin and crack; the Hitlers and Stalins of this world. Ultimate justice matters enormously, and this Psalm is about that ultimate justice.

Even in heaven, the martyrs who were tortured and killed for their faith cry out to God, 'How long, Sovereign Lord, holy and true, until you judge the inhabitants of the earth and avenge our death?' (Rev.6:10). So with sober and solemn hearts, we read this Psalm and we bow before God, and like David, we take Abraham's words on our lips and say, 'Shall not the Judge of all the earth do right?'

d) With David, we Commit our Cause to God

In a way, it is wrong to say we commit our cause to God, because it is not our cause but God's cause. Nevertheless, as we too are at times persecuted for our faith, as we too are called upon to suffer for the sake of Christ, as we have to carry a cross that can be painful and costly, we commit our cause to God.

We take no action ourselves. David himself refused to lift a finger against the man he is praying about in this psalm, King Saul. He had Saul in his power on more than one occasion, but he knew that Saul was in God's hands. It is in this that David, even in Psalm 109, faintly reflects Jesus Christ. He too bared his back to the scourging. He opened his hands to receive the nails. But, unlike David, he prayed as they hammered those nails in, 'Father, forgive them . . .'

In conclusion, let us learn to walk with God. I am told that a Scottish preacher who recently died suggested that once in heaven, David received something of a rebuke from his Saviour for writing this Psalm. Be that as it may, I hope we have seen enough to give us a little further insight into the heart and soul of a persecuted suffering believer, who lived on the far side of the cross, but whose head is now lifted up to see his Redeemer and to enjoy him forever.

The Personal Presence of God in Scripture: The Origin and Nature of the Bible

Howard Taylor

When I began attending Holyrood Abbey Church in the late 1960s, I found, as James Philip expounded and preached the Bible, the powerful and deeply personal presence of God. God was with us in holiness and great love. Yet too we felt that this exposition of the Scriptures did not just engage us as individuals but addressed in profoundly personal ways nations and peoples and spoke to generations past, present and future. This presence of God, more than anything else, brought souls to Christ and sent missionaries out into the world. If James Philip had used his gifts to expound any other book we might have been educated, enlightened, entertained and even inspired but we would not have met with God. It is the Bible as the mediator of the presence of Christ, and therefore of God himself, to all creation that is the subject of this chapter.

The Bible tells us that the Word of God is established eternally in heaven.[1] However it is not the Christian claim that the Bible itself has existed eternally in heaven, or that the Bible will be needed once God's people leave this world and go to heaven. (This contrasts with the Muslim claim about their sacred book the Quran.) The New Testament makes clear what is implicit in the Old Testament, namely that the eternal Word is not a 'thing' (a book) but the very personal expression (the Word) of the Mind of God who sustains all creation and works out the plan of salvation for the world.[2] In the New Testament

---

1. Ps. 119:89.
2. John 1:1-2.

the eternal and personal Mind or Word of God came among us clothed in our full humanity so that we might know him face to face.[3] The Bible is both the account, and the result, of this very real and personal engagement of God's eternal Mind with the history of the world. Through this very personal self-disclosure by God the Bible was written. Unless we use the Bible to receive knowledge of the eternal Word we will never really understand it. Here is an interesting comment about the Bible from a learned Hindu.

> I can't understand why you missionaries present the Bible to us in India as a book of religion. It is not a book of religion - and anyway we have plenty of books of religion in India. We don't need any more! I find in your Bible a unique interpretation of universal history, the history of the whole of creation and the history of the human race. And therefore a unique interpretation of the human person as a responsible actor in history. That is unique. There is nothing else in the whole religious literature of the world to put alongside it.[4]

So then the Bible claims to be the record of God's very personal revelation of himself to humankind. How can we understand and assess this claim? How should we study it?

I use an example from another branch of knowledge - astronomy. (Examples could be taken from any number of branches of knowledge.) Let us imagine a team of technicians coming to examine a great telescope and make sense of it, without realising that its purpose is to view distant objects in the skies beyond it. They will all try to work out what this gadget and that gadget are for, and write many learned papers about them. If they are writing independently of one another they will all have different ideas about which parts of the instrument are useful and which are useless, which were original and which

---

3. John 1:14-18.
4. Quoted in Lesslie Newbigin, *A Walk Through the Bible* (London, 1999), 4.

were later additions, which are fundamental and which are merely superficial. What is certain is that they will never be able to make sense of it as a whole until they discover what it is for, and they will not find that until they actually look through it. Once they have made this fundamental discovery, then they will gradually be able to make sense of the whole. As they actually use the telescope for its purpose of viewing reality beyond it in the heavens, then it will, as it were, be able to unfold its many and varied resources to them and they will see it as a wonderful inter-related unity. If they refuse to take into account the purpose of the telescope in their investigations, we would have to say that the whole basis of their work is irrational, even though it has the appearance of being scientific.

Similarly our understanding of the Bible can only come when we use it for its true purpose, namely to lead us to personal knowledge of God. If we resist such life-changing knowledge we will never be able to assess the truth of the Bible. We cannot be detached observers or listeners.

The Bible is the account of the relationship of God with all creation. Although the Bible writings were all complete in the first century AD, its story, in both Old and New Testaments, looks ahead to the end of time. The Bible therefore encompasses the whole of reality and does not allow us the dualist way of thinking that would seek to break up knowledge into disconnected parts. It cannot be considered as if it were just a religious book divorced from such subjects as history or science. More of this later.

God is therefore revealed in the Scriptures as deeply personal, and so something must be said here about personal knowledge. Personal knowledge of one another is not gained primarily through looking at one another but through listening to one another.[5] It is through speech that we reveal what is really on our heart and mind. Thus God's revelation of himself is in terms of 'Word' rather than picture. We must not seek to make any

---

5. I owe some of the wording of this paragraph to Lesslie Newbigin.

image of him. We know him as Person as we know all persons. Personal knowledge always has at its heart trust and love and therefore a willingness to receive and give and to be changed by our growth in understanding of other persons.

Because God is Person it belongs to the heart of the message of the Bible that our response to him must be faith and obedience rather than human wisdom or works of the law. Philosophical discussions, words of wisdom and codes of law do find their essential place in the Bible, but only as servants of that true knowledge of God that comes through faith. We should not seek to discover truth by extracting doctrines from the text of Scripture and then merely comparing them with one another. The doctrines that we find in our Bible study must only be considered in relation to that profoundly personal knowledge of God that is revealed in his personal relationship with his people. Indeed it is common to hear conversion testimonies from men and women who say that they once found the Bible meaningless but when they experienced openness to God himself, the Bible came alive.

The story of redemption as told in the Bible particularly concerns God and humankind. Because the nations and peoples are many, God chose one people, to represent all peoples, who would be the human bearers of God's purposes in redemption. They, the chosen people, were given a land – the promised land – in which God would work out his purpose for the world.

Because they were uniquely to be the ones who would receive the divine Word, God's deeply personal relationship with humankind became particularly intense in his relation with the Jewish people (Israel). They like the rest of us were and are sinners. Hence the special intensity of God's relationship with them drew out of them the best and the worst that we see in the human race. Furthermore their encounter with other nations brought and brings the Gentiles into contact with God's revelation. Therefore the nations' reaction to the Jewish people reveals both the best and the worst, not only in the Jews, but also in the wider world as well. (This is the deepest way to

understand the historic and ever-present mystery of anti-
Semitism.) [6] In the story of Israel we see, as in a magnifying
mirror, the story of all peoples and the story of our individual lives.

When we reach the New Testament we find that God has
not just drawn near to Israel, but his Word has actually come
into their midst. 'The Word became flesh and dwelt among us.'[7]
The particularly intense relationship that draws out of them both
the best and the worst now reaches its dramatic climax. It is in
this climax that God is able fully to reveal his Person to us. It is
at the cross that God's heart of love and righteousness is fully
made known. This final revelation is foreshadowed in all his
past relationship with Israel as recorded in the whole Old
Testament.[8] That is why the New Testament draws upon Old
Testament words spoken to Israel and applies them to Jesus.
Since Israel embodies before God all peoples, it also is right for
preachers to use such passages and relate them to the wider
world, the church and individuals.

It is in the culmination of meeting between God and Israel
that the worst and best about his people is finally seen. The best
is seen, for example, in the life of the apostles (all Jews) who
accept Christ, and begin to take the Word of God into all the
world, thus fulfilling God's calling to Israel to be a light to the
Gentiles. The worst is seen in the Jewish religious leadership
who reject Christ and in doing so reject the very Person of God
himself. Yet it is here that we see the wonderful sovereign love
of God for us all – a great theme of James Philip's preaching.
Not only does God use their good response to Christ, but he
needs and uses also their rejection of him too. Indeed their
rejection of him is the means by which he fully makes himself
known to us as he bears all our sins in his body and 'takes away
the sins of the world'.[9]

---

6. See Ps. 44:15-22.
7. John 1:14
8. Luke 24:44.
9. John 1:29.

Both Old and New Testament tell us that God had actually purposed to use the sin of Israel as the means of bringing light to the world.[10] His righteous love is seen in the context of the sin of his people. Although the cross of Christ is the place where this is accomplished, it is seen too in the Old Testament. Here also the wonderful love and forgiveness of God are demonstrated in the context of the sin of Israel. It is only in that context that such books as Jeremiah could have been written at all.[11] This is a major theme of Paul's epistle to the Romans. Here he argues that it is human unfaithfulness to God that brings out his faithfulness and that is the way he had purposed it from the beginning.[12]

It is out of this very real and dramatic relationship between God and Israel that Old and New Testaments came to be written. The writings of the Scriptures are the response to all that has happened as the life of God meets the people of Israel. The Bible is the result of God's really embedding himself in the humanity of his people. Those who were most intimately caught up in the drama record that divine initiative and human response for us. They were not detached observers.

Thus the writing of the Bible can be considered from the perspective of both the divine and the human. However it must never be forgotten that its ultimate origin is God, not man. It is not as though part of it is divine and part human. It is entirely divine and entirely human. It is in the very human words of the biblical writers that the divine Word is heard in all its fullness. The bond between the divine and human is always the Holy Spirit. That is why the human authors of the Scriptures, writing with all their varying degrees of good or bad Hebrew, Aramaic or Greek, nevertheless through the inspiration of the Holy Spirit, really are enabled to bring the Word of God to the world. That is what the Bible is.

---

10. Isa. 42:18-19, Rom. 11 (whole chapter).
11. See for example Jer. 30 and 31.
12. Rom. 3:1-6.

God raises Christ, having died as a Jew at the hand of Jews and Gentiles, in a new recreated humanity that breaks the human division between Jew and Gentile. In the resurrection of Christ, then, Israel is reconstituted and the church that embraces both Jew and Gentile becomes through Christ God's new temple. This is a major point made by Paul in Ephesians.[13] In Romans 11 Paul goes on to discuss the future for both the church and Jewish Israel – another of James Philip's great interests. Paul argues that it is precisely because God had purposed that Jewish Israel be disobedient for our sake that he has not abandoned the purposes for them that are revealed in the Old Testament prophets. Thus the Bible tells us about the future destiny of the church, Jewish Israel and the world. It is not, though, three separate purposes. Rather through the final restoration of Israel to its land and eventually to Christ, the church itself will be blessed and, in turn, the world will experience 'life from the dead'.[14] This does not mean that all will be saved, for although the resurrection of Christ embraces all creation there are many, both Jew and Gentile, who reject the grace of God. There will be both a resurrection to eternal life and a resurrection to condemnation.[15]

Paul also makes clear that the Christian church should never look down upon the continuing Jewish Israel, because the very sins of self-righteous pride that led them to reject Christ are in danger of affecting the church too. Indeed he goes on to imply that if the church does not live up to its position it will not succeed in its calling to lead the Jewish people to Christ.[16]

Thus although the Bible story is focused in Israel and then Christ, its story enfolds the whole of reality from the beginning to the end of time. Is there any external indication that the story it tells is a true story, a true history? Let us ponder briefly the human subject of the story, the people of Israel.

---

13. Eph. 2:14ff.
14. Rom. 11:15.
15. John 5:29.
16. Rom. 11:17-24.

Over and over again the Old Testament prophets tell us that the history of the Jews will be unlike the history of any other people, and that towards the end of time, after great suffering, the Jews will return to the promised land, where they will become the centre of hostility. This hostility will affect the whole world. Eventually God will reconcile them to their Messiah, cleanse them from their sin, judge the nations who have hated them, and make them a blessing to all peoples.[17] The New Testament is not silent about this purpose of God.[18]

Many, Jews, Christians and agnostics have written about the Jewish story and commented on its uniqueness. Here is a Jewish view:

> By the standards of others, once they had lost their country, the Jewish people should have fallen into decay long ago. But instead, *uniquely*, they continued to maintain themselves as a nation, and by so doing became in the eyes of others an uncanny and frightening people.[19]

Mark Twain expressed an agnostic view:

> The Jews constitute a tiny percentage of the human race. Properly the Jew ought hardly to be heard of; but he is heard of, has always been heard of. He is as prominent on the planet as any other people, and his commercial importance is extravagantly out of proportion to the smallness of his bulk. His contributions to the world's list of great names in literature, science, art, music, finance, medicine and abstruse learning are also way out of proportion to the weakness of his numbers. He has made a marvellous fight in this world, in all the ages; and has done it with his hands tied behind him. He could be vain of himself, and be excused for it. The Egyptian, the

---

17. Isa. 43:49; Jer. 30-33; Ezek. 36-39; Zech. 12, 13, etc.
18. For example Luke 21:20-24.
19. David Vital, *The Origins of Zionism* (Oxford,1975), 128, summarising the writing of Yehuda Leib Pinsker.

Babylon and the Persian rose, filled the planet with sound and splendour, then faded to dream-stuff and passed away; the Greek and the Roman followed, and made a vast noise, and they are gone; other peoples have sprung up and held their torch high for a time, but it burned out, and they sit in twilight now, or have vanished. The Jew saw them all, beat them all, and is now what he always was, exhibiting no decadence, no infirmities of age, no weakening of his parts, no slowing of his energies, no dulling of his alert and aggressive mind. All things are mortal but the Jew; all other forces pass, but he remains. What is the secret of his immortality? [20]

Here are two Christian views. Karl Barth, who did not like proofs from nature for the Christian faith, said of the history of the Jews:

In fact, if the question of a proof of God is raised, one need merely point to this simple historical fact. For in the person of the Jew there stands a witness before our eyes, the witness of God's covenant with Abraham, Isaac and Jacob and in that way with us all. Even one who does not understand Holy Scripture can see this reminder. Don't you see, the remarkable theological importance, the extraordinary spiritual and sacred significance of the National Socialism that now lies behind us is that right from its roots it was anti-Semitic, that in this movement it was realised with a simple demonic clarity, that *the* enemy is the *Jew*. Yes, the enemy in this matter had to be a Jew. In this Jewish nation there really lives to this day the extraordinariness of the revelation of God.[21]

The Anglican theologian and distinguished churchman, Alan Richardson, wrote as follows:

---

20. In an essay entitled 'Concerning the Jews' quoted by Lance Lambert in *The Uniqueness of Israel* (Eastbourne,1980), 57.
21. *Dogmatics in Outline* (London,1949), 75-6.

> In view of the remarkable history of the Jewish people . . . it
> ought not to seem strange to us that they should have some
> unique destiny to fulfil in the providence of God . . .The history
> of other nations provides not even a single remote parallel to
> the phenomenon of Jewish existence down the ages and to-
> day. What other nation of antiquity has preserved its identity
> and character as the Jews have done, though exiled from their
> homeland and dispersed throughout the world? . . . Throughout
> centuries of persecution the Jewish race has survived the
> catastrophes which have so often destroyed the national identity
> of other peoples . . . Religious or secularised a Jew remains a
> Jew *malgré lui,* a voluntary or involuntary witness to the truth
> that is symbolised in the story of God's Covenant with
> Abraham. This striking fact of the persistence of the Jewish
> race has long been recognised as important evidence of the
> truth of the biblical interpretation of history.[22]

As for the history of the church, the New Testament leads us to
expect that, like the churches of the New Testament, it will
have a wonderful life mixed with appalling faults.[23] Towards
the end of the age many will fall away from the faith and the
love of many will grow cold. Nevertheless, by the grace of God,
the gospel will spread to all nations.[24] In other words, as this
age draws to its close, parts of the world where the church has
been strong will see a major decline in godly faith and parts of
the world where the gospel is new will see a major expansion
of the faith of Christ.

As for the destiny of the world, the Bible leads us to expect
that wars and natural disasters will be a constant feature of world
history. Towards the end of the age we can expect an
intensification of these things. Jesus tells us that as the time of
his second coming draws near, wickedness, knowledge and
travel will greatly increase.[25] Evil will not, though, have the

---

22. *Christian Apologetics* (London,1947), 141-2.
23. Acts 20:29-30.
24. Matt. 24:9-14.
25. See Isa. 24, Joel 2:28ff., Mark 13, Rev. 6:13.

final say in the destiny of creation; for beyond the death of Christ was resurrection – a resurrection that enfolds all creation.[26]

Although it would be foolish to use science to prove the Bible's world-view, it cannot but be heartening to discover that the Bible's teaching about the essential nature of reality sits more easily with modern science's discoveries about the natural world than would have been possible with the presuppositions of an earlier science. Twentieth-century scientific discoveries about the foundations of the natural world cry out more and more for a Creator and Sustainer. They further reveal a view of created reality in which the heart of the Bible's message can make sense. They are very briefly summarised here:

- The universe gives strong indications that it is finite.
- Space-time itself is not just the container of objects and events but part of the fabric of the natural world.
- Physical existence has at its base mathematical information.
- Although the natural world is ordered it is not a deterministic system.
- Even across the bounds of space and time, physical being, at its foundations, is relational. It is not a collection of separate particles.
- Life itself is based on information technology way beyond that invented or imagined by human effort.
- The consciousness of animals and the self-consciousness of humans cry out for a non-materialistic understanding of animal and human experience.

The Bible's world-view is that:

1) God is the ground of the rationality of nature. In modern terms we can say that the laws of electricity, magnetism, gravity etc., which are fundamental to the behaviour of all physical

---

26. Col. 1:15-20.

things, did not just happen to be what they are, but owe their origin to God. The foundation of these laws is the Logos or Word of God that expresses the mind, will, grace and love of God.

2) God is not only the Creator of all things but also their Sustainer. The universe was not merely created and then left to continue in its own way independent of the Creator. At its foundations – as many think is implied by quantum mechanics – the universe is an open system that seems to depend on a greater order beyond itself. Its continuing existence depends upon the grace of God; 'he upholds everything by the word of his power.'[27]

3) Although God is the Creator and Sustainer of all things, he has granted freedom to nature and especially to humans. We really are free. We do not live in a deterministic universe rigidly controlled by physical or divine laws.

4) God has given to humankind the freedom and authority to rule the earth. Our use of freedom really does influence for good or bad the world of nature with which we come in contact.

5) There is a continuing interaction between God and nature, God and the history of the world, and God and the story of our individual lives. God speaks, loves, calls to us, and expects a response.

6) The gospel of Christ is that God has made himself known to humankind in the redemption of the world. This redemption holds together all of space and time so that, even though we are individually responsible for our actions, yet also we are related across the bounds of space and time with God, one another and the natural world through the great archetypal figures of Adam and Christ.

I end this paper with an analogy which should not be pressed too far but might just be helpful. What about the relation between the living Word and the written Word? It might be useful to

27. Heb. 1:3.

think (*mutatis mutandis*, of course) of the relation between the wave of information and the particle in quantum theory. In the wave-particle duality of the fundamental structure of nature, it is the wave of information that is primary. It is brought into concrete reality when it interacts with nature and is observed.

Could this be an analogy of how we should regard the relationship between the eternal Word of God who is the source of creation and redemption, and the written Word which comes to us through him? As he interacts with men and women in the history of Israel and the world, the Scriptures come to be written. It is by reading the written Word that we discern the eternal Word. Although the written Word cannot enclose him, we also must say that there is no other medium outside the written Word through which we hear him. The divine and human come together by the inspiration (or breath) of God in his Holy Spirit.

Medicine and Faith in the Third Millennium

Nigel Cameron

It is a very special privilege to be invited to celebrate Jim Philip and his ministry. Shenach and I met at Holyrood Abbey back in the twilight of the 1960s, we married there in 1974, our five children (Anastasia, Lydia, Daniel James Philip, Miriam, and Alice) were baptised there, and there too I served variously as locum and associate minister. Now we have been ten years in the United States, and our time at Holyrood seems long past. Yet we treasure memories and friendships, and we salute our esteemed former minister and our friend.

These reflections on the state of medicine and bioethics at the outset of the third millennium attempt an overview in the light of the biblical revelation and our consistent calling to engage the culture for Christ the King.

In the past decade both medicine and its stepsibling biomedicine have witnessed extraordinary advance. Yet despite the continued momentum of bioethics, a field whose time has surely come, our moral uncertainties as a civilisation grow at an even faster pace than the nexus of science and medical practice that holds us in such anguished awe. For as new questions are raised, and old are given sharper focus and renewed circulation, the capacity of our culture to discover answers that will command a consensus and give us a basis for our common life, continues to diminish. The predicament of the West as the global leader in both technology and morals is impossible to exaggerate. As our scientific knowledge, especially in the biosciences with their attendant medical-technological capacities, maintains its exponential growth, our moral knowledge and our capacity therefore to channel and constrain these capacities in the service of humankind continue to diminish. It is perhaps the supreme and tragic irony of western history that, at that moment when the demand for moral vision is at its greatest, its supply is found at its lowest ebb for many hundreds of years. The grounding of our culture in the Christian vision of human nature is less sure with every year that passes.

This view is offered in the knowledge that the painter is using a broad brush. The point is to offer perspective, and to do so in a context in which perspective is so often what has been found to be wanting in contemporary discussion. There is a need for fine brushwork also, and some of it is to be found in the pages that follow. Yet what we need above all is a sense of the general direction of things; for our medical-scientific culture is in process of a shift of tectonic proportions. All the many debates and changes in which we are engaged – from the restructuring of healthcare delivery and costing, to the human genome project and its fruit – are fundamentally inter-connected. Only by grasping that fact and its dynamics will we be able to gain perspective on the many particular questions under discussion.

In my book *The New Medicine*[1] I sought to develop a powerful framework of understanding within which these many questions could be seen to fall into place. The framework, as the subtitle 'Life and Death After Hippocrates' suggests, is that of the Hippocratic medical tradition, to be precise the tradition of 'Christian Hippocratism' that has dominated and determined the medical tradition of the western world down nearly two thousand years of history, and that continues, despite very serious challenges, to be an immense influence for good at the turn of the third millennium. By 'Christian Hippocratism' I mean that amalgam of classical Hippocratic medical values and the Judeo-Christian worldview that has formed the mainstream medical tradition of the western world. It is probably best to use the term 'amalgam', since one of the curiosities of the western tradition and, at the same time, a cause of disquiet

---

1. London, 1991; new edition, Chicago, Bioethics Press, 2001.

among Christians today, is the degree to which the pagan origins of Hippocratism were permitted to survive its adoption by Christendom. That in turn has led, among those who have sought in recent years to revive interest in the Hippocratic Oath, to a spate of revisions and re-writes that excise the overtly pagan element. In general, and while we recognise the problem posed by the pagan character of the Oath, this practice is to be discouraged, since it has left us with several fragmented versions of the Oath at a time when fragmentation is at the heart of our problem.[2]

As we enter the third millennium, the incipient collapse of the Hippocratic tradition is leading to the development of a 'new medicine' in which the moral vision that has driven medicine is being displaced. Many of the major questions under current discussion are directly related to the Hippocratic collapse, especially those that cluster around the question of the sanctity of life, and that other and seemingly disconnected set that concern the nature of the medical profession and the 'delivery' of what is increasingly and unfortunately termed 'healthcare'.

The life issues encompass both the old questions of abortion and euthanasia – ancient vices that our ancestors believed the spread of Judeo-Christian values had put to flight, but that have come back to haunt us as we move beyond the Judeo-Christian moral consensus – and new questions that offer fresh versions of these ancient vices for the brash and pragmatic technological society of the twenty-first century: options such as deleterious research on the human embryo, and in its latest twist the re-statement of that option in the context of both cloning and research on human embryonic stem-cells.

The rapid shifts and uncertain direction in the financing and provision of medical care in many countries, and especially the United States, offer a window on one of the most crucial and yet neglected issues in the modern world, the fate of the professions. By a curiously American irony the rise of 'managed

---

2. See BioethicsWeb.com for further discussion and various versions of the Oath.

care' in the United States, quite the most significant feature of which is its concentration of medical provision in the hands of corporations, has delivered Americans from the putative horrors of 'socialised medicine', yet by turning medicine into a corporate product. It is a complex and interesting task to weigh the moral and other merits of the varied systems of medical provision. The chief criterion of any such weighing will always be that of 'professional alignment' – the degree to which the system upholds or undermines the professional character of the enterprise. By such a criterion, it is hard to avoid the conclusion that the corporatisation of medicine is that option least friendly to the professional idea, and arguably more damaging to its flourishing than the more humane and intelligent models of social provision. Thus, when the National Health Service was introduced in the United Kingdom in the aftermath of the Second World War, one of the best decisions taken was to leave family practitioners as self-employed professionals. While the system moved to a single-payer model, its main body of physicians were protected from the worst aspect of such a model in that they did not become civil servants. By the same token, it was the sheer illiberality of the failed Clinton plan of the early 1990s that helped secure its doom, with threats, for example, of criminal sanctions for those who sought to deliver and receive medical care outside the ambit of its provision.

Let me restate: the central question is that of professional alignment; to what degree is the professional character of medical provision aided or undermined by the systems of financing and management in which it subsists? One reason for posing the question in that manner is to draw attention to the problematic character of traditional western models of medical provision, where the traditional 'fee-for-service' approach that was focused on an individual physician in general practice offers an estimable paradigm and yet does so in a context in which the growth of knowledge means that specialisation, exponentially increasing costs, and hospital-based practice must also find their place in the medicine of tomorrow.

Needless to say, it is particularly unfortunate that in the many debates of the 1990s about the delivery of medicine, especially in the US and the UK, concern for the professional criterion has been rarely voiced. That is not to say that physicians' 'professional' organisations have been silent or inactive. But their concerns have in general related only tangentially to the professional question.

There may seem to be little connection between the corporatisation of medicine and key bioethics issues such as the morality of embryonic stem-cell and related research, but in fact the connection is close. For these questions are being raised in the highly fragmented context of contemporary medicine. Were their location firmly within the professional model, the character of the discussion would be altogether different. But these issues are coming into discussion from one or both of two other directions. At one level, of course, they are posed by developments in the biosciences. While members of the bioscience research community are sometimes physicians as well as researchers, the connection is increasingly accidental. And secondly, they come to their sharpest focus in their corporate context. The biotechnology companies are increasingly setting the pace not simply in their more traditional role of developing the fruit of basic science research, but – more in the manner of pharmaceutical development – now finding themselves at the forefront of basic science. The implications of this development are huge. Among other things, it breaks the near-monopoly of public funding for basic work in the biosciences, and thereby sharpens the issue of the role of public policy. The current US debate over public funding for deleterious research on human stem-cells is a case in point. A prohibition of funding for embryo research had severely curtailed such work in the US. It is now proposed to use stem-cells from privately-funded embryo destruction for publicly-funded research. Or again, take the role of Celera Genomics in rivalling the publicly-funded Human Genome Project as the work of mapping the genome has accelerated toward completion. In this context, professional supervision of the basic science and application development is entirely absent, and supervision through public policy becomes increasingly difficult. The corporatisation of the biosciences stands in parallel with that of medical provision through the 'profession'. Medicine is being steadily redefined as a consumer product, and corporate structures put in place to shape, market, and deliver the product to its consumers.

In the past decade, everything has changed and yet nothing has changed. The gears of massive cultural shift continue to grind. In every nation that traces its roots to the amalgam of classical and Judeo-Christian civilisation that we call 'the West', the seemingly inexorable process of transformation into a new cultural pattern continues. The trend toward post-Hippocratic medicine moves, however erratically, forward. At the same time, what we might refer to as the clinical heart of medicine – its classic work of therapeutics and palliation – is giving place in both the public imagination and the informed mind of the culture to a fresh centre of focus, as the capacity of technology to delight, to impress, to dazzle, and to scare, is demonstrated afresh every day.

Cloning, for example, was a mere sci-fi debating point in 1990. After unprecedented publicity in 1997, when the cloning of Dolly the sheep was announced from Roslin, outside Edinburgh in Scotland, a major opportunity has opened for bioscience research, commercial development and ultimately medical practice. The challenge to public policy was fundamental and immediate. Efforts to ban the birth of cloned babies were unsuccessful at the level of federal legislation in the USA, though they led to the addition of a special protocol to the European Convention on Biomedicine and Human Rights. Efforts to prevent the use of somatic-cell nuclear transfer technology to facilitate deleterious research on human embryos are meeting with difficulty, especially in light of the new interest in research on human stem-cells, for which an embryo, cloned or otherwise, offers a prime source. Most outrageously, in the UK the government has moved to use the cloning technique to increase the flow of research embryos.

This is not the place to engage that debate, or to anticipate the incipient challenges from the exploitation of the vast library of information that is even now being mined open-cast in human genetics. Yet these matters lie ahead, on the near horizons of the human race. What should be noted is the extraordinary pace of technological change, and the fact that while technology does not change the basic moral questions that confront its potential beneficiaries, it re-shapes them in such a fashion as to render them both more complex and also more threatening. Never have the questions so elegantly raised by Hippocrates in the centuries before Christ been more relevant than in the third millennium AD. Yet, as couples search for their best choice of gametes on the internet while they 'plan' their 'family', and as the stem-cell debate seems to have moved beyond any serious interest in the age-old weighing of ends and means, we sample the moral culture of tomorrow. A recent article suggested that computing power in the first thirty years of the new millennium might increase by a factor of one million. The exponential character of developments in the biosciences, correlated as they are with both information technology and venture capitalism, offers a startling prospect. And they throw down the gauntlet to public policy at every level, at a time when we have less and less confidence as a community in the possibility of moral consensus as the basis for our common life.

Yet Hippocrates remains the patient's friend, locking every aspect of medical practice into the transcendent web of moral vision that brings the human and the divine into a common embrace, holds physicians accountable one to another in the guild-profession that is thereby constituted; and sets the sanctity and dignity of human life at centre-stage. Only thus has humane medicine flourished, and it is hard to see how in any other way it will flourish again.

The theological underpinnings of the Christian vision for medicine have never been clearer. In stark contrast to the efforts of Peter Singer to call us 'speciesists' because we believe that human beings are special, we stand firm on the biblical declaration that men and women are made in the image of God, and that from their creation they derive the dignity that gives them 'rights' and requires that we treat them – however young, old, damaged, or deformed – in accordance with that unique status. As the new issues of bioethics unfold – moving from 'bioethics 1', concerned with taking life, to 'bioethics 2', in which making life by design takes centre stage – the central significance of the doctrine of creation looms ever larger over our contemporary debate.

* * * * * * * * * * * * * * * * *

Resources related to *The New Medicine* will be found at BioethicsWeb.com and TheCloningDebate.com together with links to bioethics centres and other sites. The Centre for Bioethics and Public Policy in London, which started life as the Rutherford House Bioethics Project in Edinburgh, is accessible at bioethics.ac.uk. The best-stocked Christian website is cbhd.org, the Centre for Bioethics and Human Dignity (Bannockburn, Illinois).

Calvin on the Lord's Supper and Communion with Christ

Sinclair Ferguson

Some three decades ago, at the close of a conference in St Andrews, I sat transfixed as James Philip preached on Revelation 5:12 and then led us to Christ at the Lord's Table. The taste of Christ's grace that day has lingered with me throughout the years. This memory, and the fact that his preaching has often reminded me of what John Calvin's must have been like, prompts me to offer this brief essay on Calvin's teaching on our fellowship with Christ at the Lord's supper as a small expression of my deep gratitude and affection.

> As long as Christ remains outside of us, and we are separated from him, all that he has suffered and done for the salvation of the human race remains useless and of no value to us.

So Calvin notes in a famous passage at the beginning of *Institutes* Book 3, and adds that this saving union with Christ takes place only through 'the secret energy of the Spirit, by which we come to enjoy Christ and all his benefits'.[1]

Central to this understanding of the role of the Holy Spirit in our salvation is the principle that the Spirit takes what belongs to Christ and makes it known to us (Jn. 16:14). The same Spirit who accompanied Jesus from conception to ascension descends on the church at Pentecost in his specific identity as the Spirit of Jesus Christ. For the correlation between the Spirit and Christ

---

1. *Institutes of the Christian Religion* 3:1:1, trs. F.L. Battles, ed. J.T. McNeill (Philadelphia, 1960), vol.I, 537. All quotations from the *Institutes* are taken from this translation.

is now such that all that Christ has done for us lies in the possession of the Spirit, and is brought from Christ to the church by him. Thus the empty mouth of faith eats and drinks Christ and the empty hands of faith are filled with every spiritual blessing.[2]

Furthermore, for Calvin the 'first' or supreme title of the Spirit is 'Spirit of sonship'.[3] Consequently through his work believers come to experience the assurance of God's fatherly benevolence and experience communion with God.[4]

Preaching and Sacraments

The objective channels through which this communion and assurance come are the Word of God (particularly, but not exclusively, the *preached* word) and the sacraments of baptism and the Lord's supper. Standing as he does in the Augustinian tradition, Calvin sees significant parallels between the audible word expounded in preaching and the visible word received in the sacraments.[5] Just as Christ is the *scopus*, the goal and, indeed, the focus of the Scriptures, so he is also the *scopus*[6] as well as the focus, the matter and substance[7] of the sacraments. Thus, for example, baptism is into the name of Christ, because he is its *scopus*. Its whole strength (*virtus*) lies in him. In this dynamic relation between the sacrament and Christ, a double movement takes place in which the meaning of the sacrament

---

2. See, for example, Calvin's *Short Treatise on the Lord's Supper* (Geneva, 1541), 10; tr. J.K. S. Reid, *Calvin: Theological Treatises* (London, 1954), 148.
3. *Institutes* 3:1:3.
4. Cf. his comments on 1 Cor.2:12 in *The First Epistle of Paul the Apostle to the Corinthians*, trs. J.W. Fraser (Edinburgh, 1960),60.
5. Cf. *Institutes* 4:14:6.
6. Cf. his comments on Acts 10:48 in *The Acts of the Apostles*, trs. J.W. Fraser and W.G. McDonald (Edinburgh, 1965), vol. 1,319: 'Christ is the proper goal of baptism (*proprius Baptismi scopus*).'
7. *Institutes* 4:4:16.

opens out towards Christ and in that event Christ makes himself known to and communicates (engages in communion) with the believer.

In the preached word, then, Christ speaks to us and we respond in faith to his living voice. This in itself is enough for us; but God recognises that our faith is weak and in need of his strengthening. So he further provides the visible words of baptism and the Lord's supper where Christ puts his grace on display in order to bring us into a more assured communion with him through the Spirit's work and our responding faith.[8]

Focus on Christ Himself

Here already we have a hint of the theme which constantly underlies Calvin's thinking and gives rise to the polemical thrust in his teaching: Christ himself is the heart of the sacraments. They should not be expounded in terms of the *res* (the element in itself – water, bread or wine), but in terms of the *persona* (the person who is presented to us, i.e. Jesus himself). If attention is focused on the sacramental 'thing' (water, bread and wine), and hearts are not lifted beyond the sign to the person of Jesus signified in the sign and revealed by the Spirit through the sign, then the true meaning of the sacraments is bound to become distorted.

This understanding of how sacraments 'work' explains Calvin's concern to expound the role of the Spirit in their administration. It is directly analogous to his role in preaching. The Spirit does not transform the words of the Bible but employs them to bring us to Christ; so too, in the administration of the sacraments, the elements are not transformed, but rather employed by the Spirit to realise in us all that is symbolised to us. Nothing 'changes' the elements.

This note is particularly dominant in Calvin's teaching on the Lord's supper. For, in his view, while men can employ the *res* of the Lord's supper, breaking the bread and offering the

---

8. *Institutes* 4:14:8.

wine, only the Divine Spirit is qualified to communicate the person of Jesus Christ to us by these means.

A Christo-Dynamic View of the Supper

For Calvin, then, sacraments are not mere or bare signs (*signa nuda*) but, like the audible 'signs' of the words of Scripture, when received in faith they function as communicative signs. By means of them the very realities they symbolise are actually communicated to and experienced by the recipients as they respond in faith. The Spirit is the connection, the bond (*vinculum*) between the *res* (bread and wine), the *persona* (Jesus himself), and ourselves as the recipients.

If we fail to grasp this, error and confusion follow: either (i) the sign is confused with the thing signified, and an *ex opere operato* doctrine of the sacraments results, as though we could receive Christ simply by the act of eating and drinking; or (ii) the sign is divorced from what it signifies (Jesus Christ, clothed in the gospel) and the supper thus tends to be little more than an *aide-mémoire,* falling far short of Spirit-given communion with Christ.

Calvin's Christo-dynamic view of the sacraments (if we may thus describe it) constantly seeks to turn the recipient's eyes to Jesus Christ himself. The communion in view is with Christ, and the feasting is on Jesus himself. What the sacramental signs externally signify is internally effected by the Spirit.[9]

This understanding protects us from the implications of the two errors noted above:

(i) It prevents us from adorning the sign (possibly even adoring it!), as though the sign itself were or could become the reality it represents (the danger of an *ex opere operato* view, in which the priest's action is sufficient of itself to make Christ present,

---

9. See his comments on Titus 3:5 in *The Second Epistle of Paul to the Corinthians, The Epistles of Paul to Timothy, Titus and Philemon,* trs. T.A. Smail (Edinburgh, 1964), 382-3.

apart from the free, sovereign and dynamic activity of the Spirit). (ii) It safeguards us from emptying the sign of its ability to bring us to Christ when so employed by the Spirit. This is the danger of *signa nuda* reducing the bread and the wine to 'bare signs', in which human faith alone is active and nothing is attributed to the Spirit.

Calvin here distances himself from Rome on the right and the Anabaptists on the left, but also by implication from both Luther and Zwingli. Self-consciously he provided a *via media* between the latter two. He did so, however, not by adopting the common factors between them but by expounding what he saw as a biblical, that is a pneumatic (Holy Spirit-empowered), doctrine of the sacraments. Only this, he believed, preserves the biblical conjunction of the sign and the reality of the thing (or better, person) signified, and safeguards the necessity of the Spirit's ministry and also of our faith. Without this inner dynamic in the supper, the biblical correlation between Christ, the sacramental symbols, and our faith collapses.

Thus he believes that the Roman Church (papal *magisterium* and priestly acts) has usurped, whereas Zwingli and Luther have minimised, the ministry which belongs to the Holy Spirit.

Polemical Emphases
Because Calvin expounds the doctrine of the supper in a variety of polemical contexts, his teaching is contextualised in different ways.

(i) When dealing with those who boast in the sign, he tends to stress the emptiness of the sign in and of itself.
(ii) When addressing the criticisms of both Rome and the Anabaptists (one stressing the necessity of priestly ordination and power, the other stressing the personal status of the administrant), he stresses the essential insignificance of the human administrant.
(iii) When addressing believers he stresses the dynamic

connection of the sign with what it signifies – the so-called sacramental union.

But in each of these reactions, Calvin returns basically to the same central theme: the efficacy of the sacraments depends on the dynamic ministry of the Holy Spirit uniting the recipients to the reality which the sacraments objectively signify, namely the person of Jesus Christ clothed in the garments of salvation. He enlightens the mind with faith, he seals in the heart the adoption of God, he regenerates us to new life, and he grafts us into the body of Christ so that we come to live in him and he in us.[10]

The Display of Christ, the Substance of the Supper

The function of the sacraments, then, can be summed up in two Latin terms Calvin employs:

(i) Exhibere. The signs display or exhibit Christ to the eyes and to the sense of vision, just as the word displays Christ to the ears and to the sense of hearing as the Spirit takes what belongs to Christ and shows or exhibits it to us. In this sense Calvin sees sacraments as appendices to the promise of the gospel, confirming it to faith.[11] Pictures may display what the weak in faith are not able to read easily in the word. They thus help to remove our ignorance and doubt of God's grace toward us, and strengthen our weak faith.

In this respect, it is important to notice the way Calvin balances the famous definition of faith he had given earlier in his *Institutes*[12] by what he says here about faith's existential weakness:

---

10. Cf *The Epistle of Paul to the Hebrews,* trs. W.B. Johnston (Edinburgh, 1963), 149.
11. *Institutes* 4:14:5-6.
12. *Institutes* 2:2:7: 'We shall possess a right definition of faith if we call it a firm and certain knowledge of God's benevolence towards

God's truth is of itself firm and sure enough. . . . But as our faith is slight and feeble unless it be propped on all sides and sustained by every means, it trembles, wavers, totters, and at last gives way. Here our merciful Lord, according to his infinite kindness, so tempers himself to our capacity that, since we are creatures who always creep on the ground, cleave to the flesh, and, do not think about or even conceive of anything spiritual, he condescends to lead us to himself, even by these earthly elements, and to set before us in the flesh a mirror of spiritual blessings.[13]

Calvin is therefore very far from the quasi-perfectionism he detected in some left-wing Reformation thinking that viewed the sacraments as unnecessary for those who had real faith and could feed inwardly on Christ.[14] Rather, he holds that through the visible words of the sacraments, the Spirit penetrates our hard hearts, moves our jaded affections and opens our souls to receive the Christ who is exhibited by means of the signs.

(ii) Substantia. Calvin contends that the sacraments communicate to believers the 'substance' of Jesus Christ, in his saving humanity. The precise manner in which this takes place is, as we shall see, one of the most significant and distinctive elements in Calvin's teaching on the Lord's supper, and one that has provoked considerable comment. We shall return to it.

---

us, founded upon the truth of the freely given promise in Christ, both revealed to our minds and sealed upon our hearts through the Holy Spirit.'

13. *Institutes* 4:14:3.

14. For example, Caspar Schwenckfeld. See G.H. Williams, *The Radical Reformation* (Philadelphia, 1962), 106ff.

The 'Real' Presence of Christ

As with all the magisterial Reformers, the central controversy of the Lord's supper (and subsequently the context in which Calvin enlarged on the role of the Holy Spirit) was the question of the nature of the presence of the body and blood of Christ and the manner of our communion with him. Here he seeks to avoid two opposite, if not quite equal, errors:

(i) That our communion is with the flesh and blood of Christ localised in the bread and wine of the supper.
(ii) That our communion is not with the actual body and blood of Christ, but is merely a spiritual one, in the sense that the supper prompts us to reflect back on our conversion and enables us to meditate on what Jesus Christ has done for us, or on our commitment and love to him. The supper, thus conceived, has a rather subjective orientation.[15]

Against both these positions, Calvin argues that we have true communion with the actual flesh and blood of Christ, whose *virtus*, strength, is ours by Spirit-born faith. Christ who is in heaven thus feeds those who are on the earth from his own flesh. All this is accomplished – admittedly mysteriously – through the Spirit. This, for Calvin, is the true partaking of the flesh and blood of Christ. In fact, he says, in this ministry the Spirit is like a channel 'through which all that Christ himself is and has is conveyed to us'.[16]

It is here that we can see how central to Calvin's thinking about the supper is the way he views the distinctive role of the Holy Spirit. On the one hand (over against Rome), he asserts the permanent physical absence of Christ in heaven, and denies his physical presence in the bread and wine; but equally (over against a mere memorialism) he insists that the substantial presence of Christ in the event of the supper as a whole is experienced through the power of the Spirit.

---

15. *Institutes* 4:17:7.
16. *Institutes* 4:17:12.

Implications

Three important consequences emerge as a result of Calvin's thinking:

(i) The body and blood of Christ are not, and cannot be, shut up (*inclusus*) in the bread and the wine of the Lord's supper. The ascension of Christ is a real, physical, once-for-all, irreversible, redemptive-historical event. Whatever is meant, therefore, by our communion with the body and blood of Christ, they cannot be thought of as locally present *in* the elements of the supper since they are at the right hand of God, in heaven, where Jesus has ascended. Calvin regards this much as clear on the basis of Acts 3:21 ('He must remain in heaven until the time comes for God to restore everything').

It would be a major departure from the Scriptures to hold, as Rome did, that, as a result of the priestly words *Hoc est corpus meum* ('This is my body'), an act of transubstantiation takes place so that the bread and wine are changed as to their substance into the body and blood of Christ which are consequently contained by and located *within* the bread and the wine. Calvin's fundamental objection to the idea that, while the accidents or properties of bread and wine remain, their substance has become the flesh and blood of Christ, is that it compromises the heavenly glory of Christ, and fails to give due weight to the significance of the ascension.

Rather the exhortation appropriate to communion, 'lift up your hearts' (*sursum corda*), indicates that we look beyond the physical eating and drinking to enjoy communion with an ascended and glorified Lord – in the flesh and blood he assumed and continues to possess.[17]

(ii) On the other hand, to adopt the Lutheran (so-called consubstantiation) view was an equal error. Luther held, in the light of his doctrine of the ubiquity (omnipresence) of the resurrected humanity of Christ, that his body and blood could

---

17. *Institutes* 4:17:36.

be received 'in, with and under' the bread and the wine. To Calvin this was essentially to deny the reality of Christ's humanity and its real identity with ours. For ubiquity is not a property of humanity as such. If Christ's humanity is ubiquitous, it cannot truly be 'our' humanity, and the grammatical rules which make the incarnation a saving event have been transgressed: a humanity so unlike ours cannot be the means of the salvation of the humanity which is ours.

The seriousness of the flaw in the Lutheran view, as far as Calvin is concerned, is that ultimately it undermines orthodox Christology (which stated that the two natures were united in one person, not united directly in such a way that their properties mingled with each other). The Christ of this doctrine would be a 'phantasm', and this, for Calvin, meant that a consistent soteriology and a genuine sacramental theology would become impossible. Theologically what was at stake here was not merely the doctrine of the sacraments or even the finer points of Christology, but the very possibility of salvation itself. For only one who is truly one of us can become a Saviour for us.

(iii) But again, over against a reactionary memorialism which reduces the action in the supper to that of the recipient, Calvin insists that the Spirit works in order to give believers a genuine share in Christ's real body and blood, not because of its local presence, nor by its infinite extension in space, but by the power of the Spirit. This pneumatological dimension of the supper is one which Calvin believes his opponents essentially ignore. For him, however, it is the key to the whole thing.

True Communion with Christ

How then does communion with Christ take place? In Calvin's view, the space-time gap between believers and Christ is bridged by the Holy Spirit. It is his office to unite believers on earth to Christ in heaven, bringing together realities which are spatially distanced.[18] Through the Spirit we are raised up into the heavenly

18. Cf. *The First Epistle of Paul the Apostle to the Corinthians*, 246-7.

presence of Christ and feed on him. This is the secret and wonderful work of the Spirit. We cannot measure it; indeed it would be sinful to try. Calvin himself admits this is incredible. It is beyond our understanding that the Spirit should join together things separated spatially; but nevertheless we experience the reality of it even if we do not comprehend the mystery of it. Here, far from being coldly rationalistic, Calvin subscribes to the view that certain aspects of grace are, apparently, 'better felt than telt'.

Calvin's eucharistic doctrine, therefore, in denying the local, enclosed presence of Christ, emphasises what is sometimes called his spiritual presence. But here being present 'spiritually' means 'the presence of the incarnate and exalted Son of God *by the Spirit*'. Unwilling to surrender to Rome's claim that only by transubstantiation can believers enjoy the 'real presence' of Christ in the eucharist, Calvin affirms that it is only by the Spirit that believers can know Christ's real presence in the sense of his 'true presence' as a body-and-blood-presence.

Calvin's concern here is to expound the mystery of personal communion with a physical (flesh-and-blood), but glorified, Christ. For him *there is no other Christ*, and the polemic in his sacramental teaching draws its violence from the fact that his opponents' errors distort a true biblical Christology. After all, communion with a person does not involve eating their body carnally, but communion with that person-in-flesh-and-blood personally. Since Christ is a person, we enjoy fellowship with him in an embodied-person to embodied-person manner – through the ministry of the Spirit.

Thus our communion is not merely with the Spirit, but with the ascended, bodily Christ, not merely with Christ's benefits, but with Christ himself. 'Christ's flesh, separated from such great distance', says Calvin, 'penetrates to our flesh',[19] so that although it dwells in heaven, our spiritual life is drawn from his flesh:

---

19. *Institutes* 4:17:10.

> It is declared in my writings more than a hundred times, that
> so far am I from rejecting the term substance, that I ingenuously
> and readily declare, that by the incomprehensible agency of
> the Spirit, spiritual life is infused into us from the substance of
> the flesh of Christ. I also constantly admit that we are
> substantially fed on the flesh and blood of Christ, though I
> discard the gross fiction of a local intermingling.[20]

Language like this is now so rare that to modern ears it sounds
unexpectedly realistic, even shocking. Here, and in the *Institutes*
where he similarly speaks about life being 'infused into us from
the substance of his flesh',[21] Calvin is obviously struggling to
express in words the mystery of what the Holy Spirit actually
accomplishes in the supper. It is just at this point that he has
sometimes been criticised by theologians within the very
Reformed tradition to which he gave birth. William
Cunningham, for example, regarded Calvin's formulation as
both incomprehensible and impossible.[22] R.L. Dabney thought
it 'as real a violation of my intuitive reason in this doctrine as
when transubstantiation requires me to believe that the flesh of
Christ is present, indivisible and unextended in each crumb or
drop of the elements'.[23] It is, consequently, rare to find Calvin's
teaching expressed today.

---

20. These words are drawn from Calvin's 1561 treatise, *The Clear
Explanation of Sound Doctrine Concerning the True Partaking of
the Flesh and Blood of Christ in the Holy Supper to dissipate the
mists of Tileman Heshusius*, in Beveridge, *op.cit.*, vol. II, 502.
21. *Institutes* 4:17:4.
22. See William Cunningham, *The Reformers and the Theology of
the Reformation* (Edinburgh, 1862), 240. Cunningham calls Calvin's
views here 'perhaps, the greatest blot in the history of Calvin's labours
as a public instructor'.
23. R.L. Dabney, *Lectures on Systematic Theology* (1878; reprinted,
Grand Rapids, 1972), 182.

The Heart of the Matter

While one might hesitate to say dogmatically that Calvin's teaching has been misunderstood, it may be that the vigorous language in which he expresses himself has obscured the point he is making. For he makes it clear that Christ's flesh as such is not mingled with ours, but rather that, by the Spirit, Christ breathes his new life into us from the substance of that flesh, that is from all that he, the Son of God, now is in our humanity. This is Calvin's way of saying that as the last Adam who has become life-giving Spirit and Lord of the Spirit (1 Cor. 15:45; 2 Cor. 3:18), Christ gives to us both himself and all he has gained for us.

The essential point for Calvin here is that, at the end of the day, this is the only Christ there is. The Christ from whom all spiritual blessings flow is Christ physically risen and ascended, bearing our flesh albeit now glorified. If salvation and blessing are to be found only in Christ (Eph. 1:3ff.), then this Christ, flesh and blood as he remains, is the only possible source from which the Spirit can bring salvation and the only Saviour to whom he can unite us.

The general point made earlier, namely that the key to understanding Calvin's doctrine of the Lord's supper is found in his doctrine of the correlativity of the ascended yet still incarnate Christ and the descending Spirit, here comes into its own. Grasp this, Calvin believes, and the realism of his doctrine of the supper becomes less problematic.

What we find in Calvin's eucharistic theology is essentially what we find again and again in his writings: salvation is ours only in Christ incarnate, crucified, buried, raised, ascended and reigning – in our flesh.[24] This salvation is ours only by faith, and this, in turn, is the same as saying that salvation is ours only through the Spirit, because it is the Spirit who brings from Christ to us all that is in Christ for us, and it is the Spirit who creates the faith in Christ, by means of which all that is his is

---

24. A point made most graphically and in lyrical style in *Institutes* 2:16:19.

experientially realised in us. All that is planned by the Father
and fulfilled in the Son comes to us through the Holy Spirit.

Drawn into the Reformation eucharistic debates as he was,
Calvin makes statements both about the nature of Christ and
about our fellowship with him which may seem to be less heavily
accented elsewhere in his writings. Nevertheless his Christology
is one and the same. Only one who is genuinely incarnate,
sharing our flesh and blood, is qualified to be our Saviour. There
are no other resources in heaven or earth for our salvation than
those which are possessed by this Saviour wearing and
possessing our flesh. There is, therefore, no other source from
which salvation can be brought to us by the Holy Spirit than
from that glorified flesh of Christ. Faith communion through
the ministry of either word or sacraments is communion with
the enfleshed but now glorified Christ and none other.

Calvin's Christ is a substantial flesh-and-blood Christ. For
Calvin, salvation is a substantial, not merely a forensic, matter;
hence his thoroughgoing emphasis on Christ's union with us in
our flesh, and the resultant salvation-transformation of our flesh
in final salvation. Here he seems to combine elements of the
emphases of the Greek as well as the Latin Fathers of the church.
It should not surprise us if his view of the Lord's supper reflects
this substantial Christ.

Calvin's Christologically-focused eucharistic theology found
its way into the blood-stream of the Church of Scotland in the
sixteenth century. Thus, in his famous 1589 sermons in St Giles,
Edinburgh, Robert Bruce expressed the point perfectly when
he noted that we do not get a different or better Christ at the
supper than we get in the preaching of the Word; but because
the supper-sign is added to the Word preached by God's grace
and the Spirit's ministry, we may get the same Christ better,
and, sensing the firmness of his grasp of grace on us, get a
firmer grasp on him.[25]

---

25. See Robert Bruce, *The Mystery of the Lord's Supper*, ed. T.F.
Torrance (Edinburgh, 1958), 64.

It is this Calvin-Bruce tradition that Horatius Bonar so well
expressed in the nineteenth century:

> Here, O my Lord, I see thee face to face
> Here would I touch and handle things unseen,
> Here grasp with firmer hand the eternal grace,
> And all my weariness upon thee lean.

Thus we experience Christ gripping us in the Word and the
same Christ – incarnate, crucified, raised, ascended, glorified,
reigning and returning – made known at the table, and there
sometimes better grasped. It is something of this wonder we
have been privileged to taste through James Philip's ministry
of Word and sacrament.

The Four Forms of Calvin's Spoken Service of the Word of God, and his Sermons on Acts 1 – 7

David Wright

In what is now known as the cathedral of Saint Pierre in Geneva, a simple plaque commemorating Calvin describes him, in Latin, solely as 'servant of the Word of God'. The wording is as apposite as it is eloquently economic. For in Saint Pierre Calvin preached up to ten sermons a fortnight for much of his pastorate in Geneva.[1] However, preaching was but one of four forms of the oral communication of the Word of God which consumed Calvin's regular energies.[2] If preaching was the predominant form, as it was of the long service of the Word of God of the Revd James Philip, it will be instructive to note the other three, and to ask whether any counterpart to them may be identified in James Philip's ministry.

Calvin's first appointment in Geneva was as lecturer on the Bible, in Latin. He retained this role throughout his pastorate, which he assumed within a few months, and which entailed, of course, preaching in French. The lectures were delivered weekly right through books of the Bible, for the benefit of students, the other ministers, perhaps senior school-pupils and especially candidates for the pastorate for the churches in France. From the lectures came several of Calvin's Old Testament commentaries.[3] James Philip, to be sure, never spoke in other

---

1. See T.H.L. Parker, *Calvin's Preaching* (Edinburgh, 1992), pt. 3.
2. Parker, *Calvin's Old Testament Commentaries* (Edinburgh, 1986), ch. 1, discusses three forms, sermons, lectures, commentaries.
3. Parker, *ibid.*, 13-29; W. de Greef, *The Writings of John Calvin* (Leicester, 1993), 107-9.

than a sturdy Scots English, but we might discern in his numerous conference addresses, especially to theological students and ministers, not least at meetings of the Crieff Fellowship, a service of the Word of God somewhat akin to Calvin's lectures. It could also be said that the recovery of expository preaching has not always escaped a tendency for sermons to be something like exegetical lectures.

Calvin lectured, as he preached, without notes, with only a Hebrew or Greek Testament open in front of him on the pulpit or the rostrum. James Philip, too, was likewise ready to bring his facility in Greek to bear upon his elucidation of a word or a verse – but whereas Calvin nearly always reserved such erudition for his Latin lectures, the minister of Holyrood Abbey judged the Sunday congregation from time to time quite capable of understanding a close interpretation of a phrase or term in the original Greek. He might not always have been confident that audiences of students of theology or of ministers would lap up the Greek references with unanimous comprehension.

After the sermon and the lecture, the third form of scriptural exposition in Geneva belonged to a weekly meeting on Friday of what was known in French as the *congrégation*.[4] A straight transfer into English would mislead, for it was in essence a corporate Bible study for pastors and other appropriately qualified persons, not open to the public. Strange though it may seem, the presbytery in churches like the Church of Scotland had its origins partly in such an exercise in the Scriptures.

At the *congrégation* (it is customary to use the French term), one of the pastors would give an opening interpretation, and this must often, but certainly not invariably, have been Calvin himself. Calvin's early biographer, Nicholas Colladon, reported that Calvin's response to the introductory exposition itself often amounted to a lecture.[5] Pity some merely competent Genevan pastor, to have his best effort put in the shade by the great man's

4. Greef, *ibid.*, 117-20.
5. *Calvini Opera* [henceforth *CO*] 21, 66.

sequel! Yet there is evidence that Calvin came as much to learn as to teach, for the book of the Bible dealt with weekly in the *congrégations* was often one on which Calvin was engaged in writing a commentary. It was almost as if Calvin tried out his exposition among his fellow-pastors before consigning it to print. Unfortunately, few of the *congrégation* expositions have survived, so it is hardly possible to compare their form and content with the published commentary.

Nor do we know how freely the discussion ran – or raged – in the *congrégation*. Twice in 1551 Jerome Bolsec took advantage of its meetings to launch a sharp critique of Calvin's teaching on predestination. Although this was too basic a doctrine for Calvin to brook such public dissent, it would be remarkable if on other occasions he learned nothing from his colleagues' contributions to the *congrégation*. Twice in his lectures on Daniel, Calvin mentions interpretations suggested by a colleague in Geneva who taught Hebrew. It is not uncommon in his lectures to encounter a readiness to allow others to hold to an interpretation different from the one he prefers. To that extent, his exegesis is far from dogmatic in tone.

I do not know what form the evangelical ministers' fraternal in Edinburgh took when James Philip convened it, as he did for many years. The discussions at the Crieff Fellowship's gatherings undoubtedly reflected a conviction of the value of shared counsel, not least in the task of serving the Word of God. In informal circles like the meetings at Holyrood's manse for theological students, to whose value more than one contributor to this book bears testimony, Jim listened and imparted the benefit of his experience, biblical learning and wisdom. But it is well known that communal Bible study, for example, in congregational house-groups, did not meet with his favour. (The mid-week Bible study was in reality an exposition in form.) These would have been, however, a far cry from Geneva's ministerial *congrégations*. If the latter have their partial contemporary counterpart in the courts of the Church, James Philip did not shrink as opportunity offered from contributing in presbytery and general assembly a biblical word on matters of dispute.

If, however, we view the *congrégation* in part at least as preparation for another medium of scriptural exposition, the published commentary, then we should envisage Jim not in oral engagement with ministerial colleagues but rather surrounded by commentaries by other expositors as he laboured on his sermons for the coming Sunday. Calvin of course did something similar. Recent scholarship on Calvin's exegetical work has particularly emphasised its indebtedness to both later medieval and contemporary commentators (as well as to selected early Fathers).[6] It was, as it were, in conversation with a continuing community of biblical learning that he sought to expound Scripture faithfully in his day. For Jim Philip, Calvin himself was among his most valued predecessors, along with James Denney, Alexander Maclaren, Charles Cranfield and many another. (I do not recall his quoting Puritan expositors with any regularity.) Drawing in this way on the erudition and insights of one's fellow-servants of the Word of God, whether ancient or modern, is surely an appropriate response to Scripture's own reminder that 'no prophecy of scripture is a matter of one's own interpretation' (2 Pet. 1: 20). It has been James Philip's calling to be enlisted into that communal service of God's Word both by the influence of his regular preaching on numerous future ministers during their student years in Edinburgh and by his widely-circulated daily Bible readings, the tape-recorded services and published expositions chiefly from Didasko Press.

The fourth form of the service of the Word of God which John Calvin engaged in is only now becoming recognisable, as the minutes of the weekly consistory have begun publication. It is hinted at in the following passage from the life of Calvin by Nicholas Colladon published the year after Calvin's death:

> Calvin on his part did not spare himself at all, labouring much more than his strength and regard for his health could stand.

6. Cf. David Steinmetz, *Calvin in Context* (New York, 1995).

He normally preached every day for one week out of two. Three times each week he lectured in theology. He attended the consistory on the appointed day and delivered all the remonstrances. Every Friday in the Scripture colloquy, which we call the *congrégation*, what he added after the introductory exposition was virtually a lecture.[7]

With an accuracy that only the latest Calvinian scholarship is in a position to verify, at the head of his summary of Calvin's routine ministerial activities (the 1575 revision of Beza's life of Calvin called them 'his ordinary labours'[8]) Colladon listed what this paper refers to as the four forms of Calvin's service of the spoken Word of God. The fourth form to consider is the remonstrance (the word is the same in Colladon's French), delivered from the chair of the panel of ministers and elders assigned to meet in the consistory each Thursday 'to see that there be no disorders in the church and to discuss together remedies as they are required'.[9] This was how the *Ecclesiastical Ordinances* of 1541 introduced the role of Geneva's court of spiritual and moral discipline. They also repeatedly stipulated that 'admonition' or 'remonstrance' be administered to the impenitent or recalcitrant.

The first volume of the minutes of the consistory has been recently published both in the original French and in English translation.[10] In an important essay Robert Kingdon has drawn attention to the role of the remonstrances in this system of pastoral discipline.[11] Calvin probably delivered most of them,

---

7. *CO* 21, 66.

8. *CO* 21, 132.

9. *Ecclesiastical Ordinances* (1541), tr. J.K.S. Reid, *Calvin: Theological Treatises* (London, 1954), 70.

10. Robert M. Kingdon *et al.* (eds.), *Registers of the Consistory of Geneva in the Time of Calvin*, vol. I: *1542-1544* (Grand Rapids, MI, 2000).

11. 'A New View of Calvin in the Light of the Registers of the Geneva Consistory', in W.H. Neuser and B.G. Armstrong (eds.), *Calvinus Sincerioris Religionis Vindex* (Kirksville, MO, 1997), 21-33, esp. 24-30.

but not all. The minutes rarely provide more than a brief summary of their content. As often as not in this first volume, covering 1542-4, when many in Geneva still kicked against the pricks of the new evangelical order, those summoned to answer for their behaviour were admonished 'to frequent the sermons'.

But from a wider range of the minutes, most of which await publication, Kingdon has illustrated the way in which Calvin's command of Scripture informed such admonitions. The precise contents must in most cases have related to the nature of the offences alleged and to the course of the exchanges at the consistory, which on occasions are recorded as including disputed appeal to Scripture by persons summoned to give an account of their conduct. The remonstrances should not be assumed to have invariably consisted simply in a dressing-down, for clearly they sometimes took place in the context of reconciliation, whether between conflicting parties or with the church's representatives.

These consistory remonstrances – and the role of admonition more generally in Calvin's service of the Word – will attract further researchers. For the present we may ask whether the practice of admonishing out of the Word of God had a place in James Philip's powerful ministry of the Word. An immediate problem is the almost total absence of patterns of pastoral discipline from modern church life, although the courts of Scottish Presbyterianism, even in the national Church, from time to time cannot avoid disciplining ministers. During one recent episode in Edinburgh Presbytery of the Kirk the investigating panel included in its recommendations that the moderator should administer an admonition of rebuke to the person involved, but this got lost in the administrative procedures. The omission somehow seemed predictable.

The days are long past when the business of Scotland's kirk sessions was almost entirely taken up with disciplinary matters, in continuity with consistories like that at Geneva. The vestry or the manse or the home visit is now the more likely place to witness the corrective Word of God, which for Jim Philip may well often have consisted in the contemporary version of 'frequent the sermons'. For it has been Jim's profound conviction and oft-proved experience that the preached Word is applied with uncanny precision by the Holy Spirit to the conscience of the individual, whether impenitent unbeliever or backsliding church member. Hence if admonition or remonstrance is an appropriate dimension of the public service of the Word of God – and since 'all Scripture . . . is useful . . . for reproof, for correction' (2 Tim. 3:16) it has to be – the sermon is most likely to be its vehicle in the present day. My memory suggests that remonstrance explicitly addressed to some in the congregation – normally elders, if I am not mistaken – featured from time to time in James Philip's earlier pulpit ministry in Holyrood Abbey.

We have reviewed the four forms of the oral teaching of Scripture undertaken by Calvin in Geneva. The less well-known have naturally invited closer attention, but in truth the last word is far from having been said on all four of them. A balanced and comprehensive evaluation of the remonstrances must await publication of the full set of consistory minutes. Some of the few extant *congrégations* have yet to appear in print, but, short of fresh manuscript discoveries, the paucity of surviving texts is bound to limit the horizons of research. The lectures have all been accessible in Latin and in English translation for a century and a half, yet T.H.L. Parker in 1986 could comment that 'Calvin's lecturing is an aspect of his activity which has largely escaped study.'[12] That he significantly remedied the neglect in a book entitled *Calvin's Old Testament Commentaries* alerts us to the fact that modern students of Calvin know the lectures in the form of commentaries – a written, not an oral, genre. The Calvin Translation Society series has not helped by often omitting the rich prayers with which Calvin ended each lecture and by smoothing over the way he handled his Hebrew text extemporaneously.

---

12. *Calvin's Old Testament Commentaries*, 14.

By comparison Parker could claim that the history of Calvin's preaching is now well-known. Yet here too, for different reasons, there is more to be said. A good number of Calvin's sermons await translation into English – and not a few of them have yet to appear in print at all. In 1995 another eighty-seven sermons on Isaiah were discovered in the library of the French Protestant Church in London. So for students of Calvin's preaching the textual base continues to expand, and fresh perspectives and insights will assuredly enrich our understanding of Calvin, of Geneva and its Reformation and, please God, of his Word.[13]

Listen, for example, to an extended comment by Max Engammare, who unearthed the new London sermons on Isaiah, on their relevance to Calvin's well-known reticence about himself ('I do not readily speak about myself'). In the hundreds of Calvin's extant sermons he discerns a source comparable to the self-revealing *Table Talk* of Luther. He analyses a sermon that Calvin preached on 12 June 1559, when he resumed week-day preaching after an eight-month gap caused by illness, and then reflects:

> Not reread, ill prepared and delivered without notes, these sermons unveil the spontaneous character of his reasoning or the reality of his daily worries. In the spontaneity of an explanation, of a judgement, of indignation, even anger, Calvin reveals more than one had surmised hitherto, a part of his personality, quick-tempered certainly, tormented assuredly, generous without doubt, as this initial sermon proves, a sermon in the course of which he evokes his past torments and the hope which helped him to overcome his doubts, not hesitating to disclose more of himself than in his explanation of Isaiah.[14]

---

13. See Greef, *op. cit.*, 110-17, for the position in the late 1980s.
14. Engammare, 'Calvin Incognito in London: the Rediscovery in London of Sermons on Isaiah', in *Proceedings of the Huguenot Society* 26 (1996), 453-62, at 459.

Another angle on Calvin's preaching is sketched by William Naphy in *Calvin and the Consolidation of the Genevan Reformation* (Manchester, 1994). At times Calvin provoked interruption during the sermon and public riots after it by the unbridled directness of his attack on the degeneracy of some of Geneva's city councillors and other VIPs. The language was colourful, the sentiments intemperate, the outcome predictable. 'They no longer want that sort of gospel here', Calvin commented. The ministers should keep themselves to preaching 'salvation and the remission of their sins'. 'Does he think the promise of God ought to be preached thus? Should it not be proclaimed with sweetness? . . . Some say we are too rude and therefore God's Word is not received.'[15] Calvin was certainly pointed and explicit, and prominent citizens smarted from the barbs of his social and political critique.

If Calvin was 'too rude', he was but a human being – and a prey particularly to spasms of almost uncontrollable fury. (After one fit of anger he had to spend a day in bed to recover.) But his run-of-the-mill sermons were only rarely given to the kind of outspoken, personalised assaults which Naphy has highlighted. Part of Naphy's concern is to draw attention to neglect of the question of the effect of Calvin's preaching.

For most readers of this chapter, English translation of Calvin's works is a pre-requisite. Among the sermons awaiting an English version are those on Acts 1-7 first published in 1994,[16] begun on August 25, 1549, and completed on 11 January 1551. Calvin devoted at least sixty-six sermons to the first seven chapters of Acts. [17] This means that his treatment in the pulpit

---

15. Naphy, *Calvin and the Consolidation*, 161, 159.
16. *Sermons on the Acts of the Apostles*, ed. Willem Balke and Wilhelmus H. Th. Moehn (*Supplementa Calviniana* 8; Neukirchen-Vluyn, 1994), cited henceforth as *SC* 8. Forthcoming is Moehn's *'God Calls Us to His Service.' The Relation between God and his Audience in Calvin's Sermons on Acts* (Droz, Geneva).
17. For details, *SC* 8, xv-xix.

was probably three to four times longer than in his commentary. The extra space, however, does not ensure uniform coverage of the biblical text. For example, the commentary gives a full paragraph to the second part of Acts 1:18, 'in Jerusalem . . . and to the ends of the earth', but several columns of a sermon omit it entirely.[18]

If we compare sermons and commentary on Acts 2:42 (there is no evidence of Calvin's lecturing on Acts), a degree of parallelism is immediately evident. This is only to be expected, given the overlapping chronology of the two. Calvin had been working on the commentary on Acts during 1550 and had dealt with a third of the book by November. The two expository endeavours proceeded roughly in tandem. So after presenting, on 2:42, the importance of perseverance (at greater length in the sermon, with loose citations of 1 Corinthians 15:1-2 and Ephesians 1:13) and the apostles' teaching, mutual sharing, the supper and prayer as marks of the true church, both sermon and commentary launch into polemic against papal claims to be the church of God. Again the sermon's indictment is both far more extended and expressed in more graphic language than the commentary's – 'the synagogue of Satan', 'images of stone or wood . . . like that of St. Gertrude or someone else whose soul is in the pope's paradise, that is, hell', 'a great bordello, parading all his idolatries'.[19] Finally, both sermon and commentary return to reinforce steadfast adherence to the four features of the Jerusalem church set out in Acts 2:42. Again the preacher goes further than the commentator, stressing that contenting oneself with the word while abstaining from the sacraments makes it 'impossible for us to be the church of God'.[20]

---

18. For Calvin's commentary on Acts, see *CO* 48, 1-574; trs. John W. Fraser and W.J.G. McDonald, 2 vols. (Edinburgh, 1965-6). The commentary on chh. 1-13 has now appeared in the new edition, *Opera Omnia Denuo Recognita*, ser. II, vol. XII/I, ed. H. Feld (Geneva, 2001).
19. *SC* 8, 41-2.
20. *SC* 8, 45.

At the end of this sermon Calvin gives notice that he will have more to say on this passage next Sunday.[21] The next sermon develops another lengthy discourse on the Lord's supper. Calvin laments the infrequency – four times a year – of its celebration in Geneva as 'a major fault of ours'. Not that a return to the papal mass is on the cards, with the priest eating and drinking on his own – what here Calvin calls 'the excommunication of all'. Luke's linkage of the supper and 'communion' in this verse shows 'the true union together and the brotherly love of sharing with each other' which we should display as members of one body, that is, Jesus Christ.[22] Practices in the supper which attested this communion were the sharing of a kiss and the giving of alms. Then at last Calvin proceeds to Acts 2:43-5, his proper passage for this sermon.

There is space to consider only one more comparison of Calvin the preacher and Calvin the commentator, this time on Acts 6:1-4, a passage of no little importance for James Philip's conviction of the critical centrality of 'the service of the Word' and prayer in both his ministry and the church's life. Calvin delivered two sermons on these verses, one on 6:1-3 and the second on 6:1-6. The first is largely taken up with the menace of divisions within the Christian community, the necessity of caring for the poor and the significance of the office of deacons. Calvin explains, for example, his belief that there were two kinds of deacons in the primitive church, referring to Romans 12:8. The commentary omits this point, sending readers instead to the *Institutes*, i.e. 4:3:9. This sermon reveals Calvin's concern for the welfare of the needy in Geneva, preserving what is after all the chief focus of the passage, namely, the election of those whom Calvin never hesitated in regarding as deacons. Delivered just before the city council was due to elect an hospitaller, one of the second grade of deacons with 'hands-on' responsibility for welfare provision, the sermon goes into considerable detail

---

21. *SC* 8, 46.
22. *SC* 8, 47-8.

about the role and the qualities needed to fulfil it. The commentary's treatment of this is clear enough but very much briefer.

In the following sermon Calvin lingers on the avoidance of grievances and disunity and the right ordering of the church community. He had already identified the deacons as one of the four orders of ministry in the apostolic church. The choice of the seven was entrusted to the company of the disciples who are 'all taught of God' (Isa. 54:13; the corresponding paragraph in the commentary was inserted later, in the 1560 revised edition). Again the preacher is able to spend time contrasting false and true disciples. The word means 'learner, schooler', and the key issue is whether we have been to the school of Jesus Christ. Most so-called Christians, are 'poor creatures, without teaching, without instruction'.[23] There is none of this in the first edition of the commentary.

Eventually Calvin engages with v. 2, 'it is not right that we should neglect the word of God'. He embarks on some revealing reflections about what the service of God's Word involves in time and effort. 'Many think that one has only to mount the pulpit and talk and chat there for an hour (!), and that's all.'[24] Calvin has already deduced, in order to ward off the inference that the apostles had in reality been 'neglecting the word of God', that 'they often spent four or five hours teaching and declaring the Word of God'. He based this on the interval between the judgement on Ananias and on Sapphira in Acts 5:7 – three hours during which the believers 'persevered attentively to the teaching of the gospel declared to them by the apostles'.[25] (This features neither in the commentary nor in the earlier sermon.)

---

23. *SC* 8, 209.
24. *SC* 8, 211.
25. *SC* 8, 210.

This charge [of preaching] is by no means as easy as it seems
. . . It is true that word will always mean word, but we must
enquire whether this word is handled as it should be, with the
wisdom to apply it to people's needs and to what has to be
corrected and rebuked in respect of prevalent sins and the
scandals one observes daily. This is not at all easy. If the
apostles, who were endowed with such excellent graces of God,
found it so great a difficulty, what about us? As Paul wrote,
'Who is adequate for this?' Having said there that, in order to
proclaim this teaching, we must have a living and penetrating
word to imprint upon human hearts and that the Holy Spirit
issues from our mouth, like a blazing fire to inflame
consciences with the love of God, like a sword to excise all
evil passions and to put men and women to death in order to
make them new creatures – then he writes, 'Who can cope
with that?'[26]

Calvin continues at some length on the demands of faithful
service of God's Word, in terms that would elicit a hearty
'Amen' from James Philip's long devotion to the task.

In the first place, we must declare the Word of God faithfully,
without adding anything of our own. It's a matter of the zeal
and passion we must have, so that each person is brought to
the knowledge of God to receive pardon from him and reach
salvation. We must be concerned to apply this teaching to its
proper use, so that this word has its full and entire effect and
we don't simply cast it on the wind without bothering how.
There are many who would like me to preach with my eyes
closed, without regard for where I am, in what place, at what
time – as if all who are charged with proclaiming the message
of God have done nothing of what I've been doing, as if it
were the same in the time of the apostles. It's as if the prophets
never applied to their time the law of Moses, and the apostles
never followed the same line . . . We are required to apply this
teaching in the light of the scandals we notice, the decay, the
vices, the excesses among us. Now, as I have said, these are

---

26. *SC* **8**, 211.

matters of such importance that a mortal man must not presume he can carry them through while encumbered by numerous other concerns.[27]

Readers will know how to apply *this* message to more than one contemporary issue. It is a timely word, for in my judgement inadequate application to today's world and experience remains a weakness of too much expository preaching.

Calvin rounds this sermon off by contrasting the apostles' dedication with 'this miserable papacy'. 'The pope, his bishops and all his vermin' are busy with blessing organs, baptising bells, consecrating vestments and ornaments, but preaching? 'That's trivial stuff, they'll not deign to touch it. That's for the mendicants, the friars.'[28]

The student of John Calvin finds very little of this in his commentary on Acts, and yet there is sufficient in common between sermons and commentary which cry out for a thorough comparison. This chapter has focussed on oral exposition, whereas the written commentary is the most prominent of Calvin's vehicles of non-oral exposition. Today's preachers and teachers who draw upon Calvin's rich and extensive labours in the service of the Word would do well to give greater attention to his sermons, recognising the limitations of his commentaries. After all, they today seek to preach, not to write commentaries! It is true that, compared with his commentaries, much less of the Bible is covered by sermons of Calvin that are (a) extant, (b) in print, and (c) translated into English. But given that the plurality of these forms of service of the Word of God that Calvin engaged in has today very largely been reduced to the single form of preaching, it is especially to Calvin's sermons that we must resort to appreciate the vivid, vigorous, colourful, securely earthed flavour of a truly contemporary and applied service of God's Word.

---

27. *SC* 8, 212-13. Just below the middle of this passage, the French text is a little uncertain.
28. *SC* 8, 213, 214.

Worship in the Word:
The True Mark of Worship in the Church of Scotland since the Reformation *

William Philip

The centuries since the Reformation have seen considerable changes in the particular outward modes of public worship in the Scottish church. It is perhaps unsurprising that in the national church such changes should be closely connected with the history of political and social flux in the realm as a whole, particularly in view of the vicissitudes of the church-state relationship over the years. So, whereas some eras, such as the comparatively settled times from the early eighteenth century right through to the mid-nineteenth century, experienced a remarkably slow and gradual evolution of liturgical style, others by contrast have witnessed immense fluctuation and rapid change. The tumultuous years of the latter half of the seventeenth century, from the time of the Covenants through to the Revolution and establishment of Presbyterianism in 1690, is a notable example of the latter – a time when men's passions were deeply stirred and the blood of many martyrs was shed over issues at the very core of what it meant to worship God in the freedom of biblical faith. Less bloody, but arguably no less revolutionary, have been other distinct periods of innovation in liturgy, such as the influence of the Romantic revival and Catholic renaissance during the late nineteenth century, or the impact of ecumenical and charismatic movements during the later decades of the twentieth century.

---

* This is an abridged version of a fuller article which may be read at www.wphilip.com

Nevertheless, within the Church of Scotland seminal principles rooted in the Reformation period have produced a continuity that has been discernible in its worship ever since, despite the various modulations (and at times perhaps adulterations) of form and emphasis different epochs have espoused. Undoubtedly the most conspicuous element in this tradition has been the central place of the Word of God in worship, and in this essay we shall briefly sketch some of the salient features governing the place of preaching as 'the core of public worship'[1] in the post-Reformation Kirk.

Reformation Principles: Living Communion with Christ in the Word

Although the worship in the Scottish church was influenced from the earliest period of the Reformation by traditions from both Germany and England, undoubtedly the predominant inspiration emanated from Calvin's Geneva. For Calvin and his fellow Reformers, preaching was at the forefront of all corporate worship and pastoral work alike precisely because real and vital communion with a living, glorified Christ was at the heart of all Christian experience. The central place of the Word of God, and also of the sacraments, in the life of the church clearly flows directly from this understanding of communion with Christ, because for Calvin

> they are to us what Jesus and his Word and works were to those who received His grace during the days of his flesh. They are for us the 'flesh' of Jesus Christ, the lowly humble form He takes in revealing himself and apart from which we cannot come to know his glory or experience the power of His resurrection. The Word and Sacraments are thus the chief treasure of the Church. They are the signs of the presence of Jesus in the midst, the 'form' in which He 'appears' before men, and the veil through which the rays of His glory are

---

1. G. Donaldson, in *Studies in the History of Worship in Scotland*, eds. D. Forrester & D. Murray (Edinburgh, 1984), 37.

refracted so that men can come to know Him as One who, when He comes, does not come to destroy those who have sinned against Him, but gently stretch out His hands to invite them to Himself. 'We have in the Word (in so far as is expedient for us) a naked and open revelation of God.' 'There God shows Himself, as much as is expedient for us.'[2]

The glory of the gospel is that this same, self-revealing Lord of glory confronts men and women in his church today, and communes with them in a way every bit as real and satisfying as when he spoke face to face with his disciples. And the proclamation of the Word of God, and the sacraments as a visible form of that Word, are 'the forms of abasement which Christ the Mediator today assumes in confronting us with His grace and challenge'.[3] And 'even the Apostles when confronted by the glory of God shining through the risen Jesus were not privileged any more than the ordinary Christian of today who hears the Word and is invited to the Lord's table.'[4]

With such an exalted confidence in the power of the preached Word, it is not surprising that Calvin himself marvels at God's condescension to work through 'the foolishness of preaching', when he exclaims that

among the many noble endowments with which God has adorned the human race, one of the most remarkable is that he deigns to consecrate the mouths and tongues of men to his service, making his own voice to be heard in them.[5]

'The Word goes out of the mouth of God in such a manner that it likewise goes out of the mouth of men; for God does not speak openly from heaven but employs men as his instruments.'[6]

---

2. R. S. Wallace, *Calvin's Doctrine of the Word and Sacrament* (Edinburgh, 1995), 23.
3. R.S. Wallace, *Word and Sacrament*, 22.
4. R.S. Wallace, *ibid.*, 25.
5. *Institutes* 4:1:5.
6. Calvin, *Comm.* on Isa. 55:11.

Thus, a man 'preaches so that God may speak to us by the mouth of a man'[7] and in hearing the preacher it is as if the congregation 'hear the very words pronounced by God himself',[8] 'as if Jesus Christ himself spoke to us in person'.[9] Just as in the days of the prophets in Israel when 'the message of the prophet obtained as much power as though God descended from heaven, and had given manifest tokens of his presence', so we may conclude of preaching today that 'the glory of God so shines in His Word, that we ought to be so much affected by it whenever He speaks by his servants, as though He were nigh to us, face to face.'[10]

In this view of preaching the Reformers were careful not to identify the human word with the living Word of God, but rather saw the relationship as a sacramental reality. Just as in the communion, through the Holy Spirit, the supper becomes a vehicle of the real presence of Christ, so in preaching, by similar operation of the Holy Spirit, 'the voice which is itself mortal, is made an instrument of eternal life'.[11] All power of action in the proclaimed Word 'resides in the Spirit himself, and thus all power ought to be entirely referred to God alone.'[12] And so while the Word of God in preaching is not distinguished or separated from the words of the preacher, at the same time the servant of the Word is never to be confused with the Master whose Word he speaks. 'We must view the minister as one that is a servant, not a master—an instrument, not the hand; and in short as man, not God.'[13] It must also be emphasised that

---

7. Calvin, *Sermons on I Timothy* 22, on 3:1-4 *(Calvini Opera* 53, 266).
8. Calvin, *Institutes* 1:7:1.
9. Calvin, *Sermons on Ephesians* 25, on 4:11-12 *(Calvini Opera* 51, 566).
10. Calvin, *Comm.* on Haggai 1:12.
11. Calvin, *Comm.* on 1 Peter 1:25.
12. Calvin, *Comm.* on Ezek. 2:2.
13. Calvin, *Sermon on Luke 1:16-18*, quoted in R.S. Wallace, *Word and Sacrament*, 91.

preaching for the Reformers was also indissolubly bound to Scripture, for just as Christ and the Scriptures were inseparable, so preaching was unthinkable that was not expounding the written Word of God. This was given by God as the unique and final revelation for the church so that 'the only authorised way of teaching in the church is by the prescription and standard of his Word.'[14] The task of the preacher was therefore to

> *expound the scripture* in the midst of the worshipping church, preaching in the expectancy that God will do, through His frail human word, what He did through the Word of His prophets of old, that God by His grace will cause the word that goes out of the mouth of man to become also a Word that proceeds from God Himself, with all the power and efficacy of the Word of the Creator and Redeemer.[15]

Moreover, the preacher must preach, and the congregation listen 'in the expectancy that Christ the Mediator will come and give His presence where the Gospel is preached'[16] and cause his own voice to be heard through the human vehicle of the preacher's words.

Reformation Practice: The Word at Work

In total contrast, then, to the subtlety and complexity of the medieval, scholastic *artes praedicandi* ('arts of preaching') this profound belief in the power of the living Word of Christ in the preaching of the biblical gospel led to a return to the simple homiletic style of Scripture exposition which had been virtually unknown since the time of Chrysostom and Augustine. It was not that the pre-Reformation churches were without eloquent and learned preachers, nor that the Reformed ministers merely offered a radically new style of preaching. What was revolutionary was the substance: a systematic preaching of the

---

14. Calvin, *Institutes* 4:8:8.
15. R.S. Wallace, *Word and Sacrament,* 83 [italics mine].
16. R.S. Wallace, *ibid.,* 83.

content of the Scriptures. The effect was dramatic as the Word of God, which had been locked up in the language of the scholars and clergy, was let loose among the ordinary men and women of Europe. The great purpose was to 'lay bare and interpret the Word of God in Scripture',[17] and so the Reformers, inspired by the example of many of these rediscovered Fathers, threw themselves into consecutive expositions of books of the Bible on a phenomenal scale, day by day, week by week. We are told that when Ulrich Zwingli began his ministry in Zurich as the continental Reformation was just beginning in 1519,

> He started out by taking the Gospel of Matthew and preaching through it verse by verse, day after day for a whole year. Every man, woman and child who could possibly get there crammed into Zurich's Great Minster to hear him.[18]

Later, John Calvin was to follow this same characteristic pattern of expounding the Scriptures 'in course' – systematically and consecutively – in Geneva. His output was prodigious, covering virtually the whole Bible through his almost daily lecturing and preaching. He was unquestionably the most outstanding exegete of his day, acknowledged by friend and foe alike, yet surely the secret of his appeal is that never did he 'allow the pure scholar in him to oust the preacher entrusted with the cure of souls'.[19] His aspiration to lucidity led him to abjure fruitless philosophical discussion and fanciful interpretation, and he sought to deal honestly with Scripture, refusing to miss the wood for the trees, and desiring always to allow the truth of the Word of God to speak for itself. In doing so he rescued a truly sane and sound exegesis from the spell of scholastic methods, endeavouring always, as he put it, 'to exclude from it all barren refinements

---

17. T.H.L. Parker, *The Oracles of God* (London, 1947), 21.
18. Quoted by E.P. Clowney, 'Presbyterian Worship', in *Worship: Adoration and Action*, ed. D.A. Carson (Carlisle, 1993), 113.
19. A.M.Hunter, *The Teaching of Calvin* (Glasgow, 1920), 33.

however plausible and fitted to the ear, and to preserve genuine simplicity, adapted solidly to edify the children of God, who, being not content with the shell, wish to penetrate to the kernel.'[20] For Calvin this was never a cold, academic exercise, but always it was suffused with his own experience and with the warmth of personal and practical devotion. His main business in life was to open up Scripture to the common people. It was a matter of nourishment, heart knowledge as well as head knowledge, always endued with a profound spiritual imperative. What the Bible was to himself – food, light, comfort, assurance – he succeeded in making it for countless multitudes across Europe through his preaching and writings, and in so doing did more to shape the spiritual diet of the sixteenth-century church than any other.

An important factor in Calvin's widespread influence was Geneva's liberal policy towards refugees, unlike that of Basel, Zurich and Berne. This brought those of Reformed persuasion from all over Europe, often fleeing persecution, to see for themselves the applied Christianity of Calvin's city. It was thus that John Knox, having fled England following the accession of Mary in 1553, came under the tutelage of what he called 'the most perfect school of Christ that ever was on earth since the days of the Apostles'.[21] That Knox was at one with the Genevan emphasis on the priority of the Word of God made known through scriptural exposition can be seen clearly by his injunctions in *A Most Wholesome Counsel* (1556), where he urges his brethren in Scotland to preach the Bible widely, 'ever ending such books as you begin', and to 'join some books of the Old, and some of the New Testament together; as Genesis and one of the Evangelists, Exodus with another, and so forth.'[22]

---

20. Calvin, *Comm.* on Hosea (in the *Epistle Dedicatory*).
21. In a letter to Mrs Locke, 9 Dec. 1556, quoted in H.Y. Reyburn, *John Calvin: His Life, Letters & Work* (London, 1914), 274.
22. Quoted in J. Philip, 'Expository Preaching: an Historical Survey', in *Pulpit and People*, eds. N. M. de S. Cameron and S.B. Ferguson (Edinburgh, 1986), 12.

Preaching, therefore, became more prominent in the corporate worship of the new Reformed church than it had been for more than a millennium. But this was not in a stifling, deadening way that made a passive audience of the congregation. Certainly an intellectual effort was demanded, but also demanded – more crucially – was the participation of faith. For, as T.H.L. Parker says, 'In the sermon the congregation was gathered into the participation of worship in the sermon. For the sermon is as much an act of worship as the Eucharist and as central to the Church's service. God speaks; man believes – and rejoices with thanksgiving. The sermon, we might say, is the audible Eucharist, the Lord's Supper, the visible Eucharist.'[23]

Theology and Practice in the Congregations of Scotland

The revolution in congregational worship which fructified in the post-Reformation church in Scotland was rooted in this theology of corporate participation in the real presence of Christ, the living Saviour and Mediator who delights to dwell among his people and nourish them continually by faith. It likewise had its practical focus firmly in the exposition of the Scriptures as the living Word, the breath of the Spirit, through which that communion with the risen Lord is known, and by which he sustains, equips and directs his church in all its response and witness to that revelation – in short, in its life of 'rightly understood worship'.[24] Hence the Scots Confession[25] declared two of the marks of a true Kirk to be the preaching of the Word of God and the right administration of the sacraments 'quahilk man be annexed unto the Word and promise of God, to seale and confirme the same in our heart'. The *Book of Common Order* of 1564, which established the regulation of public worship in

---

23. T.H.L. Parker, *John Calvin* (Tring,1975), 114 [italics mine].
24. Rom. 12:1, my translation of *logiken latreian*.
25. Following Calvin closely, though actually elevating his emphasis on rightly administered discipline into a third mark of a true church.

the Church of Scotland until it was superseded by the *Westminster Directory* in 1645, shows 'how the theology of the Scots Confession and regulations of the *First Book of Discipline* (1560) were expressed in worship'.[26] This provided a common order for corporate worship rather than a set liturgy, somewhere between a prayer book and a directory. The structure of weekly Sunday worship was heavily shaped by the stress on centrality of the congregation gathered around the Word, the sacraments of both communion and baptism only ever annexed to the preaching, never apart from it. Monthly communion was recommended, although due to a lack of available clergy, and a certain degree of popular resistance, this became less frequent, and so in fact the preaching became even more central and pivotal to the weekly congregational services.

Following Knox's liturgy, then, the next major development came with the Westminster *Directory for Public Worship*, which issued from the Assembly of Divines convened in 1643 by the English Parliament, but was influenced considerably by the small number of Scottish commissioners who attended under the aegis of the Solemn League and Covenant. In 1645 the *Directory* was enacted by the General Assembly as the standard for public worship in the Church of Scotland, having already been approved by the Parliament for England and Ireland in the same year. Throughout the tumultuous years that followed the *Directory's* publication, from the Commonwealth period through the Glorious Revolution of 1688, there was a great deal of confusion in the politics of church and nation alike. But even during the Restoration period following 1660, with Charles II's imposition of episcopacy which demanded that the *Directory* be 'laid aside and not used',[27] there is evidence that it continued to exert considerable influence in worship at grass-roots level,

---

26. *Dictionary of Scottish Church History and Theology,* eds. N. M. de S. Cameron, *et al.* (Edinburgh, 1993), 896.
27. See Donaldson's essay in *Studies in the History of Worship in Scotland,* 57.

for, as one historian of the time noted, 'presbytery and episcopacy might come and go, but the Kirk Session . . . went on.'[28] After the Revolution of 1688 when Presbyterianism was established, the *Directory* was once again enjoined by the General Assembly, and it remains the standard of worship for the Church of Scotland to the present day.[29]

Although the *Directory* did surrender some of the practices of the Scots tradition in favour of the (illusory) ideal of Anglo-Scots conformity, it certainly maintained the centrality and dominance of the preaching, with the vast majority of the section on the public worship devoted to the sermon, and the preceding and following prayers. It was not prescriptive in determining the Scripture for the weekly preaching, but its description of preaching stands firmly in the expository tradition of the Reformers, and would-be contemporary preachers could scarcely do better than heed the instructions it gives. Following the Summons to Worship and a Prayer of Approach to God there were to be readings and psalms, then confession, and the sermon, in which the subject was urged to be 'some text of scripture . . . chapter, psalm or book' which was to be expounded 'in plain terms' with 'illustrations . . . full of light' so as to 'convey truth into the hearer's heart with spiritual delight'. The servant of Christ when preaching is not to trouble his flock with 'obscure terms of art' but must speak 'plainly, that the meanest may understand', avoiding 'unprofitable use of unknown tongues, strange phrases and cadences of sounds and words' and rather 'wisely framing all his doctrines . . . with loving affection, that the people may see all coming from his godly zeal, and hearty desire to do them good.' Following this was the great intercession (concluding with the Lord's Prayer) and the Blessing. The communion, when celebrated, followed on afterwards.[30]

---

28. *Ibid.*, 62.
29. Though, sadly, it has largely fallen into obscurity in practice.
30. *Westminster Directory*, 29-37.

Changing Tides

In terms of the outward form of church worship, there was thereafter remarkably little change for nearly two centuries, until the liturgical renaissance of the latter nineteenth century. Spearheaded by the Church Service Society, the movement in some aspects paralleled the Tractarian influence in England, and brought Eastern and Roman influence alongside the Kirk's own traditions in the eclectic liturgy of a new service book, the *Euchologion*, which really became the forerunner of the various service books of the twentieth century. Nevertheless, despite the many changes in corporate worship, such as the introduction of hymn-singing and organs, variety in patterns of service and observances of Christian festivals, the central place of the sermon in Scots worship always remained. What did change gradually from the Reformation period onwards was the form and substance of the preaching, and as a result also the collective liturgical nature of the preaching which had so characterised the Reformation worship. From the seventeenth century onwards the sermon passed from the simple homiletical ideals of the Reformers (closely mirrored in the *Directory*) into the realm of literature, such that conformity to prevailing literary standards was required of the preacher, whose style was carefully evaluated (and criticised) by discriminating hearers. One author perceptively notes the paradox that 'the congregation which had been rescued [by the Reformation] from the position of mere spectators became mere auditors.'[31]

Even within the Calvinistic Puritan tradition there was little of the ranging expository emphasis of Calvin and Knox, and sermons tended to make short texts of Scripture subservient to the subject of a particular doctrine. By the nineteenth century the Enlightenment influence had spurred an increase of intellectual preaching, with a developed rhetorical style, and sermon preparation became a craft with conventions of its own,

---

31. David Read, 'The Scottish Tradition of Preaching', in *Studies in the History of Worship in Scotland*, 133.

regardless of the theology. Liberals tended to minimise Christian doctrine except as a support for ethics, and sermons became little more than moral essays, while the evangelical revivalists for their part tended towards pietism, their brand of purely evangelistic 'gospel' preaching aimed solely at the saving of lost souls through a particular variety of conversion experience. These forms of – preaching of whatever theological hue – which continued into the twentieth century, were all far removed from the simple homiletic style of the Reformers, and, ironically, bore striking resemblance to the medieval 'arts of preaching' which, in the pre-Reformation Church, rendered the ministry so empty and powerless and resulted in such spiritual decay.

Biblical Expository Preaching Rediscovered

So, since the latter half of the twentieth century, in a manifest age of spiritual and ecclesiastical decay in Scotland (as in much of the vestiges of western Christendom), one of the most hopeful signs of restoration and revival in the church has been a renewed emphasis on systematic and continuous exposition of the Scriptures, exactly in line with the practice of the early Reformers that did so much to transform church and nation in the sixteenth century. This expository ministry movement is rightly described as 'one of the most important ecclesiastical phenomena of the twentieth century'.[32]

The pivotal figure was William Still (1911-97) who, by his own admission, discovered such systematic expository preaching almost by accident,[33] yet through his remarkable 52-year ministry in Aberdeen had an impact that was far-reaching in the recovery of the centrality of such preaching both in Scotland and far beyond. His vision inspired many, his ethos clearly resonating Knox as he bid prospective preachers

32. D. F. Kelly, 'The Recovery of Christian Realism in the Scottish Expository Ministry Movement', in *Pulpit and People*, 22.
33. Read his account of the early days in Gilcomston in *Dying to Live* (Fearn, Ross-shire, 1991), 120ff., where he describes how he 'literally stumbled on it, surely by divine providence'.

> Preach the whole Word, however you do it. Whether you do it
> by following the Church Year . . . or preaching through the
> Bible book by book, chapter by chapter, judiciously alternating
> Old and New Testaments and different parts of each, the law,
> the prophets and the writings, the Gospels and Epistles . . .
> Whatever plan you adopt, preach the whole Word. Do not leave
> it to chance.[34]

James Philip was no less a figure in the recovery of such
ministry, and the breadth of his influence is witnessed to by
this volume, and the compass of its contributors. Though he
would be the first to acknowledge his debt to William Still,
who led him to Christ while they were students together in
Aberdeen in the early years of the Second World War, in fact
William Still's debt to him was no less great. Over half a century
of ministry together, James Philip's measured theological
insight, scholarly acumen, pastoral wisdom and strategic
discernment lent more direction and substance to the Gilcomston
ministry than was perhaps ever realised (or admitted!) by the
more charismatic incumbent of its pulpit. But it was from his
own pulpit, and his own pen, that he both exemplified and
articulated an understanding of the Word of God and the worship
of God that rings with the same emphasis on living, experiential
union with Christ that we have seen in the Reformers, and in
Calvin and Knox in particular.

The Word and True Worship

Worship, he loved to point out, is 'worth-ship', 'and to worship
God is to give Him his rightful worth and his rightful place in
our lives.' It is all to do with the attitude we have towards God,
and the worth of our position in relation to his. 'He is God, and
He is worth the highest place, we are His creatures, and our
rightful place is one of humble obeisance before Him.'[35] Thus

---

34. Words addressed to Licentiates of the Presbytery of Aberdeen in
April 1963, from 'A Charge to Students', *Theological Students
Fellowship Bulletin* (Spring, 1964), 29-30.
35. J. Philip, *Worship* (personal manuscript).

worship is fundamentally a spiritual matter, not an aesthetic one:

> The deeper reaches of worship are attained not by the mystics or those that are temperamentally suited or inclined to rapt adoration and wonder, but by those that are poor and of a contrite spirit, that tremble at His Word (Isa. 66:2); and for this reason, that the issues involved are not mystical primarily, but moral, a matter not of temperament but of character.[36]

And herein lies the fundamental problem for man. For sin has inverted the natural order of this 'worthship'; we have thrown off God's yoke and usurped his place. It is, in fact, impossible for natural man to worship God at all in any meaningful sense of the term. For even to begin to worship God in this true sense requires something decisive to happen to us, and in us, to restore the natural order that has been lost.

> Until a man is converted – which means that his proud ego is broken and he takes his proper place in relation to God – he remains the centre of his world, and even God Himself is kept on the circumference. For God to have His rightful place means that we must also take our rightful place; only then is worship in the true sense a possibility . . . The words with which we begin every service, 'Let us worship God' are, strictly considered, best taken as an invitation to get right with God, to take one's proper place in relation to Him, to bow the knee before Him.[37]

William Temple's famous definition that 'to worship is to quicken the conscience by the holiness of God; to feed the mind with the truth of God; to purge the imagination by the beauty of God; to open the heart to the love of God; to devote the will to

---

36. *Ibid.*
37. J. Philip, *The Westminster Confession of Faith: An Exposition* (Edinburgh, 1984), 48.

the purpose of God' amply demonstrates the magnitude of the revolution in the heart of sinful man that must be effected before true worship may even begin. And it is when we consider how God brings conscience, mind, imagination, heart and will into obedience to himself that we realise what the real centralities in worship are; for it is by the Word of God that the work of restoring men to obedience is effected.

> It is therefore the living Word of God that is *the* great promoter of worship and its chief inspiration. Only through the action of the Word upon our souls can we be brought into a right relationship with God, and only as our response to that Word becomes greater and fuller does our worship deepen.[38]

And this is no remote or merely cerebral thing, because it is in the Word that the Lord Jesus Christ himself meets with us;

> it is here chiefly that He chooses to make Himself known to us, here that we 'see' Him, and hear His voice, here, so to speak, that He shows us His hands and His side, to draw from us, as from Thomas, the wondering response, 'My Lord and my God'. Where else then, but in and through the living Word of God, can worship find its true expression?[39]

For James Philip, then, as for Calvin, worship is not a question of outward demeanour but of an inward relation to God, issuing from an ongoing communion with the living Christ, through the living Word in the Scriptures. Christ and the Scriptures are inseparable, 'in the sense that it is only in and through the Scriptures that Christ can be known. Therefore to communicate a whole Christ and mediate a whole salvation, a whole Bible is necessary, for Christ is in all the Scriptures.'[40] Worship and

---

38. J. Philip, *Worship.*
39. *Ibid.*
40. J. Philip, 'Expository Preaching: an Historical Survey', in *Pulpit and People*, 13.

preaching are therefore also inseparable. 'In preaching it is precisely not man, but God, who is speaking.' When Paul said in 1 Corinthians 1:21, 'It pleased God by the foolishness of preaching to save them that believe', 'he meant that the voice of the living and life-giving God was in the preaching'.[41] And so in this sense preaching the Bible is revelation, as Christ himself speaks through the preacher's human words, 'revealing Himself through them and using them as the vehicle of his grace'.[42]

> *In feeding upon the Scriptures we are coming to the living Christ* and thereby enabled to offer true worship. We have a similar association of ideas in Psalm 95, one of the purest expressions of worship in the Psalter, 'Come, let us worship and bow down: let us kneel before the Lord our Maker . . . *today if ye will hear His voice, harden not your heart . . .*' This is why it is so perverse, and a misunderstanding of biblical teaching, to suppose that worship is something that can exist independently of and in indifference to the preaching of the Word, or that liturgical forms which relegate preaching to an increasingly insignificant and diminutive place could ever constitute worship in the biblical sense of the term.[43]

To sum up then, 'It is the preaching of the Word, and the response of faith in the human heart to that Word that creates what the New Testament means by worship.' Since this is so, it must be clear that for the life of the church, 'preaching is not only an integral part of worship, but its most important part'. [44]

Far from resulting in passivity and dryness, this understanding of the nature and function of expository preaching animated a ministry characterised by true congregational participation in the living Word of God. Along with an emphasis

---

41. J. Philip, *Westminster Confession*, 53.
42. J. Philip, *Pulpit and People*, 13.
43. J. Philip, *Westminster Confession*, 53.
44. *Ibid.*, 54,55.

on corporate prayer it issued in a fresh and dynamic living worship, 'rightly understood' and fruitful worship 'through which the God of all grace meets his people, transforms their lives, changes their culture, and glorifies his Son'.[45] It was a matchless privilege to live and know from earliest memories this kind of worship – worship wherein the preaching of Christ in all the Scriptures brings the dead to life, sheds his glory into the hearts and minds of men and women, and brings them to a life of joyful obedience that changes the church through grace and makes an impact upon the world in love. This is what it meant to worship as the congregation of Holyrood Abbey Church. Together, as a fellowship in communion with a living Saviour, *we worshipped in the Word*. And the 'sacrifice of praise – the fruit of lips that confess his name'[46] – was visible in the stream of men and women called into the service of the church of Christ, and scattered throughout the land and to the far flung places of the earth, with his message in their hearts and on their lips. Moreover, it was also audible in the ceaseless corporate response of prayer in the congregation as they gathered weekly to pray for those sent out, and many others beside, that through them the Word 'may have free course, and be glorified'.[47]

It is therefore my great personal hope that those who share my father's vision of such a dynamic potential in preaching this gospel, who truly stand in the tradition of the Fathers and the Reformers, will exercise an increasing influence in the *real* worship of the Church of Scotland as the twenty-first century begins. Would that there were more of them. And if there are any who in reading this essay sense something of the thrill of such a ministry, and glimpse the possibilities of such a ministry, and feel drawn to such a ministry – then who knows, in the loving providence of God, but that you may have come to the kingdom for such a time as this!

---

45. D. F. Kelly, in *Pulpit and People*, 28.
46. Heb. 13:15.
47. 2 Thess. 3:1.

Praying Societies and Praying Churches

Monty Barker

In my article 'Praying Societies in Scottish History'[1] I quoted the words of Dr A. Skevington Wood, 'The formation of praying societies represented a spiritual force in Scotland, the ultimate repercussions of which can hardly be calculated.'[2] Drawing from some old journals in the Hay Fleming Reference Library in St Andrews, I sought to sketch out more fully the history, development, spiritual impact and apparent decline of these societies. The Revd Shirley Fraser, twenty-five years later, covered some of the same ground and updated the references in her article 'A Re-examination of the Role of Praying Societies in Scottish Church Life'.[3] She re-echoed some of my misgivings about the loss of the praying societies in Scotland, but drawing upon Dr Arthur Fawcett's scholarly and thrilling account of the Cambuslang Revival she referred to the evidence for the influence of the praying societies of Cambuslang in the formation of Jonathan Edwards' Concert for Prayer, which in turn had its impact upon William Carey and the foundation of the Baptist Missionary Society.[4] The request to participate in this volume gives me the opportunity to reflect on my earlier paper and give a broader view on praying societies and praying churches specifically relating to the ministry of the Revd James Philip in Holyrood Abbey Church of Scotland.

---

1. M.G. Barker, 'Praying Societies in Scottish History', *The Christian Graduate*, 16 (Mar. 1963), 1-8.
2. A. Skevington Wood, *The Inextinguishable Blaze* (London, 1960), 125.
3. S. Fraser, 'A Re-examination of the Role of Praying Societies in Scottish Church Life', *Rutherford Journal of Church and Ministry*, 5:1 (1998), 20-23.
4. A. Fawcett, *The Cambuslang Revival* (London, 1971), 213-19.

Although meetings for prayer, Bible study and mutual spiritual encouragement became widely established as the class meetings of Methodism in the eighteenth and nineteenth centuries, there is a much longer history of voluntary religious societies going back to the earliest days of the Reformation and continuing in various forms to the present. There has been a tendency for these to be viewed as 'little churches within the church', consisting of groups of men and women seeking to be faithful and conscientious Christians within the larger church structures which contained many or even a majority with apparent nominal adherence to biblical faith. Luther, Knox and such as Samuel Rutherford approved of such societies, and the Lollards of Kyle in the south-west of Scotland could be seen as a pre-Reformation praying society.

However, it was in the latter part of the seventeenth century and in the eighteenth century that the praying society or fellowship flourished most. Many accounts have come down to us in biographies and diaries and an occasional book of minutes has survived. Thomas Boston when still a schoolboy of eleven years of age was a member of such a society of three children. They existed at every level of society including the aristocracy, professional classes and weavers and ploughmen. The evangelical ministers of the day often supported such groups and would attend their meetings, not as presidents but as members. William McCulloch of Cambuslang and Alexander Stewart of Moulin, both of whose names are associated with local spiritual revivals, were examples. Others such as Ebenezer Erskine of Portmoak actually organised praying societies throughout their parishes, there being ten when Erskine left Portmoak. Thomas Hog of Kiltearn, himself influenced by an informal society when at university in Aberdeen, started praying societies in the Highlands for the purpose of helping his young converts. From his work what was essentially a Lowland phenomenon spread to the Highlands where there are vestiges today. The development of 'the Men' famous in Highland religion stems from this beginning. Many of these societies had long lists of rules, regulations and restriction of numbers. Growth beyond a certain point meant formation of a further society. Their topics for debate and study have come down to us and include such questions as dealing with wandering thoughts in prayer, the meaning of conversion and how to deal with periods of barrenness in one's Christian experience. Some of the societies had a long history over decades and even two centuries. One praying society founded in 1740 during the great revival in Kilsyth was still functioning when further times of revival came in 1839 under the ministry of W. C. Burns.

In the nineteenth century men like Robert Murray McCheyne, ministering in a new church extension charge in Dundee, had their general church prayer meeting but also encouraged private praying societies. His friend Andrew Bonar, struggling with a hard and difficult rural parish in Angus, started cottage meetings and later kitchen meetings when he moved to his church extension charge among the new tenements of Glasgow. These meetings tended to have a double function in gathering the faithful and converted together for instruction, as well as providing a place to which the members could bring unconverted and unchurched friends. By the late nineteenth century, however, in spite of a short stimulus to such meetings after the 1859 revival and the Moody campaigns, the praying society or fellowship meeting was becoming extinct. Church magazines of the day bewailed the state of the church prayer meeting, not only in the Established Church or its giant sisters the Free Church and United Presbyterian Church, but also in the revered Original Secession Church which had sprung from such groups. Prayer meetings still existed but no longer in the everyday life of the parish church.

The praying societies were not unique to Scotland. Dr F.W.B. Bullock gives a comprehensive account of religious societies on the continent of Europe. He devotes one page to praying societies in Scotland and their 'expansion' at the time of the evangelical revival around 1730. Although ministers of the Church of Scotland encouraged these societies, the opposition of the General Assembly of the Church of Scotland as well as the resistance to the evangelical minority within the Church led to some of these societies becoming dissenters and congregationalists.[5] Nevertheless the praying societies made a significant contribution to the growth of the evangelical party within the Church of Scotland during the eighteenth century and beginning of the nineteenth century. They were not mere pietist groups who had a loose and fickle attachment to the national Church. Even though they were unsupported or actively opposed and persecuted by ecclesiastical authority, they kept alight an evangelical faith which was both Reformed and rooted in personal experience. While the cold grip of Moderatism extended its hold over Scotland in the eighteenth century, these men and women would sometimes walk miles at the end of a full day's toil that they might meet with others seriously concerned about spiritual matters. To them peace of soul, piety and a close walk with God mattered more than the wranglings of the ecclesiastics. Some of the societies were specifically founded to pray for their land in a day of spiritual torpor.

Not only did they keep alive evangelical religion in dark days but they encouraged a sturdiness of faith and knowledge of the Word, so that even those with limited education acquired an astonishing knowledge and familiarity with the Scriptures and an ability to pray readily and fluently. As for the influence of these groups they are to be found encouraging not only personal holiness, a ministry of mutual encouragement and challenge spiritually but also a desire for the outreach of the gospel to their own communities and further afield. Scotland has been fortunate in experiencing remarkable outpourings of God's Spirit in each century and contemporary documents point to the praying societies having a place of prime importance in the preparation and continuance of these revivals from Kirk o'Shotts in the mid-seventeenth century to the Lewis revival in

5. F.W.B. Bullock, *Voluntary Religious Societies 1520-1799* (St Leonards-on-Sea, 1963), 227.

the mid-twentieth century. Their strategic influence within the student population and the flowering of missionary zeal in Scottish history has been recorded by Drs Piggin and Roxborogh in their book *The St Andrews Seven*, among whom was the celebrated Dr Alexander Duff.[6]

So much for the history – but what relevance has this to the ministry of the Revd James Philip? He himself has made no secret of his wariness of private groups for prayer within the church fellowship. His own experience of the tendency to fissiparousness and exclusivism within some church groups in the north-east of Scotland may have contributed to his attitude. There can however be no doubt that his own spiritual heritage owed much to the tradition of praying societies and their association with spiritual awakening and the deepening of personal holiness. In the Holyrood *Congregational Record* of November 1965, he wrote of the death of his mother who

> was reared and nurtured in the glow and warmth of spiritual awakening during the second movement of the great revival which began in 1858 and continued until 1904. . . She was born in a little village in the heart of rural Aberdeenshire called Lumsden, in a district which had already witnessed the mighty labours of the evangelist Duncan Mathison . . . In the last two or three decades of the nineteenth century the whole area experienced the visitation of God in a remarkable way. . . Such, then, was the spiritual environment which surrounded my mother's early life. She had spoken to us of childhood memories of meetings held in the keep of Craig Castle (her father was a gamekeeper on the estate, and a lay preacher in the district) and the sense of solemn awe with which she referred to them is some indication of the deep and lasting impression they left upon her mind and spirit.

---

6. S. Piggin and J. Roxborogh, *The St Andrews Seven* (Edinburgh, 1985).

My own first meeting with James Philip was at a Christian Union preterminal conference at Strathkinness near St Andrews in October 1956. On re-reading my notes of his first talk I see that he began by referring to the history of revival in the north-east of Scotland and particularly to those times of spiritual awakening in Gardenstown in the early years of his ministry there.

On his moving to Holyrood Abbey Church of Scotland in Edinburgh in January 1958 we maintained our friendship and his correspondence included a copy of the first Bible Study Notes in November 1959 which he described as 'our latest venture'. The intention was to create a church fellowship which would be acquainted with and grounded in the whole of Scripture and not reliant only upon a weekly sermon. Quite apart from the discipline and labour that this involved for himself, the notes had a special quality which arose out of the ongoing life of the church with all its tensions, struggles, joys and aspirations. They introduced a way of handling Scripture and applying it to one's daily life in a systematic and pastoral way which was new and spiritually refreshing to many, even among those who were familiar with daily Bible reading notes. The demand for these notes increased not only within the congregation itself but from others who had contact with the fellowship and then had moved elsewhere. In April 1964 there was a new development with the incorporation of the first Congregational Letter accompanied by news of members and adherents of the congregation who were engaged in the service of the church at home and abroad. This material was included in order to keep contact with such people but also to 'stimulate interest and promote intelligent prayer'. Others will bear testimony to the stimulus which these congregational letters have given to prayer and the challenge to Christian service to many who are now scattered throughout the world. Just as the weekly letters by the William McCulloch of Cambuslang stimulated prayer for the Lord's work in Cambuslang and the wider work of evangelism and the support of those preaching and ministering, so have the congregational letters had a similar effect over the past four decades. These letters along with similar ventures in other churches have effectively produced a 'Concert of Prayer', to borrow the phrase of Jonathan Edwards. It would be of interest to know how many over the years have been encouraged and sustained during difficult times by the knowledge that they have been upheld in prayer not only by the fellowship at Holyrood Abbey but by many others who formed part of that concert of prayer worldwide, even though they may never have been formally linked with the congregation of Holyrood Abbey Church.

The focus for this exchange of information and concentration of prayer was the Saturday evening prayer meeting. This commenced fairly soon after Mr Philip came to Edinburgh but he wished to make it central to the life of the fellowship and not an optional extra. In the *Congregational Record* of October 1965 there is a discussion about what was meant by 'real membership'. This arose out of a recent Presbytery report which recommended more lay participation in the conduct of worship. In his comments Mr Philip drew a distinction between

a religious group or society which can never be a church, precisely because it tends to be composed of one kind of people rather than many; one age group rather than all; one stratum of society rather than a cross-section; and those who try to make it one inevitably suffer spiritually . . . In a loose association of individuals, each may well remain not only independent of the other but also indifferent to the other; nor is there any essential bond existing between them to lay mutual obligations upon them. But in membership of a body there is an organic bond which obliges us to be interested in one another, and lays upon us the duty of mutual consideration and care. What then, are we to say of those believers who are regularly present with us week by week, feeding on what they themselves have sometimes called 'the finest of the wheat' but who nevertheless do not become involved in the real life of the fellowship. . . but remain detached, reserved and, even after some years, still comparative strangers to those who want to share fellowship with them in the things of God. . . . Either we are content to regard Holyrood as a preaching station, a kind of spiritual 'self service' store where you help yourself to anything than happens to appeal to you, or we submit to the biblical teaching about membership of the body and take our responsibilities towards one another seriously. . . . We need one another. This is the meaning of the fellowship. There is a healing, sanctifying and enriching power in the true fellowship of the Spirit. Most people would be surprised to learn how many needs there are that nothing but the love of the saints in fellowship can meet and solve.

It is here that we can observe an emphasis which shows a development from the traditional praying society of the past to a church fellowship which prays. In the past there had perhaps been too great a readiness to accept little churches within the church (*ecclesiolae in ecclesia*). Rather the emphasis of James Philip and others of like mind in Scotland was to encourage the understanding that a company which prays together in a committed, sharing, outward-looking way is at the heart of what it is to be a church.

This is a theme which received even more specific attention in the *Congregational Record* of September 1981. In it he outlined again what he believed to be the pattern for the Holyrood fellowship:

A ministry of the Word at depth, not merely in terms of the recovery of biblical exposition, but particularly in terms of a determination to allow all the vital thrust of that Word to do its costly work in men's lives for the production of Christian character and wholeness; an incisive pastoral ministry, helping the Word home in personal application; the establishing of a life of corporate prayer as the powerhouse of the work and battleground on which a significant advance in the work is made.

He expressed concern that some who had been blessed by the ministry seldom found their way to the congregational Prayer

Meeting and stated that 'time for corporate prayer has to be bought back from other things – at a price, the price in this case being our Saturday evenings'.

Both in this letter and in the letter in the *Congregational Record* of January 1995 he sought to trace the establishment of evangelical fellowships as opposed to evangelical ministries being in measure attributed to the building up of fellowships where 'real participation takes place when the members of the body share in the real burden by a spirit of prayerful intercession, praying the Word out into the hearts of men and women'. The combination of 'a godly ministry and a praying people' was reflected in the change of scene within the Edinburgh Presbytery. Whereas there had been 130 charges within the Edinburgh Presbytery in 1958, almost 40 years later there were only 89, reflecting a substantial decrease in church membership and 'the dwindling influence of the Church in Edinburgh'. By contrast Mr Philip had seen himself as a 'lone conservative voice in the Presbytery' in 1958 but by 1995 shared a common 'witness to the evangelical cause' with some seventeen others.

Praying society, or a church which prays? The praying societies have never had a uniform structure or composition of membership but have always had a common purpose. That purpose is summed up in the words of the writer to the Hebrew Christians where he exhorts his readers to make a point of meeting together in order to challenge each other to love and good works as well as to encourage one another.[7] These words can too easily be applied solely to the meeting for public worship. But it was the special meeting specifically for prayer not only for deepening of spiritual life but also to pray for all who shared in the task of godly ministry, whether lay or ordained, at home or abroad, which has been associated with times of spiritual renewal. Occasionally there have been dramatic awakenings over a short period of time. Sometimes there has been slow progress only made clear after decades.

---

7. Heb. 10: 24-25.

There have been differing emphases between those who would seek to meet apart from church structures and jealous for exclusively lay leadership and participation. Others have striven to exert tight ministerial control within church structures. Both approaches have their dangers. But the pattern which James Philip and others of like mind fostered and encouraged must surely have its special place in the history of the praying societies of Scotland. It is a pattern not of a society of praying folks on the edge of the church but a fellowship of praying folks at the heart of the church sharing their burden of prayer for the whole work of ministry within their own fellowship, with an ever increasing remit to pray for all those who had shared in the fellowship and ministry of Holyrood at many different levels and were engaged in service in Scotland and worldwide in a variety of professions. Critics there have been and will continue to be, often with a cry of exclusivism or sectarianism. But this volume of essays I am sure will go part way to vindicate the spiritual heritage and fruit of 'a godly ministry and a praying people'.

On Parishes, Preaching and Prayer

Francis Lyall

Unlike most contributors to this volume, I am not theologically trained (for which I am occasionally thankful), I am not a minister (for which I am eternally grateful), and I have not sat regularly under the ministry of James Philip (which I regret). I am an academic, and of that genus, a Public Lawyer. My interest is in organisations, particularly the state, its elements, constitution and workings, and as it happens I have a special interest in the relationship of church and state and the constitution of churches. I see churches as human institutions, more or less approximate to the ideal in a fallen world, and have a strong sympathy with Calvin's view expressed in Book 4 of his *Institutes of the Christian Religion*, although I think that I would have found residence in the Geneva of his time quite intolerable.

The longest consecutive period I sat under the ministry of James Philip was a series of studies at an Inter-Varsity Fellowship Easter Conference at Netherhall, Largs, in 1958, but I still recall elements of some of the messages, including one which has been an occasional and necessary source of strength, emphasising as Jim then did that a person is not passive, but can choose which input shall prevail amid the conflicting and confusing voices with which one (especially a young Christian, in all senses) is surrounded. Irregularly thereafter I visited Edinburgh, or he Aberdeen, and always the Word was clear and logically arranged. The style was distinctively different from that of William Still, my own minister in Gilcomston South, Aberdeen, for forty years. That variety was refreshing, and underlined the willingness of God to speak through many different instruments. My wife, Heather, comes from Glasgow, and visiting her and her family allowed me occasionally to sit under George Philip. There also

God spoke, again through a different personality and style. And it is that element of diversity of style and personality which has triggered what follows: for it is a gross error to move from diversity to an indifference as to messenger. The parish system in the Church of Scotland invites such error. On the contrary, not all ministers are clear channels through which we sheep are fed. The ministries of James Philip, George Philip, William Still and others in the last half century show that we sheep are willing to travel to feed and be fed, and we are not necessarily hefted to a particular building. So, are parishes necessary? Probably not.

The Minutes of the Church of Scotland's Presbytery of Aberdeen for 6 February 2001 lay out the boundaries of the parishes of the Presbytery following upon recent re-adjustments occasioned by the dissolution of a number of congregations. The delineations are precise – the mid-line of certain streets, both sides of others, footpaths, and identifiable objects, such as rivers and streams, bridges and railway lines. Within each parish there is a church, a minister, a kirk session, a financial court of one kind or another, and a congregation. Inside the boundary of the parish the minister has both authority and duty. Other Church of Scotland ministers should not intrude into the parish for religious purposes without the consent of the minister of the parish, unless to attend to the needs of a member of their congregation. Similarly a congregation cannot without Presbytery approval engage in general activities in another parish. Of course, the visiting of members of a congregation in their homes wherever situated does not require the permission of the territorial parish. Such rules are all that remain of what used to be a very important institution – the parish.

A parish is a territorial area. It seems that the first territorial divisions for ecclesiastical purposes were the dioceses of bishops, the parish unit coming later as the sphere of responsibility of a priest. In its origin the word itself has no necessary ecclesiastical connotations: *para* = near, *oikos* = house, *paroikia* = a neighbourhood. The concept of the territorial unit, however, has implications of administration. As far as

Scotland is concerned, the parochial divisions established before the Reformation were not only taken over into the reformed Church's administrative structure, but also were integral to civil administration for centuries. In line with the *First Book of Discipline* of 1560-61,[1] every parish had a school and every parish had responsibilities for the poor of that parish. There are fascinating cases that deal with disputes in each area, as well as legislation more clearly spelling out the rights and duties these responsibilities entailed. Titles to land and buildings were recorded in terms of parishes. Thus, until the recent introduction of a modern system of registration of title, heritable property in Aberdeen west of Union Terrace and north of Loch Street was registered in the 'Books of Council and Session for the Parish of Old Machar', because the parish of the cathedral church of Old Aberdeen (i.e. Old Machar) swept round that of St Nicholas, the church of 'New Aberdeen'.[2]

Equally importantly in terms of civil administration, the parish was a tax unit. The heritors of a parish, those owning land within it, were liable to pay for the parish schoolmaster, and any poor relief over what the parish church itself provided from collections. The heritors were also liable for the minister's maintenance, and for the upkeep of the fabric of the church. The matter of teinds – tithes – was important.[3]

---

1. J.K. Cameron, ed., *The First Book of Discipline* (Edinburgh, 1972). The proposals of the *Book* were not legislatively enacted, but many parishes complied almost immediately, and the parochial school system prospered, giving the world many keen minds.
2. Thus also, the original 'Free Church' Gilcomston came out of the Gilcomston founded as a chapel-of-ease out-station of St Machar's Cathedral in order to provide services for the Denburn/Woolmanhill area that grew outside the technical limits of 'New Aberdeen' in the eighteenth century.
3. See J. Connell, *The Law of Scotland regarding Tithes and the Stipends of Parochial Clergy*, 3 vols. (Edinburgh, 1815, 1830); W.G. Black, *What are Teinds? History of Tithes in Scotland* (Edinburgh, 1893); A.J.H. Gibson, *Stipend in the Church of Scotland* (Edinburgh, 1961).

It was that importance of the civil aspects of the parish which led, very soon after the Reformation, to the church losing its authority to create new parishes entirely of its own will. As early as 1592, following the establishment of Presbyterianism as the form of church government, Acts of Parliament created new parishes. From 1617 the responsibility for new parishes was given to commissioners for the plantation of kirks and the valuation of teinds – a jurisdiction entrusted to the Court of Session in 1707 (c.9: *Thomson* c.10) just before the Union of the Parliaments, and exercised by the Lords of Session sitting as the 'Court of Teinds'. The organs of the state were therefore built into the matter of parishes, dealing in principle with matters of the proper organisation of the Kirk, but in practice with more concern being paid to the proper division of civil liability rather than spiritual welfare, as the reference to the 'teinds' in the very title of the court made clear. The teinds were set every year for the area, and varied with the local price for wheat, oats and bere barley of the harvest. Other income from the glebe or any mine etc. was part of the stipend of a parish, but not part of the teind income.

In the history of the Church of Scotland, the Disruption of 1843 was hugely important. This is not the place to rehearse its legal intricacies, but it will suffice to note that the question of parishes played a major part. Indeed, although I accept that as a matter of politics the position of patronage was crucial, the other cases on the creation of new parishes *quoad sacra* (i.e. for church purposes only), the so-called chapels-of-ease, were legally more intriguing. The General Assembly was claiming the right to make new parishes with spiritual functions only. The older *quoad omnia* parishes were to retain their rights and duties as to schools, poor law, etc. But it was held that the Church's Chapel Act went beyond the powers of the Kirk. New parishes, with their minister having the right to sit in presbytery, were a matter governed by civil statute alone. In short, when an enthusiasm for the Word of God began to lead the Kirk to adapt its parish structure to meet the population changes of the

eighteenth and nineteenth centuries, by the creation of
'preaching stations', those opposed to such development and
having a patrimonial (financial) interest were able to get the
civil courts to strike down the church legislation on the matter.
Civil elements overrode spiritual. This is not to say there were
no new parishes 'properly' constituted through the Court of
Teinds, but the Kirk's authority in such matters was held
subservient to that of the state.[4]

Successively, however, all the civil aspects of the parish have
diminished, dissolved or been abolished.[5] Newer structures of
civic government have taken over. Education became a state
function by the Education (Scotland) Act 1872. Poor relief has
been entrusted to state organs rather than Kirk Sessions of *quoad
omnia* parishes.[6] Yet when the bulk of the United Free Church
united with the Church of Scotland in 1929, the parish system
was retained. But since, following the Disruption in 1843, it
had been the largely-fulfilled intention of the Free Church to

---

4. See my own *Of Presbyters and Kings: Church and State in the
Law of Scotland* (Aberdeen, 1980).
5. There was quite a body of law involved: see the three editions of
A. Dunlop on *Parochial Law* (Edinburgh, 1830, 1835, 1841), the
four editions of W.G. Black on the *Parochial Ecclesiastical Law of
Scotland* (Edinburgh, 1888, 1891, 1903, 1928), and his *Parochial
Law of Scotland other than Ecclesiastical* (Edinburgh, 1893). There
are also the four editions of W. Mair's *A Digest of Laws and Decisions
Ecclesiastical and Civil relating to the Constitution, Practice and
Affairs of the Church of Scotland*, (Edinburgh, 1887, 1895, 1904,
1912 and with Supplement, 1923)(better known as *Mair's Digest of
Church Laws*). Those interested in the present inter-relationship of
church and state should see *The Laws of Scotland: The Stair Memorial
Encyclopaedia,* vol. 3, paras 701-1687, title 'Churches and other
religious bodies', and vol. 5, paras 679-705, title 'Church and State'.
My own book (see n.4) takes matters only down to 1980.
6. On the old Poor Law, see A. Dunlop, *Poor Laws of Scotland*
(Edinburgh, 1825, 1828, 1854) and R.P. Lamond, *The Scottish Poor
Laws* (Edinburgh, 1870, 1892).

provide one Free Church for every parish Church of Scotland, the result was a large number of small parishes in most areas of significant population numbers. The problem was, and remains, particularly acute in the centre of major towns and cities. Every church had to have a parish: some parishes were very small, and as towns and cities expanded, the move to outlying areas depopulated city centre parishes. And the Union of 1929 carried with it another legal change. Implementation of the Church of Scotland (Property and Endowments) Act 1925 meant the standardisation of teinds in money terms, rather than the previous variability possible by reference to market prices, and their payment to a central fund, rather than to the minister of the relevant parish. In this way the link between property ownership and a duty to contribute to local church funds was significantly weakened. The sums involved are in modern terms insignificant.[7]

In effect, therefore, the concept of the parish has been stripped of its civil and legal connotations in general law, and its importance as an area within which the preaching and prayer life of a congregation belongs has been revealed once more. But does the parish system still make sense? That there have been proposals to modify it, if not to do away with it entirely, is to be welcomed. The divergent patterns of church life envisaged or implied in certain reports to the General Assembly of 2001,[8] if adopted, will increase the varied nature of Church of Scotland congregations and ministries, as some concentrate on certain activities, while others place a higher store on preaching and prayer. As a result, where there are a number of readily accessible churches, divergent in their emphases, church

---

7. See W.M. Gordon, *Scottish Land Law* (Edinburgh, 1989), 10-50 to 10-77.
8. Cf. *Reports to the General Assembly of the Church of Scotland, 2001*: Assembly Council (Rpt. 11/2001); Board of Parish Education (Rpt. 28/2001); and 'A Church without Walls', the Report of the Special Commission anent Review and Reform (Rpt. 36/2001).

members will choose (as they do already) to go past the church of their parish of residence to sit under a more congenial ministry and take an active part in congregational social and other activities.

A parish area may make some sense outside the towns so as to ensure that to some extent the Church discharges its self-imposed duty to bring the ordinances of religion to the whole country, but that is a poor reason for retention of the concept. Indeed, it may not be effective. One may doubt whether the numerous linkages and unions that require three or more Sunday services in different buildings from one minister, or fortnightly or monthly staggered services in different churches widely located, really serve the purpose. That system smacks more of a formalism and a trust that a 'service' will do some brief magic than of proper care of a community. But in wide areas, perhaps some boundaries should be set. No matter: my point is that within the towns and cities, parishes make no sense.

The parishes of Edinburgh Holyrood Abbey, Glasgow Sandyford Henderson Memorial and Aberdeen Gilcomston South formally exist. We in Aberdeen, Gilcomston South are coming to terms with an extended parish, which has a residential population as well as numerous licensed premises in the new part. Certainly to have a territorial area as a responsibility is a challenge. But the ministries of James Philip, George Philip, and William Still, as well as of others including Eric Alexander at the Tron, Glasgow, were not territorial, albeit they all showed care for the immediate community. Though some may have come to these churches from within the parish, that was without a causal relationship. It has been the faithful preaching of the whole Bible that established those ministries and has produced the fruit now evident. When I started going to Gilcomston regularly in 1957 there were few such ministries. The ministries of James and George Philip were regularly prayed for. Others, such as Tom Allan and the Tell Scotland movement, did things otherwise, and were blessed in what they did. But the real transformation within the Church of Scotland in the latter half of the twentieth century is to a considerable extent attributable to ministries such as that of James Philip, which attracted men and women from a wider area than the nominal or immediate parish. These ministers made ministers. These ministers produced a praying people, active in evangelical concern.

The decline in numbers of the Church of Scotland, both in ministers and in congregational statistics, has continued as foreseen in Wolfe and Pickford's *Survey* of 1980.[9] Evangelical congregations have not been immune from numerical decline, but there is more hope for them than for others. The age profile of most evangelical congregations is good, and their finances are healthier in cash-flow terms, if not necessarily in endowments, than many others. Other congregations are acquiring ministers whose attitude to ministry reflects that of James Philip, and are, sometimes after some teething troubles, starting to develop health. Prayer is becoming more important. I note with appreciation that the new Moderator of the Presbytery of Aberdeen, an elder, elected in May 2001, has set aside twenty minutes at the start of each presbytery meeting for open prayer.

In the 1960s, the late Professor John M. Graham of the University of Aberdeen, and sometime Lord Provost of Aberdeen, was asked to convene a committee to advise how to strengthen the Church within the Presbytery of Aberdeen, and particularly in the centre of Aberdeen. His solution was to suggest that parishes within the Presbytery should be grouped into larger areas,[10] and that members of the Church of Scotland

---

9. J.N. Wolfe and M. Pickford, *The Church of Scotland: An Economic Survey* (London, 1980). See also *Prospects for the Eighties* (London, 1980), and P. Brierley and F. Macdonald, *Prospects for Scotland* (Edinburgh, 1985) and their *Prospects for Scotland 2000* (Edinburgh, 1995). Cf. R. Currie, A. Gilbert and L. Horsley, *Churches and Church-Goers: Patterns of Church Growth in the British Isles since 1700* (Oxford, 1977).

10. The idea is not unlike that of the 'maxi-parish' spoken of in the 'Scottish Church Initiative for Union: Second Interim Report', and

should attend the church of the enlarged parish in which they resided. If one did not, one could not hold office or be a member of whichever Church of Scotland one attended. Such an intrinsically formalistic attitude to church attendance was amazing to read of, and, of course, the suggestion did not get very far.[11] On the contrary, that church members travel across parish boundaries is simply a fact of life that has to be lived with. Sometimes people attend a church remote from their residences for family reasons, or because they have moved residence but wish to retain their existing church connection. In other instances, a ministry will gather a people hungry to hear the Word of God faithfully and fully preached, who will pass the door of less satisfying outlets. To continue the 'hunger' imagery: the assumption occasionally encountered that ministers and ministries are interchangeable is blate. Not all breads are the same, and the recent rediscovery of variety, apparent even in the supermarkets, shows that customers discriminate. More and more church members are nowadays making choices – either to come to sit under a living ministry, or to let membership lapse. The overall age profile of the Church of Scotland indicates a rapid shrinkage in membership, and therefore probably also in finance. Children are not being taught.

In my view the strength of the Church these past decades, and, given 'post-modernism' and our current spirit of the age, our hope for the future, lies with ministries similar to those of James Philip, George Philip and William Still. That the preaching of the Word and faithfulness in prayer should be the keystones has been demonstrated in those ministries. Other

---

particularly Appendix IV, 'The Structure of a United Church' sec. 2; among the *Reports to the General Assembly of the Church of Scotland 2001*, also available on the Church of Scotland website, www.churchofscotland.org.uk.
11. In fact the relevant Report of the Central Area Survey Committee was torpedoed (albeit politely) by the Presbytery at a special meeting on 30 April 1968.

ministries which basically are unqualified social work activity, or divert into political involvement, and congregations which essentially are *fora* for social engagement and nothing else, have no foundation that will last. And parishes make no sense in such a context. It should be enough that a minister is inducted to a charge. That charge should not have territorial limits. Indeed, the remaining trappings of the parish should be done away with. In particular, it is grotesque that ministers should be required to take parish funerals, of people with no connection with the parish church at all: the option should be there, but not a duty.

Some sheep look up, and have been fed. Thank you James Philip, George Philip, William Still and your successors.

Publications of James Philip

'Conversion and Sin-Consciousness', in *Theological Students' Fellowship Terminal Letter* (Spring 1958), 6-8

The Christian Faith in the World of Contemporary Thought, (Edinburgh, n.d.); includes reprint of 'Evangelism and the Intellectual', in *Theological Students' Fellowship Bulletin* 33 (Summer 1962), 1-4

'Creation, I: The Biblical Doctrine', in J.D.Douglas (ed.), *The New Bible Dictionary* (London: IVF,1962), 269-70 (and in 2nd and 3rd editions)

Repentance, its Meaning and Implications (London: Tyndale Press, 1963)

(With G.M. Philip and Eric Alexander), *Speeches in the General Assembly, May 1964,* resisting the re-interpretation of the Christian use of Sunday (Edinburgh, 1964)

Christian Maturity; The Fact and Experience of Sanctification (London: IVP, 1964; second edition 1973), later republished as *The Growing Christian* (Christian Focus Publications, Tain, Ross-shire, 1989), also translated into Spanish and Mandarin

The Westminster Confession of Faith: an Exposition, four parts (Edinburgh: Holyrood Abbey Church, 1966); revised, enlarged and republished in two volumes, 1983-84

'Exposition: The Ministry of the Word in the Church', in *Themelios* 3:2 (1966), 1-7

Unchanging Truth in a Changing World (Edinburgh: Holyrood Abbey Church, 1969)

Temptation and Trial (Edinburgh: Holyrood Abbey Church, 1970)

By Their Fruits: Sermons on 'Things That Accompany Salvation' (Edinburgh: Holyrood Abbey Church, 1971)

Good Christian Men Rejoice: The Meaning of Christmas (Edinburgh: Holyrood Abbey Church, 1971; enlarged edition 1977)

By the Rivers of Babylon: Studies in the Book of Daniel (Aberdeen: Didasko Press, 1972)

The Christian Warfare and Armour (Victory Press, Eastbourne, 1972; reprinted, Tain, Ross-shire: Christian Focus Publications 1989); recently also translated into Thai

Union with Christ (Edinburgh: Holyrood Abbey Church, 1973)

Bible Characters and Doctrines, vol. 8, pt.2: *The Person of Christ* (London: Scripture Union, 1973), reprinted separately as *Jesus as God* (London: Scripture Union, 1978; Grand Rapids, Michigan: Eerdmans, 1978)

Spiritual Depression (Edinburgh: Holyrood Abbey Church, 1974)

The Church, God's New Society (Edinburgh: Holyrood Abbey Church, 1974)

The Death and Resurrection of Christ (Aberdeen: Didasko Press, 1974) (first published as two books under the titles *The Meaning of the Cross* and *The Meaning of the Resurrection*)

'The Doctrine of Baptism', in *Three Studies on the Biblical Basis of Infant Baptism* by H.A.G. Tait, William Still and James Philip (Aberdeen: Didasko, 1975), 15-25

Except the Lord Build the House: Sermons on Personal Relationships (Edinburgh: Holyrood Abbey Church, 1976; 2nd edition revised and expanded, 1982)

The Epistle to the Romans (Aberdeen: Didasko, 1976); later published as *The Power of God: An Exposition of Paul's Letter to the Romans* (Glasgow: Nicholas Gray Publishing, 1987)

Modern Illusions and Christian Certainties (Edinburgh: Holyrood Abbey Church, 1976)

A Time to Build: Studies in the Book of Ezra (Aberdeen: Didasko Press, 1977)

'The Call to the Ministry' in *Ministers for the 1980s*, ed. Jock Stein (Edinburgh: Handsel Press, 1979), 22-31

The Vision of God (Edinburgh: Holyrood Abbey Church, 1980)

On This Rock: Addresses on the Doctrine of the Church (Edinburgh: Holyrood Abbey Church, 1981)

The Epistle to the Philippians (Edinburgh: Holyrood Abbey Church, 1982)

'A Personal View' in *The Westminster Confession in the Church Today,* edited by Alasdair I.C. Heron (Edinburgh: St Andrew Press, 1982), 124-31

'The Ministry of the Word' in *Journal of Christian Reconstruction: Symposium on Christian Reconstruction in the Western World Today,* vol. 9 (1982-83), 24-58

Jesus Paid It All: The Atonement (Crieff Trust, 1985)

Building for God: Nehemiah (Edinburgh: Holyrood Abbey Church, 1986)

The Death of Christ (Edinburgh: Holyrood Abbey Church, 1986)

'Expository Preaching: An Historical Survey' in *Pulpit and People. Essays in Honour of William Still on his 75th Birthday,* edited by N.M.de S. Cameron and S.B. Ferguson (Edinburgh: Rutherford House, 1986), 5-16

Christ In Our Place (Edinburgh: Holyrood Abbey Church, 1987)

Numbers (The Communicator's Commentary) (Waco, Texas: Word, 1987)

'James Denney', 'Fellowship', and 'Salvation Army' in *New Dictionary of Theology,* ed. S.B. Ferguson, D.F. Wright (Leicester: IVP, 1988), 190-91, 254-5, 611-12

'The Sanctity of Life: the Christian Consensus', in *Medicine in Crisis*, ed. I.L. Brown and N.M.de S. Cameron (Edinburgh: Rutherford House, 1988), 14-25

(With G.M. Philip and W. Still), *Review of the Ministry. Its Ethos Practice and Goals* (Crieff Trust, 1989)

Up Against It: Conquering Your Spiritual Afflictions (Tain, Ross-shire: Christian Focus Publications, 1991)

Recovering the Word: The Need for Expository Preaching Today (Northwich: Fellowship of Word and Spirit, 1993)

'Preachers', in *Dictionary of Scottish Church History and Theology,* ed. N.M.de S. Cameron, D.F.Wright *et al.* (Edinburgh: T & T Clark, 1993), 665-7

The Lordship of Christ in Relation to World-wide Mission (Sevenoaks, Kent: Overseas Missionary Fellowship, n.d.)

Bible Study Notes: Old Testament (for Pastors, Evangelists and Sunday School Teachers etc.) (Calabar, Nigeria: Hope Waddell Press, n.d.)

Temptation, and the Way of Escape (Edinburgh, n.d.)

Tapes of James Philip's Ministry

The master tapes of James Philip's ministry from Holyrood Abbey Church have been passed to The Proclamation Trust, and in course of time will appear in their Tape Catalogues. In the meantime many tapes are available from two sources and enquiries may be made to the following:-

The Proclamation Trust Tape Ministry
Willcox House, 140-148 Borough High Street,
London, SE1 1LB (Tapes are for sale or loan)
Voicemail: 020 7407 0563
e-mail: tapemin@proctrust.org.uk
website: www.proctrust.org.uk

Mr J. Bruce Laing
Tapes from Scotland
177 Hamilton Street, Broughty Ferry
Dundee, DD5 2RE.
Send S.A.E. for catalogue of available tapes.
(Tapes are for loan only, donations cover expenses.)